Fourth edition

D1647399

New Headway

Intermediate Student's Book

Liz and John Soars

OXFORD

UNIVERSITY PRESS

CONTENTS LANGUAGE INPUT

SKILLS DEVELOPMENT

READING	LISTENING	SPEAKING	WRITING
Worlds apart *Welcome to our world* The lives of two families from different parts of the world (jigsaw) p10	**A world in one family** Ana from Spain and her son, Xabier talk about living in England p12	**A class survey** Lifestyles p9 **Exchanging information** Comparing two families from different parts of the world p10 **What do you think?** Discussing the pros and cons of bringing up a family in another country p12 **Roleplay** Acting out everyday situations p13	**An informal letter** Correcting mistakes (1) Finding and correcting mistakes in a model letter *I do mistakes WW* **Writing a letter to a friend, correcting each others' letters** p103
Charles, Prince of Wales *The life of a hard-working future king* – the private and public man p18	**Who earns how much?** How much do different jobs pay? p17 **Spoken English – giving opinions** *I reckon … I'd say …* *I think so, too. Actually …* p17	**Talking about you** How often do you do things? p15 **Project** Interviewing someone about their job p16 **Discussion** Which job deserves most money? p17 The role of monarchy p19 **Exchanging information** Talking about your free time activities p20	**Letters and emails** Differences in formal and informal writing Beginnings and endings of letters and emails *I am writing in response …* *Give my regards to Robert.* **Emailing an old friend with news** p104
A Shakespearean Tragedy *Romeo and Juliet* The love story in cartoons p26	**The first time I fell in love** Three people talk about their experiences of early love p28 **Dictation** Transcribing a summary of an interview p24	**A Shakespearean Tragedy** Retelling the story of Romeo and Juliet from pictures p26 **What do you think?** Shakespeare and his plays p26 Falling in love – Who do we fall in love with? Which couples are well-suited? p28	**Telling a story (1)** Two stories: 'The farmer and his sons' 'The Emperor and his daughters' Linking ideas *as soon as* *However* **Writing a folk tale or fairy tale** p105
Kids then and now *Kids who have it all* Bringing up kids in the 1970s and now p34	**Rules for life** Three people talk about their personal philosophies p33 **Spoken English – *have got to*** *I've got to go now. Bye!* p33 **Song** *I believe,* by Ian Dury p33	**Discussion** Laws in Britain and your country p32 What's important to you in life? p33 **What do you think?** Bringing up children Household rules p34	**A biography** Mother Teresa of Calcutta Combining sentences *Her father, who was Albanian, died, leaving her mother to bring up the family.* **Researching facts about a famous person and writing a biography** p106
Life fifty years from now *Life in 2060* An international group of scientists make their predictions p42	**World weather warnings** Five weather forecasts from around the world p40 **Rocket man** Steve Bennett, scientist and space traveller p41 **Spoken English – *pretty*** *The weather was pretty bad.* p41	**Discussion** Talking about changes in the environment p39 **What do you think?** Space tourism p41 Predictions about the future p42 **Roleplay** Making arrangements to meet p45	**Writing for talking** – my cause for concern A talk by a teenager about the influence of video games on children *The thing I'm concerned about …* *Let me explain why.* **Writing a talk about an issue that concerns you** p107
The heart of the home *My Kitchen* Three women's kitchens in three different countries (jigsaw) p50	**My closest relative** Five people talk about who they feel closest to in their family p52 **Spoken English – adding emphasis** *My father I don't get on with.* *What I like about her is …* *The thing I love about him is …* p52	**Project** Your most treasured possession p49 **Talking about you** Your kitchen p50 **Discussion** First-born/second-born children Who do you feel closest to in your family? p52	**Describing a place** – a description of a room Relative pronouns *who / that / which* Participles *I spend hours listening to music.* **Writing about your favourite room** p108

LANGUAGE INPUT

SKILLS DEVELOPMENT

READING	LISTENING	SPEAKING	WRITING
Football – a global passion *The Beautiful Game* Football past and present p58	**An interview** Jack, aged 10, talks about Harry Potter p55 **Things I'm passionate about** Five people talk about their passions p60	**Roleplay** Interviewing Calvin Klein p57 ***Have you ever …?*** Conversations about your life experiences p57 **What do you think?** Your feelings about football and its place in the world p58 Things you feel passionate about p60	**Describing a person** – Facts and opinions My crazy uncle Joe *in his mid 20s He's more like a big brother.* **Writing a description of someone in your family** p109
Dangerous journeys in history *Hannibal crosses the Alps Mao Zedong on the Long March* Remarkable journeys made by two famous leaders (jigsaw) p66	**Fears and phobias** Three people talk about what they're afraid of p65 **The psychologist's view** A psychologist explains phobias and their treatment p65	**Talking about you** True and false facts about your life p64 **What do you think?** People and their phobias p65 **Exchanging information** Comparing the journeys of Hannibal and Mao Zedong p66	**Telling a story (2)** – 'The *Titanic*' Organization, information, creating interest, and descriptive language **Writing the story of *The Trojan Horse*** p110
The victim meets the burglar *I'm sorry* How restorative justice can help criminals and their victims (jigsaw) p74	**A social conscience** Five people describe a difficult situation – what did they do? p73 Spoken English – *just I've just read a great book. I'm just tired, that's all. I just love your coat!* p73	**Talking about you** What would you have done in the same situation? p73 **Exchanging information** Comparing the stories – a burglar and his victim p74 **What do you think?** Forms of punishment and aims of imprisonment p74	**Pros and cons** – Is childhood the best time of your life? Arguing for and against *In my opinion … Another point is that …* **Writing a discursive essay** p112
Architecture old and new *Meet me at St Pancras* London's new *Eurostar* station p82	**What do you do on the Net?** Five people talk about what they use the Internet for p81 **Descriptions** Identifying objects p85 Spoken English – *also, as well, too I'm also selling some of my old stuff. I update my Sat Nav system as well. I get traffic reports too.*	**Talking about you** Websites you like, and what the Internet represents p81 **What do you think?** Your favourite building p83	**A famous town or city** – From notes to writing Completing a description of New York City from notes *History – Dutch 1614* **Researching a city and writing a description** p114
The adventures of Sherlock Holmes *The Three Students* A detective story p90	**A discussion of optical illusions** Two people talk about a set of optical illusions **What on earth has happened?** A telephone conversation about a burglary p88 **A radio drama** Part 3 of the Sherlock Holmes detective story p90	**What do you think?** Modern methods of crime detection p91 **Telling the story** Retelling a story round the class p91	**Expressing attitude** – An informal letter Linking ideas using words and expressions *anyway, naturally fortunately, nevertheless* p116
People who changed the world *Movers and shakers* Famous people, their ideas, and their impact on how people think (jigsaw) p98	***She didn't say that!*** Spotting inaccuracies in five conversations p96 **What the papers say** An interview with the singer Jamie Seabrook p100	**What do you think?** People from your country who changed ideas p98 Newspapers in your country p100 Talking about a current news story p100	**A thank-you email** Correcting mistakes (2) in a model email **Writing a thank-you email** p117

Verb patterns p158   **Irregular verbs** p159   **Phonetic symbols** p159

1

A world of difference

Tenses • Auxiliary verbs • What's in a word? • Everyday situations

 STARTER

1 Each question has one word missing. Write it in.

1 Where do you ‸*come* from?
2 When and where you born?
3 You live in a house or a flat?
4 Why you studying English?
5 Which foreign countries have you been?
6 What you do yesterday evening?
7 What are you going do after this lesson?

2 Ask and answer the questions with a partner.

> Where do you come from?
>
> Slovakia.

3 Tell the class about your partner.

> *Zuzana comes from Slovakia. She's studying English because...*

I DIDN'T KNOW THAT!
Tenses and auxiliary verbs

1 Answer the questions in the *One World Quiz*. Discuss your answers with a partner.

2 **T 1.1** Listen and check your answers. Make notes about the extra information you hear for each one. Discuss this as a class.

> **GRAMMAR SPOT**
>
> **1** Read the questions in the quiz again. Identify the tense in each one. Which two are passive?
>
> **2** Answer these questions. Give examples from the quiz.
>
> Which tenses use the auxiliary verbs *do/does/did* to form questions and negatives?
>
> Which tenses use the verb *to be* (*is/are/was/were*)?
>
> Which use *have/has*?
>
> ▶▶ **Grammar Reference 1.1–1.5 p133**

Write your own quiz

3 Work in two groups.

- Do some research and write six questions about the world, past and present.

- Ask and answer the questions with the other group. Which group are the winners?

ONE WORLD QUIZ

1 In which country **do** men and women **live** the longest?

a Japan   b Germany   c The USA

2 In which year **did** the world population **reach** 6 billion?

a 1989   b 1999   c 2005

3 If you **are standing** on the equator, how many hours of daylight do you have?

a 12   b 16   c 24

4 Where **does** most of the world's oil **come** from?

a Russia   b Saudi Arabia   c Iran

5 Which of these seven wonders of the world **is** still **standing**?

a The Lighthouse of Alexandria
b The pyramids of Egypt
c The Colossus of Rhodes

6 Why **didn't** dinosaurs **attack** humans?

a Because they were vegetarian.
b Because they became extinct before humans were on the earth.
c Because they didn't run fast enough.

7 Where **was** the Titanic **sailing** to when it sank?

a Southampton   b Rio de Janeiro   c New York

8 How long **has** Elizabeth II **been** Queen of England?

a since 1952   b since 1959   c since 1963

9 How many people **have won** the Nobel Peace prize since it started in 1901?

a 26   b 58   c 94

10 How long **have** people **been using** the Internet?

a since 1969   b since 1976   c since 1984

11 How many languages **are spoken** in Switzerland?

a 3   b 4   c 5

12 In which country **were** women first **given** the vote?

a Canada   b Liechtenstein
c New Zealand

PRACTICE

You're so wrong!

1 Correct the information in the sentences.

1 The Pope lives in Madrid.
He doesn't live in Madrid! He lives in Rome!

2 Shakespeare didn't write poems.
You're wrong! He wrote hundreds of poems.

3 Vegetarians eat meat.

4 The Internet doesn't provide much information.

5 The world is getting colder.

6 Princess Diana was travelling by plane when she was killed.

7 England has never won the World Cup.

8 The 2008 Olympics were held in Tokyo.

2 **T1.2** Listen and check. Notice the stress and intonation. Practise making the corrections with a partner.

's = is or has?

3 Is *'s* in these sentences the auxiliary *is* or *has*?

1 Who's making that noise?   **is**
2 She's done really well.
3 Champagne's made in France.
4 Who's been to America?
5 He's leaving early.
6 What's produced in your country?

4 **T1.3** Listen to some more sentences with *'s*. After each one say if it is *is* or *has*.

Talking about you

5 Complete the questions with the correct auxiliary verb and name the tense.

1 What time _____ you usually get up at weekends?

2 What time _____ you get up this morning?

3 How long _____ it usually take you to get from home to school?

4 Who _____ sitting next to you? What _____ he/she wearing?

5 How long _____ you known the teacher?

6 What _____ you doing when your teacher came into the room?

7 What _____ (not) you like doing in English lessons?

8 Which school subjects _____ (not) you like when you were younger?

9 Which other foreign languages _____ you studied?

10 What presents _____ you given on your last birthday?

Ask and answer the questions with a partner.

MAKING CONVERSATION
Short answers

1 **T 1.4** Ruth is collecting her children, Nick and Lily, from school. Listen and complete the conversation. Which child is more polite? In what way?

Ruth So kids, _____ you have a good day at school?

Nick No.

Lily Yes, I _____. We _____ practising for the school concert.

Ruth Oh, lovely. _____ you have much homework?

Lily Ugh! Yes, I _____. Loads. I've got Geography, French, and Maths! _____ you got a lot Nick?

Nick Yeah.

Ruth Nick, _____ you remembered your football kit?

Nick Er …

Lily No, he _____. He's forgotten it again.

Ruth Oh, Nick you know it needs washing. _____ you playing football tomorrow?

Nick No.

Ruth Lily, _____ you need *your* sports kit tomorrow?

Lily Yes, I _____. I've got a hockey match after school. We're playing the High School.

Ruth _____ they beat you last time?

Lily Yes, they _____. But we'll beat them tomorrow.

Nick No, you _____! Your team's rubbish.

Ruth Ok, that's enough children. Do up your seatbelts! Let's go!

SPOKEN ENGLISH Sounding polite

1 In English conversation it can sound impolite to reply with just *yes* or *no*. We use short answers with auxiliaries.

'*Did you have a good day?*' '*Yes, I did/No, I didn't.*'

2 It also helps if you add some more information.

'*Do you have much homework?*' '*Yes, I do. Loads. I've got Geography, French, and Maths.*'

3 Reply to these questions. Use short answers and add some information.
  1 Did you have a good day?
  2 Do you like pizza?
  3 Did you enjoy the film?
  4 Has it stopped raining?

▶▶ **Grammar Reference 1.6 p133**

---

2 Rewrite Nick's lines in exercise 1 to make him sound more polite.
  T 1.5 Listen and compare the conversations.

3 Work in groups of three. Look at T1.4 and T1.5 on p118. Practise them, sounding polite and impolite.

PRACTICE

1 Match a line in **A** with a short answer in **B** and a line in **C**.

A	B	C
1 Did you hear that noise?	No, I haven't.	They didn't have my size.
2 Are you doing anything tonight?	No, I'm not.	I think it was thunder.
3 Have you seen my mobile phone anywhere?	Yes, it is.	Thank goodness!
4 Did you get those shoes you liked?	Yes, I did.	Do you want to come round?
5 Is it time for a break?	No, I didn't.	Have you lost it again?

T 1.6 Listen and check. Practise with a partner. Pay attention to stress and intonation.

A class survey

Find out about the students in your class.

2 Read the class survey and answer the questions about you. Add two more questions.

3 Work with a partner. Ask and answer the questions in the survey. Give short answers in your replies and add some information.

> Are you interested in any sports?

> Yes, I am. I often go skiing in winter and I like playing tennis.

4 Tell the class about each other.

> Milo's interested in two sports – skiing and tennis. He often ...

5 What can you say about your class?

> Nearly everyone is interested in at least one sport. Most of the boys love football. Some of us like skiing.

Check it

6 There is one mistake in each sentence. Find it and correct it.

1 Rae comes from Canada and he speak French and English.
2 Which subjects Susan is studying at university?
3 'Do you like football?' 'Yes, I like.'
4 Did you watched the match last night?
5 What does your parents do at the weekend?
6 I think is going to rain.
7 What was you talking to the teacher about?
8 I don't think John's arrive yet.

CLASS SURVEY

1 ARE YOU INTERESTED IN ANY SPORTS?

2 HAVE YOU GOT A PET?

3 DOES MUSIC PLAY AN IMPORTANT PART IN YOUR LIFE?

4 DO YOU USE THE INTERNET MUCH?

5 DOES ANYONE IN YOUR FAMILY SMOKE?

6 DID YOU STUDY ENGLISH IN PRIMARY SCHOOL?

7 HAVE YOU EVER BEEN TO ENGLAND?

8 ARE YOU STUDYING ANY OTHER FOREIGN LANGUAGES?

9 ....

10 ....

READING AND SPEAKING
Worlds apart

1 Discuss these questions about your family.
- Who is in your immediate family?
- Name some of your extended family.
- Who are you close to?
- Who do you live with now?
- Who did you grow up with?

2 Read the PROFILES of two families from very different parts of the world. Who is in the family? Where do they come from? What do you know about their countries?

3 Divide into two groups.

> **Group A** Read about the **Kamau family** from Kenya.

> **Group B** Read about the **Qu family** from China.

4 In your groups answer these questions about the Kamaus or the Qus.
1. Where do they live? What are their homes like?
2. How long have they lived there?
3. What jobs do the parents do? Do they earn much money?
4. What do they spend their money on?
5. What do you learn about the children? What do they do?
6. How long have the parents known each other?
7. What do you learn about other members of the family?
8. What hopes and ambitions do the parents have for themselves and their children?

5 Work with a partner from the other group. Compare and swap information about the families and their mottos.
1. What similarities and differences can you find?
2. How have their lives changed over the years?
3. What regrets or worries do they have now?

WELCOME TO
The Kamaus from KENYA
PROFILE

FATHER: Boniface Kigotho Kamau, 35
MOTHER: Pauline Wanjiku, approximately 29 (exact age unknown)
DAUGHTER: Joyce Muthoni, 8
DAUGHTER: Sharon Wanjiru, 16 months

Boniface and his wife, Pauline, live in Ongata Rongai, a small town near the capital, Nairobi. They have two daughters: Joyce, who is in her third year of school, and 16-month-old Sharon.

Their home is a two-bedroom apartment, one of 20 in a single-storey block. Boniface works as a taxi driver at the international airport in Nairobi. Each morning he leaves home at 4.30am in his white Toyota – cracked windscreen, 200,000 miles on the clock – and is back by 10pm. On a good day he finds two clients. In a typical month he takes home about £140.

'It's a hard job but I like it,' he says. 'I meet new people, so I get some experience of the world – even though I have never been outside Kenya.'

Pauline is a dressmaker but isn't working at the moment. She stays at home to look after the kids. The weekend is often the only time Boniface sees Joyce and Sharon. Boniface and Pauline met in 1994: 'We liked each other immediately,' says Boniface. 'I didn't want a woman from the city so when I learned that Pauline was from the country, I was pleased.'

They married in 1995 and at first they lived in a slum, and often didn't have a lot to eat, just sukuma wiki (a green vegetable). Then, in 1996, Boniface won £60 in a cycle race. The money helped them move house to a better area and paid for driving lessons so that Boniface could become a taxi driver.

His salary doesn't go far. Rent is £30 a month, and he gives the same amount to his parents, who don't work. Also, as the most successful of six brothers and sisters, Boniface is expected to help their families too. He says, 'I am always so stressed about money.' Joyce's school fees cost another £25 a month.

'We are trying to give our children the best education,' says Pauline, who, like her husband, never finished school. 'Joyce wants to be a doctor.'

Next year, Sharon is going to preschool, so Pauline will have more time to start her own dressmaking business. By then, the family might have a new home. 'This apartment is not a good place to raise a family,' says Boniface. 'The toilets are communal – one for every four families.' Boniface plans to build a three-bedroom house in the suburbs of Nairobi.

THE FAMILY ARE HAPPIEST WHEN they have a bit of spare money: Boniface takes them to see the wild animals at Nairobi National Park.
FAMILY MOTTO Try to do your best at all times.

OUR WORLD

The Qus from Beijing, CHINA

PROFILE

FATHER: Qu Wansheng, 44
MOTHER: Liu Guifang, 43
DAUGHTER: Chen, 17
GRANDFATHER: (Qu's father) Huanjun, 84

Qu and Liu have known each other since childhood. The most noticeable change in China since then is the size of families. Qu was the youngest of six. Liu grew up as one of five children. But they have only one daughter.

Unlike many Chinese parents, Qu and Liu are happy to have a girl. However, like most parents in China, they put the needs of their only child, Chen, first. She is trying for a place at the prestigious Beijing University. Qu, a propaganda officer at the municipal services bureau, and Liu, who works at the No. 3 computer factory, are saving every last yuan for their daughter's education.

The family have lived in their house in central Beijing for 70 years. It is in one of the capital's ancient Hutong alleyways. These are known for their close-knit families and warm hospitality. The elderly sit outside and chat. People wander to the shops in their pyjamas. It is a way of life cherished by Qu, but he can see that this relaxed routine is increasingly out of step with a nation experiencing one of the most amazingly quick changes in human history.

'We are not in a hurry to get rich,' says Qu. 'I don't want to rush around trying to make money – I am not a machine. I put my family first.'

Tens of thousands of alleyways have been knocked down in the past few years, and their house is said to be next for demolition. And when the old communities go, the traditional family structure, in which children look after their elderly parents at home, goes too.

But for now, the Qus keep the old ways. The grandfather, Qu Huanjun, 84 and frail, is the centre of the family. 'My father lives here so this is the headquarters of the family,' says his son. 'My brothers and their families come to visit most weekends. We are very close.'

They are sad that their daughter has grown up alone because the one-child policy forbids them from having any more. 'Our daughter is lonely,' says Liu. 'I always wanted to have two children.'

Qu and Liu are proud of their daughter. Chen is bright and well-balanced. She wants to study archaeology. 'University will cost a great deal of money,' says her father. 'So we try to live frugally and save for our daughter.'

THE FAMILY ARE HAPPIEST WHEN they are all together in the evening.
FAMILY MOTTO Save money, live simply, care for your friends, tell the truth.

Vocabulary work

6 Find the six highlighted words in your text. Work out the meanings from the contexts.

Match the words to the meanings in the chart.

The Kamaus
1 someone who makes clothes
2 with only one floor
3 an old house in bad condition
4 shared by a group of people
5 broken
6 worried

The Qus
1 loved and treasured
2 weak and unhealthy
3 narrow lanes between buildings
4 knocking down buildings
5 close and caring
6 economically

7 Work with a partner from the other group. Teach them your words.

What do you think?

- In what ways are these families typical of their country?
- What is a typical family in your country? Is there such a thing?
- Is your family typical? Why/Why not?

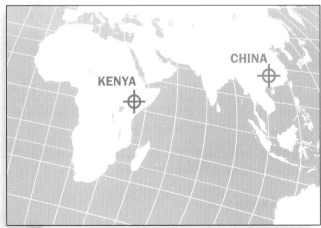

KENYA

CHINA

LISTENING AND SPEAKING

A world in one family

1 Do you know anyone who has married someone of another nationality? Do they have any children? Tell the class.

2 Look at the photo of the family. There are *three* nationalities in the family. How can this be?

Xabier Ana Teo James

3 **T 1.7** Listen to Xabier talking about his family. Read and answer the questions. <u>Underline</u> any you cannot answer.

1 What nationality are Xabier and his parents, Ana and Teo? Which city do they live in?

2 How did Xabier's parents meet? Give details. Why did they decide to live in England?

3 When and why did Xabier first notice his nationality?

4 Why weren't Xabier and James bilingual as children?

5 How many times has Xabier been to Bolivia? How old was he? How many times has James been?

6 What contact does he have with his mother's family? How long did they stay in Spain every summer?

7 What is Xabier studying? What is James going to study?

8 What is Xabier hoping to do in the future? Where is he planning to live?

9 What is James doing at the moment? What's he going to do?

10 What does Ana think are the pros and cons of bringing up a family in another country?

4 **T 1.8** Now listen to Xabier's mother, Ana. Answer the questions that you <u>underlined</u> in exercise 3.

What do you think?

• What are the pros and cons of bringing up a family in another country? Make two lists.

    + **You get the best from two cultures**   – **You don't feel completely at home in either of them**

• Discuss your lists as a class.

VOCABULARY
What's in a word?

These exercises will help you to think about how you learn vocabulary.

Meaning

1 These sentences all contain the nonsense word *uggy*. Is *uggy* used as a **verb**, an **adjective**, a **noun**, or an **adverb**?

1 My grandmother's very old and *uggy* now so she can't get out much.

2 She gave me my grandfather's gold watch. I'll *uggy* it forever.

3 The poor people lived crowded together in *uggies* in the old part of the city.

4 They can't afford to buy meat and fish. They live very *uggily* on rice and potatoes.

Can you guess what *uggy* means in the four sentences?

Which real English word goes into each sentence?

• cherish • frail • slums • frugally

Pronunciation

2 Say these words aloud. <u>Underline</u> the word with the different vowel sound.

1 /əʊ/ or /ʌ/ rose goes does toes

2 /iː/ or /eɪ/ meat beat great street

3 /eɪ/ or /e/ paid made played said

4 /ʌ/ or /əʊ/ done phone son won

T 1.9 Listen and check.

▶▶ **Phonetic symbols p159**

3 Say these words aloud. Which syllable is stressed?

mother enjoy apartment holiday **population**

T 1.10 Listen and check.

Word formation

4 Complete the word *act* in the sentences using the suffixes from the box.

-ress -ion -ing ~~-ive~~ -ivities

1 My grandfather is 84, but he's still very act**ive** .
2 My sister's an act_____. She's often on TV.
3 Act_____ is not always a well-paid job.
4 This is not a time to do nothing. It is a time for act_____.
5 We do a lot of act_____ in class to learn English.

Words that go together

5 Match a word in **A** with a line in **B**.

A	B
cosmopolitan	carelessly
well-paid	city
close-knit	in love
drive	a race
fall	family
win	job

Keeping vocabulary records

6 Discuss how you can keep vocabulary records.

- Do you have a special notebook or do you record your vocabulary electronically?
- Do you write a sentence with the new word?
- Do you write the translation? What about pronunciation?

> **📌 My notes**
>
> **records** /ˈrekɔːdz/ *noun*
> a written note of something
> - *I keep vocabulary records.*
>
> Translation = apuntes   [Remove note]
>
> **record** /rɪˈkɔːd/ *verb*
> to write down or keep information electronically
> - *I record my vocabulary electronically.*
>
> Translation = apuntar   [Remove note]

▶▶ **WRITING** AN INFORMAL LETTER *p103*

EVERYDAY ENGLISH
Everyday situations

1 Work with a partner. Where could you hear the following lines of conversation? Who is talking to who?

1 I need to make an appointment. It's quite urgent. I've lost a filling.
2 A medium latte and a muffin, please.
3 I can't make the meeting. I'm stuck in traffic.
4 Can you put in your PIN number and press 'Enter'?
5 Sparkling or still? And do you want ice and lemon in it?
6 I don't think you've met Greg. He's joining us from our New York office.
7 How many bags are you checking in?
8 The lift's on your right. Would you like someone to help you with your luggage?
9 Please hold. Your call *is* important to us. All our operators are busy at the moment, but one of them will be with you shortly *(music)* …
10 There are still tickets for the 5.45 performance but the 8.45 performance is sold out, I'm afraid.

2 Match a line from exercise 1 with a reply.

a 7 Just the one.
b ☐ Never mind. We'll start without you and brief you later.
c ☐ Hello. Good to meet you. I've heard a lot about you.
d ☐ No, thank you. I'll manage.
e ☐ That's fine. We'll have two, please, one adult, one child.
f ☐ Have here or take away?
g ☐ Oh no! I can't remember my number for this card. Oh what is it?
h ☐ If I have to listen to that again, I'll go mad!
i ☐ Sparkling, please. Ice but no lemon.
j ☐ We have a cancellation this afternoon. 2.45 if that's OK?

T 1.11 Listen and check. How does each conversation end?

3 Listen again. Pay attention to the stress and intonation. Practise some of the conversations with your partner.

Roleplay

4 Work with a partner. Turn to p147 and act out the situations.
T 1.12 Listen and compare.

2 The working week

Present tenses • Passive • Free time activities • Making small talk

Blue Monday, how I hate Blue Monday

STARTER

T 2.1 Listen to a song called *Blue Monday*.

- What is the singer's favourite day of the week?
- What's wrong with the other days?
- Which days are OK?

MY FAVOURITE DAY OF THE WEEK
Present tenses – states and activities

1 Look at the photos.
What do the people do? What are they doing?
In pairs, ask and answer questions.

What does Vicky do?   *She's a schoolgirl.*
What's she doing?   *She's doing her homework.*

2 **T 2.2** Listen to them talking about their
favourite day of the week. What is it? Why?

Vicky's favourite day of the week is . . . because she . . .

3 Listen again and complete the sentences.

1 I _____ with my parents during
term-time.
2 I _____ day today.
3 … it _____ work at all. Time
_____ by.
4 The restaurant _____ redecorated at
the moment …
5 I _____ because it's challenging, but I
_____ surfing.
6 The boards _____ in South Africa.
7 We rarely _____ at the weekend or
Christmas Day …
8 Now we're lambing, so we _____, either.

What else can you remember about each person?

Vicky likes being with her friends all the time.

4 Work with a partner. What is your favourite and
least favourite day of the week? Why?

Vicky

Terry

Dave

Jenny and Mike

1 What are the tenses in these sentences? Why are they used?

I **have** two lessons on a Monday.
I'**m having** a bad day today.

Find more examples, active and passive, in T2.2 on p119.

2 Which of these verb forms is right? Why is the other wrong?

| I **like** | my job. | I **know** | we're very lucky. |
| I'**m liking** | | I'**m knowing** | |

Some verbs are rarely used in continuous tenses. These are called state verbs. Underline the five state verbs in the box.

love understand work want enjoy cost need learn

3 Adverbs of frequency (*always*, *never*) answer the question *How often?* Find examples in T2.2 on p119.

▶▶ Grammar Reference 2.1–2.4 p134–5

PRACTICE

Questions and answers

1 Read about Dave, the police officer from p14. Which question goes with which paragraph?

How often do you go surfing?	What do you think of your job?
~~What's your background?~~	Do you have a business?
Why do you like surfing?	What hours do you work?
What's your favourite day of the week?	

T 2.3 Listen and check.

2 Complete the questions about Dave. Then ask and answer them with a partner.

Has he got any children?   Yes, two.

1 Has ... any children?
2 How often ... them?
3 Why ... morning shift?
4 How many hours ...?
5 What ... like about his job?
6 What ... think ... while ... surfing?
7 Where ... next month?
8 ... business doing well?
9 What ... on Sunday evenings?

T 2.4 Listen and check.

Talking about you

3 Make sentences about *you* using the prompts in the box.

I visit friends as often as I can.

... as often as I can.	... once a fortnight.
... eight hours a day.	... one evening a week.
... when I'm on holiday.	... twice a year.
... on a Sunday.	I hardly ever ...
I always ...	... whenever I'm not working.

4 Talk to a partner about you. Tell the class about your partner.

Dave Telford police officer and surfer

1 **What's your background?**

I'm 46, and I'm divorced. I have two kids, who I see once a fortnight. I live in Devon, in the south-west of England. I'm a police officer. I've been in the police force for over twenty years. I love my job, but my passion is surfing.

2

I work different shifts. The morning shift starts at 5.00, and I can't stand that because I have to get up at 4.30. My favourite shift is 2.00 in the afternoon till midnight because I get home about 12.30. What's good is that I work ten hours a day for four days, then have three days off.

3

My job is extremely busy and very hard. But I like it because it's challenging, and I never know what's going to happen. I like working in a team. We look after each other and work together.

4

My work is very stressful, so I surf to get away from it all. It's just me and the sea, and my mind switches off. I concentrate so hard on what I'm doing that I don't think about anything else.

5

I go surfing whenever I'm not working. Sometimes I'm on the beach before 7.00 in the morning. I go all over the world surfing. Next month I'm going to Costa Rica, and in the autumn I'm going to Thailand.

6

I've got a surf school. I teach all ages, from kids to pensioners. The business is doing well. I'm also opening two shops that sell surfboards. The boards are made in South Africa. They're the best.

7

I like Sundays best of all. I work as a lifeguard all day, then around 6.00 me and my mates barbecue some fish and have a few beers. Fantastic! I've been all round the world, but when I look around me, I think there's nowhere else I'd rather be.

Simple and continuous

1 `T 2.5` Listen to two people talking about who's who in *The Office*. What are their names? What are their jobs?

d	Simon	**Accountant**
☐	Edward	*Human Resources (HR) Manager*
☐	Anna	Managing Director (MD)
☐	Jenny	**Personal Assistant (PA)**
☐	Matthew	Information Technology (IT) Manager
☐	Christina	*Sales Director*

2 What are the people doing? What are they wearing?

Simon's sitting at the top of the table reading something. He's wearing a jumper.

`T 2.5` Listen again. What comment is made about each person?

Simon shouts a lot, but he listens as well.

3 Match a job from exercise 1 with a job description and a current project.

The MD is responsible for running the whole company. Currently, he is . . .

Job description	Current project
is responsible for running the whole company	buying new hardware
makes appointments and arrangements	*making bookings for a conference*
negotiates prices and contracts	**visiting new customers in China**
runs an IT support team	recruiting new staff
is in charge of budget and cash flow	*discussing plans and targets with the Board*
looks after employees	preparing a financial report

4 Work with a partner. Read the conversation aloud.

A What's your job?
B I'm a Human Resources Manager.
A So what do you do exactly?
B I look after the employees and their training.
A And what are you working on at the moment?
B I'm recruiting and interviewing. We're trying to find new staff for our office in Paris.

5 Make similar conversations using the jobs in exercise 1. Choose another job, for example, film director, journalist …

Project

Interview someone you know about his/her job. Tell the class about this person.

I talked to …, who's a … He …, and he starts work at … He has to … He likes his job because … On his days off he …

THE OFFICE

State and activity verbs

6 Are these sentences right (✓) or wrong (✗)? Correct the wrong sentences.

1 I'm not wanting an ice-cream.
2 Are you understanding what I'm saying?
3 I'm enjoying the course. It's great.
4 I'm thinking you're really nice.
5 What are you thinking about?
6 I'm not believing you. You're telling lies.
7 I'm knowing you're not agreeing with me.
8 She's having a lot of money.

Active and passive

7 Read the statistics. Choose the correct form, active or passive. Do any of the statistics surprise you?

STATISTICS ABOUT JOBS AND MONEY IN THE UK

1 Nearly half the population (29m) **involve / are involved** in some form of employment.

2 20% of the workforce **employed / are employed** by the state.

3 The average worker **pays / is paid** £27,000 a year.

4 The average worker **pays / is paid** £250,000 in tax in his or her lifetime.

5 Women **earn / are earned** on average 17% less than men for full-time work.

6 Children **give / are given** on average £9 a week pocket money.

7 The average household **spends / is spent** £70 per week on transport.

8 75% of British households **own / are owned** a car.

▶▶ **Grammar Reference 2.5–2.6 p135**

8 Put the verbs in the present passive, simple or continuous.

1 'Can I help you?' 'I**'m being served** (serve), thank you.'

2 A lot of manufactured goods _____ (make) in Asia.

3 'Why are you getting the bus?' 'My car _____ (service).'

4 Nearly 50% of the food we buy _____ (import).

5 The banking industry in the UK _____ (situate) in London.

6 _____ service _____ (include) in the bill?

7 The hotel is closed while the bedrooms _____ (modernize).

8 Footballers _____ (pay) far too much money.

LISTENING AND SPEAKING
Who earns how much?

1 Work with a partner. Look at the chart. Discuss which job you think goes with which salary.

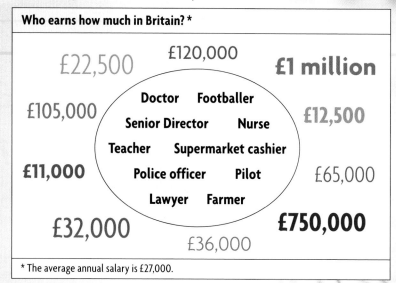

Who earns how much in Britain? *

£22,500   £120,000   **£1 million**

£105,000   £12,500

£11,000

Doctor   Footballer
Senior Director   Nurse
Teacher   Supermarket cashier
Police officer   Pilot
Lawyer   Farmer

£65,000

£32,000   **£750,000**

£36,000

* The average annual salary is £27,000.

2 You are going to hear two people discussing the chart.

T 2.6 Listen to **Part 1**. Answer the questions.

1 Which jobs do they discuss? Which salaries do they agree on?

2 Complete the sentences.
They think a doctor earns either £_____ or £_____.
They think either a _____ or a _____ earns £750,000.
They think a _____ earns about £65,000.

3 What comment do they make about … ?
• doctors   • footballers   • senior directors   • pilots

3 **T 2.7** Listen to **Part 2**. Answer the questions.

1 Who do they think are the lowest earners?
2 How much do they think farmers earn?
3 Do they agree about a teacher's and a police officer's salary?
4 What is the woman's final point?

SPOKEN ENGLISH   Giving opinions

1 Notice the ways of expressing an opinion.
  I reckon …   I'd say …   I suppose …
Find three more in T2.6 and T2.7 on p120.

2 Are these ways of agreeing or disagreeing?
  I think so too.   Definitely.   I know what you mean, but …
  I'm not so sure.   Actually, …   Absolutely.

3 What do we mean when we say … ?
  Could be.   Maybe, maybe not.   Possibly.

4 Discuss the salary chart again using some of these expressions.

---

4 Work in small groups. Turn to p147. Which salaries do you think are unfair? Are any surprising?

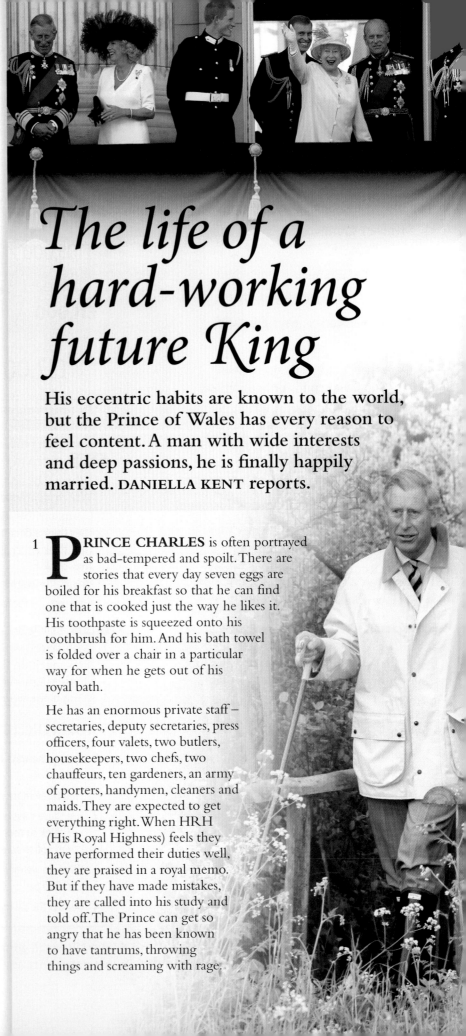

READING AND SPEAKING
Charles, Prince of Wales

1 What are the names of the people on the balcony? What is the relationship between them?

2 Work with a partner. Write down what you know about Prince Charles. Compare your ideas as a class.

He's about 60.
He's heir to the British throne.

3 What do you think occupies most of his time? Write a number 0–5 next to each activity, 0 = not at all, 5 = a lot.

☐ earning a living
☐ hunting
☐ entertaining
☐ travelling
☐ skiing
☐ performing royal duties
☐ being with his family

4 Read the article. Answer the questions after each part.

Part 1
1 What gives you the impression that Charles is extremely wealthy?
2 What happens to his staff if they do well? What happens if they don't?

Part 2
3 What is the routine when he entertains at Highgrove and Sandringham?
4 What is the private side of Prince Charles?

Part 3
5 What are some of his public duties?
6 What good deeds does he do?

Part 4
7 'Prince Charles has everything'. What does he have? What doesn't he have?
8 What is Duchy Originals? What is happening to it? What does it sell?
9 What title will Camilla have when Charles is King?
10 In what different ways is Charles referred to?
future King   Prince of Wales . . .

The life of a hard-working future King

His eccentric habits are known to the world, but the Prince of Wales has every reason to feel content. A man with wide interests and deep passions, he is finally happily married. DANIELLA KENT reports.

1 **P**RINCE CHARLES is often portrayed as bad-tempered and spoilt. There are stories that every day seven eggs are boiled for his breakfast so that he can find one that is cooked just the way he likes it. His toothpaste is squeezed onto his toothbrush for him. And his bath towel is folded over a chair in a particular way for when he gets out of his royal bath.

He has an enormous private staff – secretaries, deputy secretaries, press officers, four valets, two butlers, housekeepers, two chefs, two chauffeurs, ten gardeners, an army of porters, handymen, cleaners and maids. They are expected to get everything right. When HRH (His Royal Highness) feels they have performed their duties well, they are praised in a royal memo. But if they have made mistakes, they are called into his study and told off. The Prince can get so angry that he has been known to have tantrums, throwing things and screaming with rage.

The private and public man

2 Charles is eccentric, and he admits it. He talks to trees and plants. He wants to save wildlife, but enjoys hunting, shooting, and fishing. He dresses for dinner, even if he's eating alone. He's a great socializer. Poets, artists, writers, broadcasters, politicians, actors and singers all eat at his table. Arriving at Highgrove, his family home, on a Saturday afternoon in time for a stiff Martini, guests are entertained in the height of luxury. They are then sent on their way before lunch on Sunday, having been shown round his beautifully-kept gardens.

The Prince also entertains extravagantly at Sandringham, one of the Queen's homes, at least twice a year. There are picnic lunches on the beach, expeditions to local churches, and lavish dinners with organic food from Highgrove. Conversation is lively, but the heir to the throne has to be careful what he says, because he knows only too well that anything he says in private may be repeated in public.

The future monarch that we don't see is a man of great humour, who cares passionately about the state of the British nation, and is devoted to his two children, William and Harry. He is madly in love with 'his darling wife', which is how he refers to Camilla in public.

A dutiful life

3 Together Charles and Camilla perform royal duties, both at home and abroad. He attends over 500 public engagements a year. He visits hospitals, youth groups, performing artists, charities, and business conferences. He hosts receptions to welcome visiting heads of state and VIPs. He travels abroad extensively, as an ambassador to the United Kingdom, representing trade and industry. He works hard to promote greater understanding between different religions. He is also President of the Prince's Charities, which are active in promoting education, business, the environment, the arts, and opportunities for young people. The group raises over £110 million annually.

Camilla shares Charles' passion for hunting, and also his interest in conservation of towns and countryside. The one thing she leaves to Charles is skiing. She prefers to stay at home when he makes his annual trip to Klosters in Switzerland.

Everything except the top job

4 Since his second marriage, Prince Charles has everything he wants except, as Diana (who was killed in a car accident in 1997) used to call it, 'the top job'. Yet despite not being on the throne, he has worked hard to accomplish so much. He is concerned about the state of the country he loves, and shows his frustration that governments do little to tackle those problems about which he feels so strongly.

The Prince of Wales has his own food company, Duchy Originals. It originally sold biscuits, but is now expanding to become one of Britain's best-known and most successful organic brands, with over 200 different products, including food, drinks, and hair and body care products.

Charles, well-intentioned, hard-working, conservative and old-fashioned, continues to do his duty as he sees it. But he is no longer alone. One day he will be King, and his darling Camilla will be HRH The Princess Consort.

5 Now you have read the article, have you changed your mind about any of your answers in exercise 3?

Vocabulary work

Which of these adjectives are positive and which are negative?

hard-working – positive

~~hard-working~~	bad-tempered
spoilt eccentric	old-fashioned
sociable cautious	passionate
frustrated successful	well-intentioned

Give an example of Charles' life or behaviour that illustrates each adjective.

hard-working – He performs a lot of royal duties, and does charity work.

Discussion

- What do you know about the attitude of the British people to their royal family?
- What countries do you know that have a royal family? Are the members of the family popular? What do they do?

VOCABULARY AND SPEAKING
Free time activities

1 What do you do when you aren't working? Make a list of what you do in your free time.

go on the Net   *play golf*   *go for a run*

Who do you do it with? Where? Tell the class.

2 What activities can you see in the photos? Which of them …?

- do you do alone, or with another person
- do you do at home, or in a special place
- needs special clothes or equipment

3 Which of these things go with the activities?

a drill	a recipe
planting	serving an ace
the sales	a sleeping bag
a racket	a screwdriver
a concert	a bargain
zoom	keeping fit
sweating	meditating
wearing a helmet	a torch
sketching	weeding

4 Complete the diagram about cooking with words from the box.

boiling	to chop
to mix	a casserole dish
herbs and spices	minced meat
an oven	baking
roasting	a food processor
olive oil	to weigh

5 Choose an activity that you are interested in. Draw a similar diagram and choose the categories. Fill it in.

6 **T 2.8** Listen to John talking about his hobby. Make notes under these headings.

- Favourite hobby
- Where and when he does it
- Clothes and equipment
- What he likes about it
- The best bit

7 Work in small groups. Use the headings from exercise 6 and your diagram to talk about what you like doing in your free time.

equipment
a saucepan
_____
_____
_____

ingredients
eggs
_____
_____
_____

food preparation
to peel
_____
_____
_____

cooking

ways of cooking
frying
_____
_____
_____

EVERYDAY ENGLISH
Making small talk

1 When do we make small talk? Who with? What about?

2 **T 2.9** Read and listen to the conversation between Ann and Lars. Where are they? What is Lars doing there?

Ann So what do you think of Liverpool, Lars?

Lars *really interesting/old city/lovely buildings/people so friendly*
It's really interesting. Liverpool's such an old city, isn't it? There are some lovely buildings, and the people are so friendly!

Ann Yes, they are, aren't they? When did you get here?

Lars *… ago/plane from Oslo/a bit late/didn't matter*

Ann Oh, good. Where are you staying in Liverpool?

Lars *… Grand Hotel/convenient for the office/room not very big/OK*

Ann What a pity! Never mind. Where are you from?

Lars *Norway/born in Bergen/live in a suburb of Oslo/pretty/sea*

Ann Really? It sounds beautiful. Your English is very good. Where did you learn it?

Lars *… very kind/a lot of mistakes/school for years/been to England quite a few times*

Ann Oh, have you? How interesting! And what are you doing here in Liverpool, Lars?

Lars *… attending a conference/here for five days/home on the 17th*

Ann Oh, so soon! And have you managed to get around our city yet?

Lars *… not seen very much/a walk along the riverside/taken a ferry across the Mersey/ not seen the Beatles' Exhibition yet*

Ann Well, I hope you enjoy it. Don't work too hard!

Lars *… try to enjoy myself/bye/nice to talk*

3 What information does Lars add to keep the conversation going? How does Ann show she's interested? Find examples.

4 Work with a partner. Use the prompts to practise the conversation. **T 2.9** Listen again. How well did you do?

SPOKEN ENGLISH Softening a negative comment

1 In conversation, we sometimes don't want to sound too negative. We soften negative comments.

We were late landing.	*We were **a bit** late landing.*
My room is tiny.	*My room **isn't very big**, but it's OK.*

2 Make these comments softer. Use the words in brackets.

1 It's expensive. *(bit)*   4 They're rude. *(friendly)*
2 It's hard. *(quite)*   5 I earn very little. *(much)*
3 It's cold. *(warm)*   6 There's nothing to do. *(very much)*

---

5 **T 2.10** Listen to the questions and answer them. Make a comment and add some information. Add a question if you can.

> **Who do you work for?**

> **Siemens. I've been with them for four years. They're a good company. How about you?**

T 2.11 Listen and compare.

6 You are abroad on a business trip. Invent a name and a background for yourself.

You are at a social event. Stand up and socialize! Ask and answer questions.

▶▶ **WRITING** LETTERS AND EMAILS *p104*

3 Good times, bad times

Past tenses • Spelling and pronunciation • Giving opinions

STARTER

Play the *Fortunately, Unfortunately* game around the class.

Start: **I woke up very early this morning.**

Student A   **Fortunately, it was a lovely day.**
Student B   **Unfortunately, I had to go to school.**

VINCENT VAN GOGH

Past tenses and *used to*

1 Look at the pictures by the painter, Vincent Van Gogh. What do you know about him? Was he happy? Was he successful?

2 Read the notes below about Vincent Van Gogh. Complete the questions about his life.

Vincent Van Gogh
1853–1890

Vincent Van Gogh was born in 1853. When he was a young man he worked in London and Paris, but he was dismissed.

He tried to commit suicide.

In Paris, Vincent met many famous artists while he was ✹ .

In 1888 he moved to Arles in the south of France. Another famous painter came to live with him. He was an old friend.

One evening Van Gogh left the house carrying a ✹ . He cut off part of his ear.

After this, he moved into an asylum. Many of his most famous paintings were completed here.

In 1890, while he was ✹ , he shot himself in the chest. Two days later he died. He was buried.

When he died, he had no money.

1 Where **was he born**?
2 What . . . job?
3 Why . . . ?
4 Why . . . ?
5 Which . . . ?
6 What . . . when he met them?
7 Who . . . ?
8 Where . . . first meet?
9 What . . . ?
10 Why . . . ?

11 Which . . .
12 What . . . doing . . . ?
13 Why . . . ?
14 Where . . . ?
15 Why didn't . . . ?

T 3.1 Listen and check the questions.

The Red Vineyard was sold for 400 francs in 1890.

Self-Portrait without a Beard was sold for $71.5 million in 1998.

Irises was sold for $53.9 million in 1987.

3 Read the full text about Vincent Van Gogh. With a partner ask and answer the questions from exercise 2.

T 3.2 Listen and check.

Vincent

Vincent Van Gogh, the genius unrecognized in his own lifetime

Vincent Van Gogh was born in Brabant in the Netherlands in 1853. As a young man he worked as an art dealer in London and Paris. He was dismissed from this job because he had argued with customers about art.

In 1881 he tried to commit suicide. He was depressed because he had fallen in love with his cousin, but she had rejected him.

In 1886 he went to Paris to study art, and it was while he was studying that he met Degas, Pissarro, Seurat, Toulouse-Lautrec, Monet, and Renoir.

After two years in Paris, Van Gogh went to live in Arles in the south of France. His friend and fellow painter, Gauguin, who he had met in Paris, came to join him. The two men settled down in Arles, but there was a lot of tension between them. Vincent used to drink heavily, and they quarrelled fiercely, mainly about the nature of art.

One evening in December 1888, Van Gogh left the house carrying a razor blade. He'd been drinking, and he'd had an argument with Gauguin. He cut off part of his ear.

After this, he moved voluntarily into an asylum for the insane at St-Rémy-de-Provence. He used to wake up at six in the morning and go out to paint. It was here, in the last two years of his life, that many of his most famous paintings were completed. These included *Starry Night*, *Irises*, and *Self-Portrait without a Beard*.

In 1890 he left the warm south and moved to Auvers-sur-Oise. Here he continued working despite his growing depression. It was while he was painting outside that Vincent shot himself in the chest. Two days later, he died. He was buried in the cemetery in Auvers.

When Van Gogh died, he had no money because he'd only sold one of his paintings, *The Red Vineyard*, in his entire life. His sister-in-law took his collection to Holland, where his work was published. He was instantly recognized as a genius.

GRAMMAR SPOT

1 In these sentences, which verb form is . . . ?
Past Simple   Past Continuous   Past Simple passive

> He **worked** as an art dealer.
> He **was dismissed**.
> He **was studying** art.

Find more examples of the three verb forms in the text.

2 In this sentence, what happened first?

> He **was dismissed** because he **had argued** with customers.

had argued is an example of the Past Perfect tense. How is this tense formed? Find more examples in the text.

3 Look at the sentence.

> Vincent **used to** drink heavily.

Do you think this happened once or many times? Find another example of *used to* in the text.

▶▶ **Grammar Reference 3.1–3.7 p135–7**

Pronunciation

4 **T 3.3** Listen and repeat the weak forms and contracted forms.

/wəz/	/wəz/
What was he doing?	**He was studying.**
/wə/	/hɪd/
They were working …	**He'd had an argument.**
/ðeɪd/	/hɪd bɪn/
They'd met in Paris.	**He'd been drinking.**

5 Write the verbs from the box in the chart according to the pronunciation of *-ed*.

~~worked~~   dismissed   tried   rejected
quarrelled   moved   completed
continued   died   published   recognized

/t/	/d/	/ɪd/
worked		

T 3.4 Listen and check.

PRACTICE

I didn't do much

1 **T 3.5** Listen to four people saying what they did last night. Who said these lines? Write a number 1–4.

- [ ] I went for a drink with a couple of friends.
- [ ] We talked for a bit.
- [ ] I didn't do much.
- [ ] I got home about nine.
- [ ] I had an early night.
- [ ] I didn't get home till about midnight.
- [ ] I did some stuff on the computer.
- [ ] Quite a late night for me!

2 What did *you* do last night? Discuss in small groups.

Discussing grammar

3 Compare the use of tenses in these sentences. Say which tense is used and why.

1. It *rained* all day yesterday.
   It *was raining* when I woke up.
2. I *wore* a suit for my interview.
   She looked great. She *was wearing* a black top and tight jeans.
3. 'What *were* you *doing* when you lost your phone?'
   'Shopping.'
   'What *did* you *do* when you lost your phone?'
   'Bought a new one.'
4. When Bill arrived, | we *were having* lunch.
   | we *had* lunch.
   | we'd *had* lunch.
5. I got to the cinema. The film | *started*.
   | *had started*.
6. When I was a kid I *used to play* football with my dad.
   I *played* football with my kids last Saturday.

A newspaper story

4 Read the newspaper article. Put the verbs in brackets in the correct past tense, active or passive.
   T 3.6 Listen and check.

5 **T 3.7** Listen to a radio news item on the subject of the same accident. What do you learn that wasn't in the newspaper article?

Dictation

6 **T 3.8** You will hear a summary of the interview at dictation speed. Write it down. Compare with a partner.

SMASH!
Clumsy visitor destroys priceless vases By Tom Ball

A CLUMSY visitor to a British museum has destroyed a set of priceless 300-year-old Chinese vases after slipping on the stairs.

The three vases, which (1)_____ (produce) during the Qing dynasty in the 17th century, (2)_____ (stand) on the windowsill at the Fitzwilliam Museum in Cambridge for forty years. Last Thursday they (3)_____ (smash) into a million pieces. The vases, which (4)_____ (donate) in 1948, (5)_____ (be) the museum's best-known pieces.

The Fitzwilliam (6)_____ (decide) not to identify the man who (7)_____ (cause) the disaster. 'It was a most unfortunate and regrettable accident,' museum director Duncan Robinson said, 'but we are glad that the visitor (8)_____ seriously _____ (not injure).'

The photograph of the accident (9)_____ (take) by another visitor, Steve Baxter. 'We (10)_____ (watch) the man fall as if in slow motion. He (11)_____ (fly) through the air. The vases (12)_____ (explode) as though they (13)_____ (hit) by a bomb. The man (14)_____ (sit) there stunned in the middle of a pile of porcelain when the staff (15)_____ (arrive).'

The museum declined to say what the vases were worth.

VOCABULARY
Spelling and pronunciation

1 **T 3.9** Listen and repeat these words. What do they tell you about English spelling and pronunciation?

good /gʊd/   food /fuːd/   blood /blʌd/
road /rəʊd/   rode /rəʊd/   rowed /rəʊd/

Words that sound the same

2 **T 3.10** Listen and write the words you hear. What do they have in common? Compare with a partner. Did you write the same words?

3 Read these words aloud. Write another word with the same pronunciation.

1	male	_mail_	6	week _____
2	blew	_____	7	hole _____
3	piece	_____	8	pair _____
4	where	_____	9	allowed _____
5	caught	_____	10	weight _____

4 Write the correct spelling of the words in phonemic script.

1 /piːs/ _Peace_ is the opposite of /wɔː/_____.
2 I'm not /əlaʊd/_____ to /weə/_____ make-up.
3 I'd like a /peə/_____ of /bluː/_____ jeans, please.
4 I /wɔː/_____ the same socks for a /həʊl/_____ /wiːk/_____.
5 I had to /weɪt/_____ in the rain and I /kɔːt/_____ the /fluː/_____.

Spelling

5 Read these words aloud. Which two words rhyme?

1	(love)	move	(glove)
2	some	home	come
3	dear	fear	pear
4	lost	most	post
5	meat	cheat	great
6	boot	shoot	foot
7	eight	weight	height
8	blood	wood	flood
9	flower	power	lower

T 3.11 Listen and check.

6 These words have the same vowel sound but different spellings. Spell the words.

/uː/ t_oo_th   tr_u_th   j___ce   thr___
/ɔː/ c___t   d___n   w___   fl___
/ɜː/ ___th   w___ld   b___n   f___
/eə/ t___   f___   squ___   th___

Lost sounds

7 In some words we lose sounds.

chocolate   /tʃɒklət/ has two syllables, not three.
comfortable   /kʌmftəbl/ has three syllables, not four.

Read these words aloud. Cross out the lost sounds.

different   several
business   restaurant
marriage   interesting
vegetable   temperature
secretary

T 3.12 Listen and check.

8 Some words have silent letters. Cross out the silent letters in these pairs of words.

1	foreign	sign
2	climb	bomb
3	neighbour	weigh
4	honest	hour
5	knee	knock
6	psychology	psychiatrist

T 3.13 Listen and check.

The postman brought the male.

READING
A Shakespearean tragedy

1 What do you know about William Shakespeare?

2 Look at the list of characters in the story of *Romeo and Juliet*. What do you know about the story? How did people at that time decide who to marry? Who made the decision?

3 Read 1–6 in the story. Answer the questions.
1 Why did the Montagues and the Capulets hate each other?
2 Why wasn't it a good idea for Romeo to go to the Capulet's party?
3 What happened when Romeo and Juliet first met?
4 'Wherefore art thou Romeo?' (= *Why are you Romeo?*) Why was Juliet upset about Romeo's name?
5 How long had they known each other when they decided to get married?
6 Why did Friar Laurence agree to marry them?
7 Why did Romeo try to stop the fight?
8 Why was Juliet desperate?

4 Read 7–12 in the story. Answer the questions.
1 What couldn't Juliet tell her father?
2 What was the Friar's plan?
3 Which part of the plan worked?
4 What went wrong with the plan?
5 Why did Romeo kill himself?
6 Why did Juliet kill herself?
7 How did their families feel at the end?

5 **T 3.14** Listen to actors speaking Shakespeare's lines, and follow them in the story. Read the lines in more modern English on p148.

6 Retell the story using the pictures.

What do you think?

- Whose fault was the tragedy?
- In the play, Juliet was just thirteen. Do you think this is too young to fall in love?
- Shakespeare wrote comedies, tragedies, and history plays. What titles do you know? Do you know any of the stories?

▶▶ **WRITING** TELLING A STORY (1) *p105*

Romeo

The Montagues

Lord Montague

Romeo, son of Montague

Mercutio, Romeo's best friend

Peace! I hate the word As I hate hell, all Montagues and thee!

I Many years ago, in the ancient Italian city of Verona, there were two very rich but warring families, the Montagues and the Capulets. They had hated each other for so long that no one could remember how the feud had started. Fights often used to break out in the streets.

My heart's dear love is set on the fair daughter of rich Capulet.

...This alliance may so happy prove, to turn your households' rancour to pure love.

4 As dawn broke, Romeo raced to Friar Laurence and begged him to marry them. The Friar agreed, hoping this would uni the families. That afternoon, Juliet joined Romeo, and the lovers were wed. They parted, but planned to spend that night together.

O, think'st thou we shall ever meet again?

I doubt it not; and all these woes shall serve for sweet discourses in our times to come.

7 Next morning the lovers could hardly bear to part. When would they meet again?
More disaster was to come. Juliet learned that her father had agreed to give her in marriage to a nobleman, Paris. How could she tell her father she had already married Romeo?

Eyes, look your last. Arms, take your last embrace ...Here's to my love! O true Apothecary, thy drugs are quick. Thus with a kiss I die.

10 But Romeo never received the Friar's letter. Thinking that his beloved Juliet had died, he bought poison and went to the tomb. He saw his beautiful, lifeless Juliet. He would never leave her side. He kissed her, and drank the poison.

and Juliet *by William Shakespeare*

The Capulets

Benvolio, Romeo's cousin | Friar Laurence, a priest | The Prince | Paris, a nobleman suitor of Juliet | Juliet's nurse | Tybalt, Juliet's cousin | Juliet, daughter of Capulet | Lord Capulet

Did my heart love till now? For I ne'er saw true beauty till this night.

My only love sprung from my only hate, …

2 Lord Capulet was planning a celebration for his daughter, Juliet. Romeo, Lord Montague's son, went to the party uninvited. He saw Juliet and fell instantly in love! They touched hands. They talked. They kissed. Only then did they discover their families were enemies!

O Romeo, Romeo wherefore art thou Romeo? Deny thy father, and refuse thy name … What's Montague? … A rose by any other word would smell as sweet.

3 That night Juliet stood on her balcony and declared her love for Romeo. Romeo had climbed up a wall and was listening. They swore eternal love to each other, and promised to marry in secret the next day.

Thou wretched boy … shalt with him hence.

Now, Tybalt, … Mercutio's soul is … above our heads, either thou or I, or both, must go with him.

5 Returning to Verona, Romeo found his friends, Benvolio and Mercutio being attacked by Tybalt, Juliet's cousin. Romeo tried to stop the fight. He failed, and Mercutio was killed. Romeo had to take revenge! He fought Tybalt and killed him.

I'll find Romeo to comfort you …

O find him … and bid him come to take his last farewell.

6 The Prince, hearing of the deaths, banished Romeo from Verona. Poor Juliet! Her husband had killed her cousin, and now he was exiled. She was desperate. Her nurse brought Romeo to Juliet so they could be together one last time.

Take thou this vial, … and this liquor drink … no pulse … no breath shall testify thou livest … two and forty hours …

Give me! … Love give me strength.

8 Juliet ran to Friar Laurence for help. The Friar gave her a sleeping potion to make her appear dead for forty-two hours, so she couldn't marry Paris. The Friar would tell Romeo the plan, and he would arrive as she was waking up. They could then escape together.

O hateful day! Never was seen so black a day as this. O woeful day! …

Romeo, Romeo, Romeo! Here's drink — I drink to thee.

9 Juliet returned home and pretended to agree to the marriage. She took the drug. The next day, everyone thought she was dead. She was carried to the family tomb, from where, according to the Friar's plan, Romeo would rescue her.

What's here? A cup closed in my true love's hand? Poison, I see … I will kiss thy lips … some poison doth hang on them to make me die … Thy lips are warm! Oh happy dagger! Let me die!

11 Juliet woke up to see Romeo lying dead beside her. She wept and kissed him again and again, hoping that the poison on his lips would kill her too. Finally she took his dagger and, stabbing herself, fell dead upon her husband's body.

For never was a story of more woe than this of Juliet and her Romeo.

12 The families of the Montagues and the Capulets arrived at the tragic scene. They were overwhelmed with grief, and horrified at the pain that their families' hatred had caused. Thus they buried their feud, along with their precious children, Romeo and his sweet Juliet.

LISTENING AND SPEAKING
The first time I fell in love

1 What do you understand by these quotations?

> *'People ask what love is. If you have to ask, you don't know.'*

> *'Love is a kind of madness.'*

> *'Love is blind.'*

> *'When you're in love, 1 + 1 = everything, and 2 − 1 = nothing.'*

> *'Love is what is left when being in love has burned away.'*

> *'Love is the most beautiful of dreams and the worst of nightmares.'*

2 **T 3.15** Listen to three people talking about the first time they fell in love. Take notes and complete the chart.

	Sarah	Tommy	James
1 How old was he/she?			
2 Who did he/she fall in love with?			
3 Was it a pleasurable experience?			
4 Was the love reciprocated?			
5 How did it end?			

3 In groups, compare your answers. Listen again to check.

4 What are some of the effects of being in love that the people describe?
'He made me go all weak at the knees.'

What do you think?

- Psychologists say we fall in love with a person with whom we can form a whole, like *yin* and *yang* in Chinese philosophy. Do you agree?

- Who do we fall in love with? Someone like ourselves, or someone different? Do opposites attract?

- 'The course of true love never did run smooth.' (Shakespeare – *A Midsummer Night's Dream*)
  Think of couples, perhaps famous, perhaps not, who didn't have or haven't had an easy romance. What happened to them?

- What couples do you know who are well-suited? Why do they go well together?

EVERYDAY ENGLISH
Giving opinions

1 **T 3.16** Read and listen to the conversation. What is it about? Which two people agree with each other?

A So, what do you think of Meg's new boyfriend? He's really great, isn't he?

B Definitely! I think he's absolutely fantastic!

A Mmm. Me too. I just love the stories he tells.

B So do I. He's very funny. I really like his sense of humour.

A They get on so well together, don't they?

C Well, maybe. He's quite nice, but I don't think that he's the one for her.

B That's rubbish! They absolutely adore each other!

C Mmm. I'm not so sure.

B Come on! You're just jealous. You've always fancied her.

C Actually, that's not true at all. But I quite like her sister.

In groups of three, practise the conversation.

2 Listen again to the conversation. Answer the questions.

1 **A** and **B** agree with each other. What are their actual words?

2 **A** uses two question tags. Practise them.

He's really great, isn't he?
They get on so well together, don't they?

Is **A** *really* asking for information, or does she just want the others to agree with her?

3 Complete these question tags.

1 We had a great time in Paris, <u>didn't we</u>?

2 The weather was lovely, _____?

3 The French really love their food, _____?

4 It's a lovely day today, _____?

5 Alice and Tom are a really lovely couple, _____?

6 Tom earns so much money, _____?

7 They want to get married, _____?

T 3.17 Listen and check.

SPOKEN ENGLISH Making an opinion stronger

1 Adverbs like *very, really, just,* and *absolutely* help make an opinion stronger.

It's good. ⟶ It's **very** good. ⟶ It's **really** good.

It's bad! ⟶ It's **just** awful! ⟶ It's **absolutely** awful!

2 We can use an adverb to qualify an adjective or a verb.

He's **really great**, isn't he?

I **really don't like** his sense of humour.

Find more examples in the conversation in exercise 1.

---

4 Work in pairs to make these opinions stronger. Use a wide voice range to sound enthusiastic.

1 She's quite nice. **She's absolutely wonderful!**

2 The film was good. *just brilliant*

3 The hotel's all right. *really fabulous*

4 I like dark chocolate. *absolutely adore*

5 I quite like Peter. *really love*

6 The book wasn't very good. *absolutely awful*

7 I don't like noisy bars. *just can't stand*

T 3.18 Listen and repeat.

5 Write down some opinions on …

• the last film you saw
• something in today's news
• the weather
• the clothes that someone is wearing today
• what a celebrity is doing at the moment
• a programme on TV

6 In pairs, ask for and give opinions.

> I saw that new film last week.

> Oh! What did you think of it?

> Great! I really enjoyed it. The acting was just amazing!

4 Getting it right

Modal and related verbs • Phrasal verbs (1) • Polite requests and offers

STARTER

Look at the sentences.
Say them aloud as a class.

You	can must should have to	go.

1 Say the negative.
2 Say the question.
3 Say the 3rd person singular with *he*.
4 Which verb is different in form?

MODERN DILEMMAS
should/must/have to/be allowed to

1 Work in groups. *The Times* newspaper has a section called *Modern morals* where readers help other readers with problems. Read the problems in *Readers ask*. What advice would you give? Use these phrases:

   I think they should …   I don't think she should …   He must …

2 Read the lines from *Readers reply* on p31. Which lines do you think go with which problems?

   Read the full replies on p149. Do you agree with the advice?

3 Look again at *Readers ask* 1–7. Find the questions used to *ask for* advice. Find the verbs used in *Readers reply* a–g to *give* advice.

Modern morals

Readers ask

1 How should I deal with my difficult and disagreeable neighbour? He is in the habit of dumping his garden waste along the public footpath between our two houses.
Jim T. via email

2 Is it OK to greet people you don't know with a 'How are you?' In California (my home) it's considered friendly, but here in London some people react with a cold look. Should I be less friendly in my greetings?
Erica Fleckberg, London

3 My new PC automatically picks up wireless networks to gain access to the Internet. This includes the one belonging to my neighbour. Is it right for me to use it?
Richard Dalton, via email

4 My stepfather was disqualified for two years for drink-driving, but we have learnt that he still drives while under the influence of alcohol. Should we keep quiet or inform the police?
Stella Milne, Newcastle

5 I am a medical student. After I qualify in June, I have one month before my first job starts. My fiancée says that I am not allowed to claim unemployment benefit for this. I disagree, because I'll be unemployed. The dole is for all those who are out of work, isn't it? What do you think?
J. R. Collin, via email

6 Is it wrong for me to record CDs borrowed from my local library? I am not denying anyone the money, as I wouldn't buy the CD anyway.
Pete Rodriguez, via email

7 Is it ever permissible to lie to children? I lied to my two-year-old granddaughter to remove her from a fairground ride without a tantrum. I said: 'You must get off now because the man is going for his dinner.' She got down without a fuss. But I'm worried that if she remembers this, she won't trust me in future.
Barbara Hope, Perth, Australia

GRAMMAR SPOT

1 These sentences give advice. Which is the stronger advice?

You **should** check online.
You **must** tell your neighbour.

2 Which sentences express permission? Which express obligation?

I	can **am allowed to** **must** **have to**	go.

3 Complete the sentences with *have to*, *don't have to*, or *mustn't*.

Children _____ go to school.

You _____ ride your bike on the footpath.

People over 65 _____ go to work.

4 The past of these sentences is the same. What is it?

I must go.   I have to go.

▶▶ **Grammar Reference 4.1–4.5 p137–8**

Readers reply

a You must ring 'Crimestoppers' and report him. You don't have to give your name.

b I think you are allowed other benefits. You should check online.

c You don't have to be like the English just because you're in England.

d You've got to act with self-control. I don't think you should confront him.

e It's not only wrong, it's illegal. You are not allowed to do this.

f Not only should you lie sometimes, you often have to.

g You must tell your neighbour this. It's the only fair thing to do.

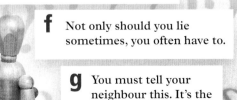

PRACTICE

Discussing grammar

1 Choose the correct verb to complete the sentences.

1 I don't get on with my boss. Do you think I *should / must* look for another job?
2 We're giving Tom a surprise birthday party. You *shouldn't / mustn't* tell him about it.
3 Please Dad, *can / must* I go to Tom's party? It'll be great.
4 You *should / have to* drive on the left in Britain.
5 Do you *must / have to* wear a uniform in your job?
6 Are you *can / allowed to* take mobile phones to school?
7 I *must / had to* go to bed early when I was a child.
8 You *mustn't / don't have to* go to England to learn English, but it's a good idea.

T 4.1   Listen and check.

Giving advice

2 **T 4.2**   Listen to three conversations. After each one discuss these questions.
1 What is the problem?
2 What is the advice?
3 Do you agree with it? Give *your* advice if it's different.

3 Listen again and complete the lines with the exact words.
1 I don't know if I _____ go or not.
2 They told her she _____ to have friends over while they were away.
3 Come on! You _____ come. It's a party.
4 Look. You _____ tell your mum and dad.
5 You _____ to smoke in here.
6 Do you think I _____ tell her to stop?
7 No, no, you _____ say anything.
8 I _____ say something.
9 I _____ go to the shops for my dad.
10 I think he _____ pay the fine.

Practise the conversations in T.4.2 on p122.

Rules present

1 Work with a partner. Read these British laws. Compare them with laws in your country. Are they the same?

In Britain . . .
1 you can get married when you're 16.   5 you mustn't use a mobile phone while driving.
2 you can't buy cigarettes until you're 18.   6 young people don't have to do military service.
3 you're not allowed to buy alcohol until you're 18.   7 there are lots of public places where you aren't allowed to smoke.
4 you have to wear seat belts in the front and back of a car.   8 many school children have to wear uniforms.

2 What other laws are there in your country? Think of places such as: motorways, parks, town centres, libraries, churches and schools. Tell the class.

Rules past

3 Read *Education in Victorian England*. Discuss with a partner which statements below are correct.

    1 In 1870 all children *had to / didn't have to* go to school.

    2 In 1880 children *had to / weren't allowed to* go to school until they were 10.

    3 In 1899 children *weren't allowed to / didn't have to* leave school until they were 12.

4 Read the *School Rules*. What do you think was true for Victorian schools? Complete them with *had to/didn't have to/weren't allowed to*.

5 **T 4.3** Listen to Jess talking about her great-grandmother's schooldays. What was the problem? Retell the story in your own words.

Do you know anything about your parents' or grandparents' schooldays? Tell the class.

Education in Victorian England
1832–1901

In Victorian England education played a very small role in most children's lives. In 1840 only 20% of children had any schooling at all. Then, in 1870 an Education Act was passed which said that children aged 5–10 should attend school. However, many parents preferred their children to work and earn money for their families. It was not until 1880 that all children had to attend school until the age of 10. Then, in 1899 the school leaving age was raised to 12.

School Rules 1880

1 Boys and girls __had to__ enter school through different doors.

2 Children _____ call teachers "Sir" or "Ma'am".

3 Children _____ ask questions.

4 Children _____ stand up to answer questions.

5 Children _____ do any sports.

6 Boys _____ do woodwork. Girls _____ do needlework.

7 Children _____ to use their left hand for writing.

8 Female teachers _____ get married.

LISTENING AND SPEAKING
Rules for life

1 **T 4.4** Listen to three people talking about their rules for life and make notes after each one.

Millie, 15
_____
_____
_____

Richard, 33
_____
_____
_____

Frank, 65
_____
_____
_____
_____

2 Discuss their ideas. Are they optimists or pessimists? Do you agree or disagree?

SPOKEN ENGLISH *have got to*

1 *Have got to* means the same as *have to* but is used more in spoken English. Look at these examples from Millie, Richard, and Frank.

They've got to employ bodyguards.
You've got to give meaning to life by what you do.
You've got to look for the good in people.

2 Complete the conversations with *'ve got to/'s got to*.

1 'Isn't your mum away at the moment?'
  'Yeah, so Dad _'s got to_ do all the cooking.'
2 'Where's my briefcase? I _____ go to work.'
  'It's where you left it. In the hall.'
3 'Mum, why can't I go out now?'
  'You _____ tidy your room first.'
4 'Won't you be late for work?'
  'Oh, goodness. Look at the time I _____ go now. Bye!'

T 4.5 Listen and check. What extra information do you hear in the answers? Practise the conversations.

▶▶ **Grammar Reference 4.2 p146**

Song – *I believe*

3 Look at the photo and read about Ian Dury. Who was he?

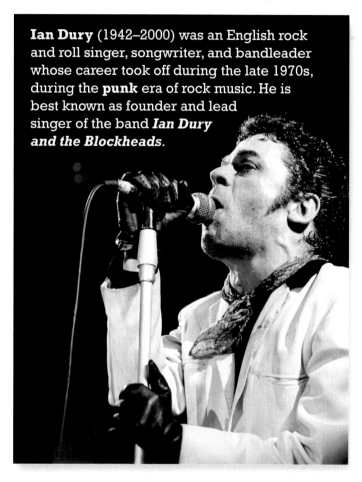

Ian Dury (1942–2000) was an English rock and roll singer, songwriter, and bandleader whose career took off during the late 1970s, during the **punk** era of rock music. He is best known as founder and lead singer of the band *Ian Dury and the Blockheads*.

4 **T 4.6** Listen to one of his songs – *I believe*. It expresses Ian's philosophy on life. Is he an optimist or a pessimist?

5 Work with a partner. Turn to p150. Read the song. Discuss which word best completes the lines.

6 **T 4.6** Listen again and check your answers. Which of the things 1–8 does he believe in?
1 Recycling rubbish.
2 Healthy outdoor activities.
3 Having lots to eat and drink.
4 Being truthful and kind.
5 Having strong opinions about everything.
6 Good manners.
7 Putting yourself first.
8 Peace not war is possible.

7 Which of the things in exercise 6 are important to you? Discuss as a class.

▶▶ **WRITING** A BIOGRAPHY *p106*

READING AND SPEAKING
Kids then and now

1 Close your eyes and imagine your bedroom when you were 10. What was in it? Were there many electronic items? Tell the class about your room.

2 Read the introduction to the newspaper article on p35. Answer the questions.

1 What did a child's bedroom use to be like?
2 Why is the bedroom of today's child like a space station?
3 Why is it sometimes the most expensive room in the house?
4 What question is asked at the end of the introduction? What is your opinion?

3 The main part of the article describes a modern-day family in an experiment done by a TV company. Look at the photo and the heading. Who are the people? What do you think the experiment was?

4 Here are some words from the article. Use them to predict each paragraph. Check new words in a dictionary.

Paragraph 1:
21st century family   Jon made a fortune
large house   huge bedrooms   hi-tech toys

Paragraph 2:
Jon's childhood   small council house
mother died   five kids   share household chores

Paragraph 3:
back to the 70s   house stripped of all gadgets
wash own clothes   battered old van   £39 a week

Paragraph 4:
tears and rows   Hannah's wardrobe emptied
Josh – piano, no TV

Paragraph 5:
learnt to appreciate small treats
baked cookies   started to save

5 Read paragraphs 1–5 quickly. Were your ideas correct?

6 Read to the end of the article. Answer the questions.

1 How did Jon make a fortune?
2 How was Jon's childhood different from his children's?
3 In what ways was his father strict?
4 How did the TV company transform their lives?
5 What did Hannah and Josh have to do that they didn't have to do before?
6 How did the kids react to the changes at first? How did their attitude change?
7 How did the kids make extra money?
8 What is Jon's advice to other parents?

Vocabulary work

Read the sentences below. Find the phrasal verbs in the text which mean the same as the words in **bold**.

1 Electronic items **increase** the value of the rooms.
2 The father, Jon, **founded** his own business.
3 He was one of five children **raised** by his father, when his mother died.
4 Josh had to **stop** watching his wide-screen television and **start** piano lessons.
5 They enjoyed the vegetables they'd **taken** from the garden.
6 We shouldn't **surrender** to our kids' demands.

What do you think?

Discuss in groups.

- Do you think a lot of children are spoiled these days?
- What household rules do you think are a good idea for families?

  You must always make your bed.
  Everyone has to help at meal times.

Write a list of rules and read them to the class.

Kids who have it all

GO BACK JUST THIRTY YEARS and look inside a child's bedroom. What do you see? Some books, a few dolls or toy cars, some cuddly animals, and perhaps a desk. Look inside the bedroom of today's kids and it's a 21st century space station.

Computers and other hi-tech toys can make a youngster's bedroom the most expensive room in the house. But it's not only electronic items that push up the value. Today's children also have sports equipment, designer clothes, and accessories such as sunglasses, watches and jewellery. Do they have everything and appreciate nothing? A TV channel tried an experiment. TANYA BOWERS REPORTS

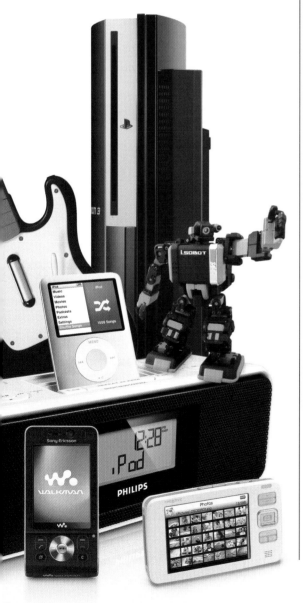

Josh · Hannah · Jon · Emma

Back to the 1970s

1 The TV company, Channel 4, transported a typical 21st century family back in time to the 1970s. The Gregory family live in a large house in Milton Keynes. Fifteen years ago the father, Jon, set up his own business and made a fortune. The children, Hannah, 12, and Josh, 10, have huge bedrooms full of expensive hi-tech toys and clothes. They don't have to help at all with the running of the house.

2 This is all very different from Jon's childhood in the 70s. He grew up in a small council house in Leeds, one of five children brought up by their father after his mother died. Discipline, order and thrift ruled his life. "We ate what we were given. We walked to school and we had to share all the household chores. We had to do what we were told. Dad was very strict."

3 The TV company transformed the Gregorys' house and their lives. For two weeks the family had to go back to the 70s and live Jon's childhood. The house was stripped of all modern gadgets and equipment. Hannah and Josh had to wash and iron their own clothes, do all the washing-up, and help dig the vegetable garden. The family car was exchanged for a battered, old VW van and they had to live on just £39 a week.

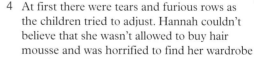

4 At first there were tears and furious rows as the children tried to adjust. Hannah couldn't believe that she wasn't allowed to buy hair mousse and was horrified to find her wardrobe emptied, leaving her with just jeans, two tops and a 'Sunday Best'. Josh had to give up watching his wide-screen television and take up the piano. They didn't have to walk to school but were filled with embarrassment when their dad drove them to the school in their 'new' van.

5 However, gradually Hannah and Josh learnt to appreciate small treats. They enjoyed eating the vegetables they'd dug up from the garden. They made some extra money by selling cookies they'd baked to their neighbours. They started to save rather than spend and understand the value of a £90 pair of trainers.

What should today's parents do?

It's difficult to get things right as a parent. Jon says: "We shouldn't give in to our kids' demands. There's no feeling like getting something you've worked really hard for." Hannah now has £30 in the bank, all earned by doing extra jobs round the house. She has learnt some valuable lessons about life and she doesn't buy hair mousse any more!

VOCABULARY AND SPEAKING
Phrasal verbs (1)

Literal or idiomatic meanings?

1 Look at the cartoons. Which two meanings of *take off* are idiomatic? Which is literal?

a His business has really taken off.

b She took her boots off.

c The flight to Singapore took off on time.

2 In these groups of sentences which two phrasal verbs are idiomatic? Which is literal?

1 a He *brought up* five children on his own.
  b The porter will *bring* your bags *up* to your room.
  c She *brought up* the subject of money.

2 a Do you think you'll *get through* your final exam?
  b I tried to ring you but I couldn't *get through*.
  c His van couldn't *get through* that narrow gate.

3 a The village was *cut off* by the floods.
  b Hello, hello? I can't hear you. I think we've been *cut off*.
  c She *cut off* a big piece of meat and gave it to the dog.

4 a Her health has really *picked up* since she moved to a sunny climate.
  b Can you *pick up* my pen for me? It's under your chair.
  c I *picked up* some Spanish when I was travelling in Peru.

Separable or inseparable?

3 These sentences all contain **separable** phrasal verbs. Replace the words in *italics* with a pronoun.

1 He turned on *the light*.   **He turned it on.**
2 She's taken off *her boots*.   **She's taken them off.**
3 He took up *golf* when he retired.
4 We picked up *Spanish* very quickly.
5 I looked up *the words* in my dictionary.
6 They brought up *five children* really well.
7 I've given up *smoking* at last.

4 These sentences all contain **inseparable** phrasal verbs. Replace the words in *italics* with a pronoun.

1 She takes after *her father*.   **She takes after him.**
2 Nearly everyone got through *the exam*.
3 We looked after *their cats*.
4 He gets on well with *his sister*.
5 I'm looking for *my glasses*.
6 They're looking forward to *the holiday*.
7 We couldn't put up with *the noise* any longer.

Talking about you

5 Complete the phrasal verbs in the questions with **one** of the words in the box. Then ask and answer the questions with a partner.

with	up	to	after

1 Who do you take _____ in your family?
2 Do you get on well _____ both your parents?
3 Have you recently taken _____ any new sports or hobbies?
4 Do you often look _____ words in your dictionary?
5 Are you looking forward _____ going on holiday soon?
6 Do you pick _____ foreign languages easily?
7 Have you got any bad habits that you want to give _____ ?

T 4.7 Listen and compare your answers.

EVERYDAY ENGLISH
Polite requests and offers

1 Match a line in **A** with a line in **B**. Who is talking to who? Where are the conversations taking place?

A	B
1 _g_ I'll give you a lift into town if you like.	a Diet or regular?
2 ___ It's a present. Do you think you could gift-wrap it for me?	b Go ahead. It's very stuffy in here.
3 ___ Pump number 5. And could you give me a token for the car wash?	c One moment. I'll have to look it up.
4 ___ Two large Cokes, please.	d I'm sorry, it's not working today.
5 ___ Can you tell me the code for Tokyo, please?	e Oh, sorry, I didn't realize that you couldn't get through.
6 ___ Could you show me how you did that?	f Yes, of course. I'll just take the price off.
7 ___ Would you mind moving your car?	g That would be great. Could you drop me at the library?
8 ___ Would you mind if I opened the window?	h Certainly. Just go to 'Systems Preferences' and click on 'Displays'.

T 4.8 Listen and check your answers.

> ### Music of English ♪♫
>
> English voice range is very wide, especially in polite requests.
>
> **1** **T 4.9** Listen and repeat.
>
> *Could you show me how you did that?*
>
> *Would you mind moving your car?*
>
> **2** **T 4.8** Listen again to the lines in exercise 1. Practise the conversations.
>
> ►► Grammar Reference 4.6–4.7 p138

2 **T 4.10** Listen to four more conversations. What is each one about?

1 _____   3 _____
2 _____   4 _____

3 Listen again. What are the exact words of the request or offer? Try to remember the conversations with your partner.

Roleplay

Work with a partner. Choose a situation and act it out to the class.

In a restaurant	In a clothes shop	At home
Student A you are a vegetarian customer **Student B** you are a waiter	**Student A** you want to buy a jumper **Student B** you are the sales assistant	**Student A** you are having a party **Student B** you are a friend, offer to help
table by the window menu, wine list ready to order vegetarian eat fish dessert coffee the bill	help jumper in the window only colour try on – my size really suits in the sale 70% discount bargain – take it	come over and help buy drinks, etc. on your way while preparing food decorate the room, blow up balloons set up the music system choose some CDs doorbell! – let the guests in

5 Our changing world

Future forms • *may, might, could* • Word building • Arranging to meet

STARTER

Scientists predict that global warming will change our world forever. Look at the photos. What do you think will happen?

I think/don't think that ... will ...

THINGS OUR GRANDCHILDREN MAY NEVER SEE
Making predictions

1 **T 5.1** Hannah and Dan are expecting their first baby. They're looking at the photos in the newspaper. Listen to their conversation. Answer the questions.
1 What is Hannah worried about?
2 Why is Dan surprised?
3 What do the scientists say about the future?
4 What examples of global warming does Hannah mention?
5 How does Dan try to reassure Hannah? What does he say?

2 Listen again and complete the lines with the *exact* words from the conversation.
1 What _____ the world _____ like when he or she grows up?
2 Don't they make you worry about what _____ happen in the future?
3 Of course, things _____ change a lot in the next hundred years, …
4 No one says it _____ get warmer or it _____ get warmer any more.
5 Scientists say that it definitely _____ warmer.
6 They say temperatures _____ rise by up to 4°C.
7 You _____ a baby soon.
8 We _____ do our bit.
9 OK, but maybe it _____ help. It _____ too late already.

What do you think will happen?

3 Work in groups. Ask questions about the future with *Do you think … will …?* Answer with *may, might, could* or *will*.

1 the earth/continue to get warmer?

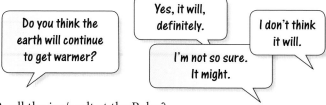

> Do you think the earth will continue to get warmer?

> Yes, it will, definitely.

> I'm not so sure. It might.

> I don't think it will.

2 all the ice/melt at the Poles?
3 polar bears/become extinct?
4 more people/travel by train?
5 air travel/banned to reduce CO_2 emissions?
6 new sources of energy/found?
7 there/be more droughts or more floods in the world?
8 lifestyles/have to change?

T 5.2 Listen and compare your ideas.

PRACTICE

Discussing grammar

1 Work with a partner. Decide which is the correct verb form.

1 A Have you decided about your holiday yet?
  B No, not yet. We've never been to Prague so we *will / might* go there.

2 A *Will you / Are you going to* take an umbrella?
  B No, I'm not. The forecast says it*'ll / might* be fine all day.

3 A Why are you making a list?
  B Because *I'll go / I'm going* shopping. Is there anything you want?

4 A Would you like to go out for a drink tonight?
  B Sorry, I*'ll work / 'm working* late. How about tomorrow night? *I'll call / I'm calling* you.

5 A What *are you doing / will you do* Saturday night?
  B I'm not sure yet. I *will / may* go to friends' or they *will / may* come to me.

6 A Are you enjoying your job more now?
  B No, I'm not. I*'m going to / will* look for another one.

7 A Your team's rubbish! It's 2–0 to United!
  B Come on. It's only half-time. I think they *are going to / could* still win.

8 A You *won't pass / aren't passing* your exams next month if you go out every night.
  B I know, I *might / 'll* work harder nearer the time. I promise.

T 5.3 Listen and check. Practise the conversations, paying attention to stress and intonation.

GRAMMAR SPOT

1 Which predictions are most sure? Which are less sure?

It **might/may/could** change.
It **is going to/will** change.

2 Which *two* answers to the question are correct? Which is not? Why?

'Can you come on Sunday?'

Sorry, I can't.	**I'm seeing** **I'm going to see** **I'll see**	my grandmother.

3 Which of these future forms expresses … ?

• an intention • a prediction • an arrangement

Our love **will last** forever.
I'm going to stop smoking next year.
We**'re meeting** James at 11.00 in the conference room.

▶▶ **Grammar Reference 5.1–5.3 p139**

World weather warnings

2 What are these extreme types of weather?

thunderstorms   floods   hurricane   heatwave   snowstorms

3 **T 5.4** Listen to five short weather forecasts from around the world.
Number the countries in the order you hear them.

Hungary	☐	The British Isles	1	Mexico	☐	South Africa	☐	Canada	☐

4 Listen again to the forecasts. Make notes about the weather in each country.

5 Work with a partner. Use your notes to describe the weather in each country.
What's the weather forecast for where *you* are for the next few days?

I think/don't think . . .

6 Make sentences with *I think . . . will* and the prompts in **A**. Match them with
a sentence in **B**.

I think it'll be a cold night tonight. Wrap up warm if you go out.

A	B
1 it/a cold night tonight	___ But we'd better get a move on.
2 I/get a new computer	_1_ Wrap up warm if you go out.
3 I/do a cookery course	___ I want a laptop this time.
4 you/like the film	___ You've got all the right qualifications.
5 we/get to the airport in time	___ It's a great story, and really well cast.
6 you/get the job	___ I can't even boil an egg.

T 5.5 Listen and check. Practise the lines.

7 Make sentences with *I don't think . . . will* and the words in **A** in exercise 6.
Match them with a sentence in **C**.

I don't think it'll be a cold night tonight. You won't need to take a jacket.

C
___ There's too much traffic.
___ I'll get lessons from my mum.
___ It may seem old-fashioned to you but it's OK for me.
_1_ You won't need to take a jacket.
___ You're too young, and you've got no experience.
___ It's not really your kind of thing.

T 5.6 Listen and check. Practise the lines and continue some of them.

Talking about you

8 Make true sentences about *you*. Say them aloud in small groups.

1 I/go for a coffee after class
2 I/go shopping this afternoon
3 I/eat out tonight
4 our teacher/tell us that our English/improving
5 it/rain tomorrow
6 my grandchildren/have holidays on the moon

I might go for a coffee.

I think/don't think I'll go
for a coffee.

LISTENING AND SPEAKING
Rocket man

1 Look at the pictures. Which rockets do you recognize?

2 Read about Steve Bennett. Who is he? What was his dream? How is it coming true? What do you understand by *space tourism*?

Rocket Man
Steve Bennett

As a little boy, like lots of little boys, Steve Bennett dreamed of becoming a spaceman, but *un*like most little boys, Steve's dream is coming true. Steve is Britain's leading rocket scientist and he's now building his own rocket. In a few years' time he's going to travel into space with two other passengers. He believes the age of mass space tourism is on the horizon.

3 **T 5.7** Steve was interviewed for a BBC Radio programme called *Saturday Live*. Close your books. Listen to the interview.
- What's your impression of Steve? Would you describe him as 'a realist' or 'a dreamer'? Professional or amateur?
- Would you like to travel with him into space?

4 Work with a partner. Read the questions below. Which can you answer?

1 Why is Steve so sure space tourism will happen? Why are Richard Branson and Jeff Bezos called 'big names'?
2 In what way does he compare space travel with the Internet?
3 How will the passengers be like the early American astronauts? What are they *not* going to do?
4 What influenced Steve as a small child? Why is his rocket called *Thunderstar*? What was he not allowed to watch?
5 What was his parents' attitude to space travel?
6 Why does he think it is necessary for humans to be in space?
7 Why is skydiving good training for space tourists? How much have the couple paid?
8 What does Steve think about every day?

T 5.7 Listen again and check your ideas.

What do you think?
- Is space tourism a good idea?
- Is space travel important to the world? Why/Why not?
- Should the money be spent on other things? Give examples.

SPOKEN ENGLISH	*pretty*

1 Look at how Steve uses *pretty* in the interview.

*I kept it **pretty** quiet . . .*
*That's **pretty** much where the human race needs to be.*

2 The adverb *pretty* is often used in informal, spoken English. It means 'not a lot' but 'more than a little'.

*She's **pretty** nice.*
*The weather was **pretty** bad.*

3 Work with a partner. Ask the questions and reply including *pretty* in the answer.

1 A Did your team win?
  B No, but they played well, all the same.
2 A You haven't lost your mobile phone again!
  B No, no. I'm sure it's in my bag somewhere.
3 A Do you enjoy skiing?
  B I do, but I'm hopeless at it.
4 A What do you think of my English?
  B I think it's good.

T 5.8 Listen and check. Practise again.

▶▶ **WRITING** WRITING FOR TALKING **T 5.9** *p107*

READING AND SPEAKING
Life fifty years from now

1 The future is difficult to predict. What things in our lives today do you think scientists fifty years ago did NOT predict?

2 Look at the text *Life in 2060*. Read the introduction and paragraph headings 1–7 only. What do *you* predict about the topics?

3 Which sentences a–g do you think go with which topic?

a Lost limbs will regrow, hearts will regenerate.

b This knowledge will help reduce suicide rates, one of the major causes of death worldwide.

c ... the most sensational discovery ever, that is, confirmation that life really does exist on Mars.

d It is now routine to extend the lives of laboratory animals by 40%.

e ... your fridge will 'know' when you are low on milk or any other item, ...

f Soon their existence will be no more controversial than the existence of other galaxies 100 years ago.

g It could cause a global revulsion against eating meat ...

4 Read the article and put sentences a–g in the right place.

5 Are these statements true (✓) or false (✗)?

1 Women will be able to give birth aged 100.

2 It will be possible to replace all the parts of the body.

3 Animal parts will be used for transplantation.

4 Scientists think that computers won't ever do the work of the human brain.

5 Scientists believe that if we can talk to animals, we won't want to eat them.

6 Alien life has already been found on Mars.

7 There could be an infinite number of other universes.

8 The walls in your house will change colour to suit your mood.

9 Your armchair will help you do your housework.

10 Pills will replace food.

What do you think?

• Read the article again and <u>underline</u> the predictions that most surprise you.
Which do you believe will definitely happen?
Which might happen?
Which do you believe won't happen?

• What predictions can you make? Choose from these topics:

transport	jobs	television	communication
the home	food	clothes	sport

Life ir

An international group of forty scientists have made some very surprising predictions about the future. They say that in the next fifty years the way we live will change beyond our wildest dreams. Here are some of their predictions. You may find some of them surprising.
BEA ROSENTHAL reports.

1 Life expectancy

Within 50 years, living to a 100 while still enjoying active, healthy lives will be the norm. Professor Richard Miller of the University of Michigan says: '⬚⬚⬚⬚⬚⬚ We will be able to do the same for humans.' So with regular injections, centenarians will be as vigorous as today's sixty-year-olds. Women will be able to give birth well into old age; their biological clocks could be extended by ten years.

2 Growing body parts

Professor Ellen Heber-Katz says: 'People will take for granted that injured or diseased organs can be repaired in much the same way as we fix a car. ⬚⬚⬚⬚⬚⬚ Damaged parts will be replaced. Within 50 years whole-body replacement will be routine.' But doctors will need huge supplies of organs for transplant. Where will they come from? Scientists say these could be grown inside animals from human cells.

3 Understanding the brain

We don't yet know how the brain gives us our awareness of being alive. 'But,' says Professor Susan Greenfield of Oxford University, 'in 50 years' time we may have a clearer idea of how the brain generates consciousness.' Studies of the brain and the nature of consciousness will bring much greater understanding of disorders such as schizophrenia and depression. ⬚⬚⬚⬚⬚⬚ Other scientists go further than Professor Greenfield. They believe that by 2060 computers will develop their own consciousness and emotions. Human beings may eventually be replaced by computers in some areas of life.

2060

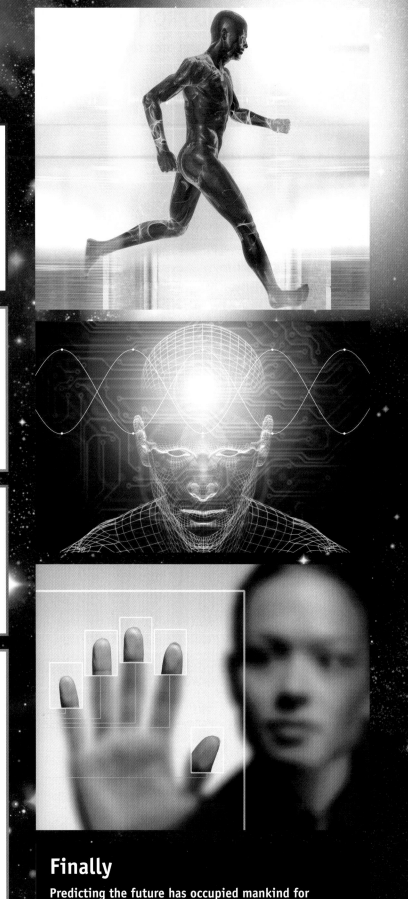

4 Understanding animals

Thanks to a device which can 'read' emotions, feelings, and thoughts, we will be able to 'talk' to animals. The story of *Dr Dolittle will be fact, not fiction. 'This could first work with primates, then mammals, then other vertebrates, including fish,' says Professor Daniel Pauly from Canada. ' [   ] , so we might all become vegetarian.'

* fictional character for children

5 Discovering aliens

A number of scientists predict that the biggest breakthrough in the next 50 years will be the discovery of extra-terrestrial beings. Dr Chris McKay of NASA says: 'We may find evidence of alien life frozen in the ancient permafrost on Mars.' Scientists hope that the current interest in space missions to this planet means that there is every chance of making [   ] Dr McKay also believes that evidence of alien life forms may even be found here on Earth.

6 Parallel universes

Advances in quantum physics will prove that there are parallel universes. In fact there may be an infinite number of them. These universes will contain space, time, and some of them may even contain you in a slightly different form. For years parallel universes only existed in the works of science fiction, but now Professor Max Tegmark says: '[   ]'.

7 Our homes

What might our houses be like in the second half of the 21st century? This is Professor Greenfield's prediction:

As you enter the living room, sensors will detect your presence and the walls will start to glow. Talk to the walls and, activated by your voice, they will change to a colour of your choice, 'pink' to 'green' to 'blue', whatever suits your mood.

Sink into your glowing cyber-armchair, relax in the knowledge that the house computer will perform all your everyday household tasks. The voice system in the chair will address you by name and advise a change in position that will be better for your spine.

In the kitchen, [   ] and it will automatically send orders to the supermarket. However, it is in the kitchen where 'new' meets 'old'. Food remains in its old-fashioned form. Pills, so confidently predicted in the 20th-century to replace food, exist, but nobody wants them. There is too much pleasure in cooking, chewing and tasting all kinds of food.

Finally

Predicting the future has occupied mankind for generations. However, not always successfully. The huge influence of many of today's technical marvels, such as the Internet or mobile phones, was never predicted.

VOCABULARY AND PRONUNCIATION
Word building – suffixes and prefixes

1 Work with a partner. Look at the information on suffixes.

> **SUFFIXES** are used to form different parts of speech.
> What endings do you notice on these words?
> What part of speech are they?
>
> act act**ion** act**ive** active**ly**

What part of speech are the words in the box?
What are the different word endings?

prediction	colourful	excitement	suitable
shorten	confidently	creative	business
automatically	imagination	qualify	careless

2 Look at the information on prefixes.

> **PREFIXES** are used to change the meaning of words. Look at these words with prefixes.
> **pre**dict **re**grow **extra**-terrestrial **dis**order
> Which means . . . ?
> *before outside again*
> Which is a negative prefix?

Choose a prefix from the box to make the words mean the opposite.

un-	in-	im-	il-	dis-	ir-

1 possible **impossible** 5 appear
2 patient 6 regular
3 lucky 7 formal
4 legal 8 conscious

3 Work in two groups. Make new words with the base words using the suffixes and/or the prefixes.
Which group can make the most words?

PREFIX	BASE WORD	SUFFIX
un- im- re- dis- mis- in-	agree arrange conscious expense happy help kind polite react success understand use	**-ness** -ment -ion **-ful** -less -able -ive

4 Complete the sentences with a word from exercise 3.

1 Bob and Jan don't get on at all. They dis_____ about everything.
2 Money doesn't always lead to h_____ness.
3 My aunt says today's kids are all rude and im_____.
4 Thanks for your advice, it was really h_____ful. I really appreciate your k_____ness.
5 My dad is u_____less at fixing his computer. I always have to help him.
6 Please don't mis_____ me. I didn't mean to be un_____. I'm really sorry.
7 Timmy fell off his bike and hit his head. He was un_____ for a few hours.
8 What was your wife's re_____ion when she heard you'd won the lottery?

T 5.10 Listen and check.

Changing word stress

5 In some words the stressed syllable changes in the different forms. Read aloud these pairs of words.

advertise advertisement imagine imagination	prefer preference employer employee

T 5.11 Listen and check. Practise again.

6 **T 5.12** Listen to four short conversations. Write down the pairs of words with stress changes. Practise the conversations.

1 _____ _____
2 _____ _____
3 _____ _____
4 _____ _____

EVERYDAY ENGLISH
Arranging to meet

1 **T 5.13** Listen to two friends, Gary and Mike, arranging to meet over the weekend. Complete the diaries.

Gary

22 FRIDAY
Morning
Afternoon
Evening

23 SATURDAY
Morning
Afternoon
Evening

24 SUNDAY
Morning

Mike

22 Friday
Morning
Afternoon   finish work early
Evening

23 Saturday
Morning
Afternoon
Evening

24 Sunday
Morning

Why is it difficult to find a time? Where and when do they finally agree to meet?

Making suggestions

2 **T 5.13** Listen again to the conversation. Complete the suggestions with the exact words Gary and Mike say.

1 I was _____ if we _____ meet?
2 I _____ meet you in the afternoon.
3 What _____ Saturday afternoon?
4 Is Saturday evening _____?
5 Why _____ we meet at the station?
_____ meet there for breakfast.
6 _____ we say about 10 o'clock?
7 Can you _____ it 10.30?

♪♪ Music of English ♪♪

1 **T 5.14** Listen and repeat the suggestions in exercise 2. Pay attention to the stress and intonation.

2 Work with a partner. Take turns to read aloud the suggestions and answer with a suitable reply from below.

Oh dear, I'd love to – but . . .
I'm afraid that's no good . . .
Er, let me see.
I can't, I've got an appointment with . . .
Sorry, the evening's out for me.
Sounds good to me.
Fine. 10.30 it is.

Roleplay

3 It is Saturday morning. You want to meet a friend over the weekend. Fill in your diary. What are you doing this weekend? When are you free?

23 Saturday	
Morning	
Afternoon	
Evening	

24 Sunday	
Morning	
Afternoon	
Evening	

4 Find a partner. Make suggestions and arrange to meet.

Are you doing anything on Saturday morning?

I'm afraid I'm going . . .

What about the afternoon?

Let me see . . .

I was wondering if you'd like to . . .

When you have finished, tell the class when and where you're meeting.

We're meeting on Saturday afternoon. We're going . . .

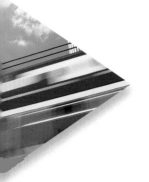

6 What matters to me

Information questions • Adjectives and adverbs • In a department store

 STARTER

1 Think of someone in the room. Don't say who it is.
The other students must ask questions to find out who it is.

Is it a boy or a girl?	*What colour is her hair?*
Has she got blue eyes?	*What sort of clothes does she wear?*

2 Do the same about someone famous.

DESCRIPTIONS
Information questions

1 Match a question with an answer.

DESCRIBING PEOPLE

1	*e* What's she like?	a	She's in her twenties.
2	☐ What does she look like?	b	She likes dancing and shopping.
3	☐ What does she like doing?	c	Five foot eight.
4	☐ How tall is she?	d	She's quite tall and pretty.
5	☐ What colour eyes has she got?	e	She's really nice. Very easy-going.
6	☐ How old is she?	f	She's fine.
7	☐ What kind of clothes does she wear?	g	Brown.
8	☐ What's her hair like?	h	It's sort of long, fair, and wavy.
9	☐ How is she?	i	Not smart. Casual. She has a lot of style.

T 6.1 Listen and check. Work with a partner. Practise the questions and answers. Cover one column, then the other.

2 Ask and answer the questions about a relative.

> *What's your brother like?*

> *He's a great guy, very kind. You'd like him.*

You can use the ideas in the box to help.

good fun	a bit quiet	very sociable	good-looking
quite dark	attractive	medium height	about 1 metre 70
in his mid-twenties	straight	short	curly

3 <u>Underline</u> the correct answer.

DESCRIBING PLACES

1 What's your flat like?
   It's quite modern, but it's cosy. / I like it.
2 How big is it?
   Yes, it is pretty big. / About 75 sq m.
3 How many rooms are there?
   Two bedrooms. / A kitchen-diner, a living room, and a bedroom.
4 What size is the kitchen?
   It's square. / Four metres by two.
5 Which floor is it on?
   Wooden. / The fourth.
6 Which part of town is it in?
   It's south of the river. / I get the 79 bus.
7 How far is it to the shops?
   Just a five-minute walk. / It takes half an hour.

T 6.2 Listen and check. With your partner, practise the questions and answers.

4 Ask and answer questions about where you live. You can use the ideas in the box to help.

in an old block   noisy   has a view of . . .
a terrace where we can sit outside
ground floor   enormous   tiny

What's your flat like?

It's quite small, but it's comfortable.

5 Look at the questions for describing things. Put a word from the box into each question.

much   How   make   of   long   for   size

DESCRIBING THINGS

1 What _____ is it? *Sony.*
2 How _____ does it weigh? *1.3 kg.*
3 What's it made _____? *Carbon and titanium.*
4 What's this button _____? *It turns it on.*
5 _____ big is the screen? *13.2 inches.*
6 How _____ is the battery life? *Eight hours.*
7 What _____ is the hard disk? *80 gigabytes.*

T 6.3 Listen and check. With your partner, practise the questions and answers.

6 Ask and answer similar questions about your laptop/ mobile/camera/MP3 player.

What make is it?

It's a Dell.

GRAMMAR SPOT

1 *What* and *which* can be followed by a noun.
   What colour/**Which** floor . . . ?
   Find examples on these pages.
2 *How* can be followed by an adjective or an adverb.
   How tall/far . . . ?
   Find examples.
3 Match a question and an answer.

| What's she like? | Very well, thanks. |
| How is she? | Very nice. Quite pretty. |

▶▶ Grammar Reference 6.1–6.2 p140

PRACTICE

Getting information

Ask questions for these situations.

1 Do you have brown bread? White bread?
   What sort of bread do you have?
2 Would you like vanilla ice-cream? Strawberry? Chocolate?
3 Do we go left or right at the traffic lights? Or straight on?
4 Is your camera a Canon? A Samsung? An Olympus?
5 Do you like pasta? Hamburgers? Spicy food?
6 Is that your sister's top you're wearing? Suzie's? Or your own?
7 Does it take 30 minutes to get to the airport? An hour?
8 Is your house 100 metres from the beach? One kilometre?
9 Do you go to the cinema once a week? Once a fortnight?
10 Do two of you want coffee? Four of you? All of you?
11 Do you take size 40 shoes? 42? 44?

T 6.4 Listen and compare.

VOCABULARY
Adjectives

1 Work in pairs. Look at the advertisements 1–3. Which advert is for …?

a date   something to eat   a holiday destination

2 Find some adjectives in the adverts.

Mamma Mia

Mamma Mia pasta sauces. From much-loved bolognaise to our latest garlic and basil. Made from the finest organic ingredients in the old-fashioned way.

**So tempting!
Just like home-made.
You'll be amazed!**

Mamma Mia Bolognaise

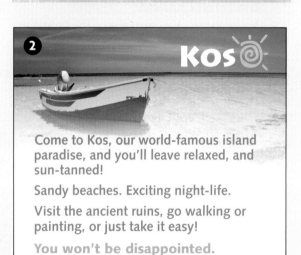

② Kos ☀

Come to Kos, our world-famous island paradise, and you'll leave relaxed, and sun-tanned!

Sandy beaches. Exciting night-life.

Visit the ancient ruins, go walking or painting, or just take it easy!

You won't be disappointed.

③ **LOVE, MAYBE?**

Pretty, slim, blue-eyed lady, 35, tired of living alone, seeks tall, dark, handsome, easy-going, charming M with great sense of humour, 30-40, for fun and long-lasting friendship. And possibly more! Box 349056

-ed and -ing adjectives

3 How do these words end in the adverts?

amaz-   relax-   excit-   disappoint-   tir-   charm-

Complete the sentences with one of these adjectives ending in -ed or -ing.

1 Having a massage is very __relaxing__ .
2 I was _____ when they offered me the job. I was sure I'd failed the interview.
3 Our holiday was _____ . It rained every day.
4 My kids are so _____ on Christmas Eve, they can't sleep.
5 The journey was very _____ . I was exhausted.
6 He says such lovely things. He is _____ . He makes you feel so special.

Adjectives and nouns that go together

4 Some adjectives and nouns often go together.

sandy beach   ancient ruins

Match an adjective and a noun. Sometimes there is more than one possibility.

adjective	noun
fresh latest pretty clear fast crowded casual close handsome straight cosy challenging	friend fruit clothes fashions hair job restaurant food woman man room sky

T 6.5 Listen and check.

Compound adjectives

5 Find some compound adjectives in the adverts.

much-loved   old-fashioned

Match a word from **A** and **B** to make compound adjectives.

A	B
well- (×2) full- hard- good- second- hand- brand-	new dressed hand behaved time looking working made

Think of a noun that goes with each adjective. What's the opposite?

well-behaved children   badly-behaved children

6 Test each other on the compound adjectives in exercise 5.

Another word for handsome.

good-looking

What sort of job is it if you work forty hours a week?

full-time

Adverbs

1 Look at advertisements 4–6. Which advert is for …?

a pain killer a watch a house to rent

2 Find adverbs that end in *-ly* in adverts 4 and 5.

simply beautifully

Find some adverbs that don't end in *-ly* in advert 6.

just too

---

❹

LOG FIRES IN DEVON

£750 pw

Live simply in this beautifully restored 16th century country cottage. Sit peacefully in front of the fire. Situated in a charming village, sleeps 6, fully equipped.

andycurran@fastnetuk.com

---

❺ You don't actually own one of our hand-made instruments. You merely look after it for the next generation.

Probably the best investment you'll ever make.

---

❻ Painful headaches that just won't go? Backache, too?

Relieve aches and pains fast with Cuprodil! Cuprodil goes straight to the pain.

You'll soon feel good again!

✧ **CUPRODIL**

Adverbs and verbs that go together

3 Some verbs and adverbs often go together.

drive carefully walk slowly explain clearly

Match a verb and an adverb. Sometimes there is more than one possibility.

verb	abverb
wait love behave shine fight leave whisper die rain dress speak breathe	badly peacefully heavily smartly patiently fluently suddenly deeply brightly passionately softly bravely

4 Mime some of the verbs and adverbs to the class.

> You're driving carefully!

> You're waiting patiently!

Adverbs that don't end in *-ly*

5 Complete the sentences with an adverb from the box.

again	fast	hard	loud	wrong
even	right	straight	together	almost

1 Peter and I lived _____ at university.
2 He's a good student. He tries _____ .
3 'Where's the town hall?' 'Go _____ on.'
4 Say that _____. I didn't hear you.
5 Don't talk so _____ ! Everyone can hear you.
6 Why do you drive so _____ ? Slow down!
7 His wife's name is Sue, not Sally! Get it _____ .
8 The holiday was a disaster. Everything went _____ .
9 This room is cool, _____ in summer.
10 'Are you ready?' '_____ . Give me another five minutes.'

T 6.6 Listen and check.

Project – My most treasured possession

1 **T 6.7** Listen to three people, Amy, Jack, and Lucy, describing what they'd save if their home was on fire. What is it? Why would they save it?

2 What is *your* most treasured possession? Prepare to talk about it.

I couldn't live without my . . .
It's important to me because . . .
It was given to me by . . .
I've had it for . . .
It reminds me of . . .

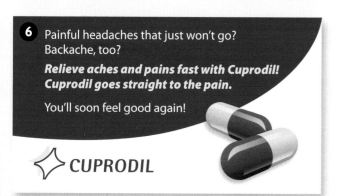

READING AND SPEAKING
The heart of the home

1 Close your eyes and think of your kitchen at home.

- Who's in it?
- What's happening?
- What are they doing?
- What can you smell?

2 Read the introduction to *My kitchen* at the top of p51. Do you agree that the kitchen is the heart of the home? Is it where *your* family get together?

3 Work in three groups.

Group A   Read about Santina, from Italy.
Group B   Read about Elizabeth, from the United States.
Group C   Read about **Lakshmamma**, from India.

Answer the questions.

1 What does she do?
2 What does her husband do?
3 Where does she live?
4 What's her house like?
5 How does she feel about her kitchen?
6 Is her life easy or difficult?
7 What does her family eat?
8 Does she seem to be happy?
9 What do you think she worries about?

4 Find a partner from the other groups. Compare and swap information.

5 Which person is most likely to say …?

1 *'I can never decide where to go swimming.'*
2 *'We have found you a very nice girl. Why won't you marry her?'*
3 *'If anyone wants me, I'm weeding and watering.'*
4 *'I'm too busy to play tennis today.'*
5 *'I live my life in tune with nature.'*
6 *'I'd love to have a new kitchen.'*

What do you think?

In your opinion, who …?

- is the wealthiest materially
- is the happiest spiritually
- is the most creative cook
- has the hardest life

Give reasons for your answers.

Speaking

1 What food do you most associate with home? Is there a particular day of the week or time of year when you eat it?

2 Talk about your kitchen. Answer questions 1–12 from the text.

 **WRITING** DESCRIBING A PLACE *p108*

My *Kitchen*

Italy

Housewife Santina Corvaglia, 61, lives in an old two bedroom farmhouse in south-east Italy with her husband, Carlo, 56, who's a mechanic. They have a 31-year-old daughter, Francesca.

1 **Q** How much is your house worth?
A About £50,000.

2 **Q** What is your kitchen like?
A It's not very big. It's my little corner of the house. It's where I belong, and where I'm happiest.

3 **Q** How big is it?
A 12 sq m

4 **Q** What's your favourite thing?
A My cupboard full of different Italian herbs.

5 **Q** How much time do you spend in the kitchen?
A About four hours every day. And the same in the garden.

6 **Q** How many meals do you cook a day?
A Three. For the three of us, and whoever comes by – friends, relatives. My family is the most important thing to me. I want grandchildren!

7 **Q** What's in your fridge and cupboards?
A Vegetables, water, wine, eggs, cheese, ham, sausages, lemonade, butter, pasta, tinned tomatoes, beans, honey, and home-made jam.

8 **Q** What would make your life easier in the kitchen?
A Nothing. I have all I need.

9 **Q** Who helps you?
A My daughter helps sometimes. My husband wouldn't dream of it, and I wouldn't want him to.

10 **Q** How often do you sit down and eat together as a family?
A Twice a day.

11 **Q** How much do you spend on groceries every week?
A I grow my own vegetables, and we have chickens and rabbits, so I only spend about £30 a week. But there is a drought this year.

12 **Q** What can you see from your kitchen windows?
A My garden, my orchard, and my olive trees.

The kitchen is the **heart of the home**. It's where the family gets together for the important things in life – food, conversation, and celebration. Three women from around the world invite us into their kitchens. PENNY ROGERS reports.

California, US

Elizabeth Anne Hogan, 45, is a lifestyle coach living in a 30-roomed house on the beach in California. It has ten bathrooms, seven bedrooms, an astronomy dome, a tennis court, a swimming pool, and a bomb shelter. Her husband, Mike, 47, is a businessman. They have two children, Hailey, 14, and Hanna, nine.

1 **Q How much is your house worth?**
   A About £6 million.

2 **Q What is your kitchen like?**
   A There are two. The beach kitchen is simple. The house kitchen is futuristic. I don't know how everything works, so it's all a bit 'alien' to me.

3 **Q How big is it?**
   A 45 sq m

4 **Q What's your favourite thing?**
   A The three ovens, but they take up too much space. The lift that brings the groceries from the five-car garage is handy.

5 **Q How much time do you spend in the kitchen?**
   A About seven to eight hours a day. But not cooking. It's the room we live in.

6 **Q How many meals do you cook a day?**
   A Two to three, if you count cereal and bagels. But only one, if you mean actually doing things with real food.

7 **Q What's in your fridge and cupboards?**
   A Fruit, vegetables, champagne, milk, yoghurt, pâté, cheeses, crisps, and cereal. Lots of take-away food. And dog food.

8 **Q What would make your life easier in the kitchen?**
   A A chef. We do everything for the kids ourselves. No nannies, housekeepers, or cooks for them.

9 **Q Who helps you?**
   A My husband and kids take food out of take-away containers and put it on plates. Does that count as helping?

10 **Q How often do you sit down and eat together as a family?**
    A Every morning and evening.

11 **Q How much do you spend on groceries every week?**
    A £300. Everything is low-fat and organic, pre-packed and prepared. It's all delivered.

12 **Q What can you see from your kitchen windows?**
    A A panoramic, 180-degree view of the Pacific Ocean.

India

Lakshmamma, 50, is a housewife living in a three-roomed mud hut near Bangalore. Her husband, Adaviyappa, 55, works on a cattle farm. They have two sons, Gangaraju, 30 and Ravi, 25, who both live at home.

1 **Q How much is your house worth?**
   A To rebuild it would cost about £1,250.

2 **Q What is your kitchen like?**
   A It's small, dark, and crumbling. I dislike just about everything about it. It's so old.

3 **Q How big is it?**
   A 5 sq m

4 **Q What's your favourite thing?**
   A The stone where I grind my spices.

5 **Q How much time do you spend in the kitchen?**
   A Six to seven hours a day – sometimes more. I'm always cooking or washing.

6 **Q How many meals do you cook a day?**
   A Two or three.

7 **Q What's in your fridge and cupboards?**
   A We don't have a fridge. On shelves I have lentils, rice, spices such as chillies, turmeric powder, some vegetables, and salt.

8 **Q What would make your life easier in the kitchen?**
   A Running water. A daughter-in-law would be good as well! But God has given me life and I am grateful.

9 **Q Who helps you?**
   A My eldest son helps when he has time. My younger son isn't well and needs constant care. My husband doesn't help.

10 **Q How often do you sit down and eat together as a family?**
    A Men eat before women in our community. We don't eat together.

11 **Q How much do you spend on groceries every week?**
    A £4. Sometimes less. It depends how much money we have.

12 **Q What can you see from your kitchen windows?**
    A I have no windows in my kitchen.

LISTENING AND SPEAKING
My closest relative

1 Discuss the statements in small groups. Are they true for your family?

- Mothers feel closer to their sons.
  Fathers feel closer to their daughters.
- The first-born child is ambitious, responsible, dominant, and insecure.
  The second child is free, independent, creative, and easy-going.
  The last-born child is the baby – spoilt, happy, confident, and secure.

2 **T 6.8** Listen to five people talking about who they feel closest to in their family. Complete the chart.

	Ellie	Simon	Julia	Tessa	Chris
I feel closest to . . .	my mum				
He/she is easy to talk to.	✓				
We do things together.					
We have a similar character.					
I like the way he/she thinks.					
We are different.					

3 Who said these expressions? What do you understand by them?

1 'We have our ups and downs, of course …'
2 'We don't really see to eye to eye about anything.'
3 'In many ways she drives me crazy.'
4 'We're like chalk and cheese.'
5 'They fight like cat and dog.'

SPOKEN ENGLISH Adding emphasis

1 We can change the order of words in a sentence to add emphasis. What is the more usual word order for these sentences?

1 *She's very open, my mother.*
2 *My father I don't really get on with.*
3 *My mother I hardly ever see.*
4 *He's pretty cool, my dad.*
5 *Me, I'm a lot quieter.*

2 Notice how these sentences add emphasis.

What I like about her is her attitude.
What I like about him is that he's interesting and interested.
The thing I love about her is the way everyone knows her.

3 What could people say about . . .?

1 Joe: his sense of humour
      the way he makes everyone laugh
2 Tina: her kindness
       the way she makes everyone feel good
3 Beth: her attitude to life
       the fact she doesn't care what other people think

Discussion

- Work in pairs. Discuss who you feel closest to in your family, and why.
- Work in groups of four. Who has a similar family relationship to yours?
- Discuss as a class. Which family member are most people closest to?

EVERYDAY ENGLISH
In a department store

1 What are the big department stores in your town? What are they famous for? Do you like shopping in them?

2 Look at the board showing where the various departments are in a store.

Where would you find ...?

- a tie
  in menswear, on the ground floor
- a wallet
- earrings
- a saucepan
- a hairdryer
- shower gel
- a doll
- a DVD player
- women's boots
- the Ladies'
- a birthday card
- a shaving mirror
- a lipstick
- a vase
- trainers
- a sofa
- sheets
- a suitcase
- a pair of tights
- a light snack

Store Guide

3 Third floor
Toys and babywear
Hairdresser's
TV, Audio, and Phones
Sports

2 Second floor
Furniture
Linen
Bathroom accessories
The Terrace Cafeteria
Toilets
Baby facilities

1 First floor
Ladies' fashions
Lingerie
Leather goods
Luggage

G Ground floor
Menswear
Stationery
Toiletries
Jewellery
Cosmetics

B Basement
Kitchenware
China and glassware
Electrical appliances

3 In which department could you see these signs?

a **Cut and blow dry £30 Highlights from £50**

b **Buy two coffee mugs, get one free!**

c **Travel in style – perfect coordinating bags for long weekend breaks or short holidays**

d *Half price! Final clearance of men's woollens before the spring!*

e **CUSTOMERS ARE REMINDED THAT ONLY FOOD AND DRINK PURCHASED ON THESE PREMISES MAY BE CONSUMED HERE**

f *Back to school! Beat the rush. Get your pens and paper and files NOW!*

4 Which of these two signs ...?
- is telling you how to take things back
- is inviting you to save as you spend

Open a loyalty card today and you will receive a 10% discount on all your purchases.

If goods are returned in their original packaging with a receipt within 28 days we will offer an exchange or refund.

5 **T 6.9** Listen to some conversations in a department store. Which department are they in? What are they trying to buy?

6 Listen again and complete the lines.

1 **A** _____ do you take?
   B Nine. That's 41, isn't it?
   A _____ 43 would be more comfortable, sir.

2 **B** I'm afraid _____. We've _____ that size.
   A Will you _____ any more _____?
   B We should _____ by the end of the week.

3 **A** Do you have _____?
   B No, Madam. They all _____.

4 **A** Would you like me _____?
   B Ooh, _____! Thank you so much!

5 **A** It _____. It's too tight.
   B Shame. It _____. What _____ of?
   A Cashmere. Its so soft!

6 **A** Keep your _____. That's your guarantee.
   B _____ is it _____ for?
   A For a year.

With a partner, practise the conversations.

7 Practise having conversations in other departments. Act them out to the class.

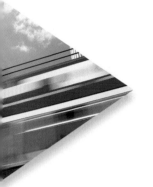

7 Passions and fashions

Present Perfect – simple, continuous, passive • Making the right noises

 STARTER

Talk about three things you have **NEVER** done.

I've NEVER been to a football match.
  Me neither. I hate football.
I've NEVER had body piercing or a tattoo.
  I have. I've got a tattoo of a rose on my ankle.
I've NEVER read a Harry Potter book.
  Really? I've read them all.

300 MILLION BOOKS SOLD!
Present Perfect – simple, continuous, passive

1 Look at the book titles. Have you read any of them or seen the films?
   Do you know anything about the author, J.K. Rowling /rəʊlɪŋ/?

   HARRY POTTER and the Philosopher's Stone (1997)
   HARRY POTTER and the Chamber of Secrets (1998)
   HARRY POTTER and the Prisoner of Azkaban (1999)
   HARRY POTTER and the Goblet of Fire (2000)
   HARRY POTTER and the Order of the Phoenix (2003)
   HARRY POTTER and the Half-blood Prince (2005)
   HARRY POTTER and the Deathly Hallows (2007)

2 Complete the questions about J.K. Rowling. Use *did*, *was*, *has*, or *have*.

   1 Where and when _____ she born?
   2 When _____ she write her first story? What _____ it about?
   3 What _____ she doing when she had the idea for Harry Potter?
   4 Where _____ she teach English?
   5 When _____ the first Harry Potter book published?
   6 How long _____ she been writing the books?
   7 How many _____ she written?
   8 How many children _____ she had?
   9 How many books _____ been sold?
   10 Which books _____ been made into films?
   11 How much money _____ she made?
   12 How many authors _____ become billionaires?

3 **T 7.1** Read and listen about J.K. Rowling. What does J.K. stand for?

4 Work with a partner. Ask and answer the questions in exercise 2.
   T 7.2 Listen and check.

$1 billion

JK Rowling
Author and billionaire

THE EARLY YEARS

Joanne Kathleen Rowling, author of the best-selling Harry Potter series of books, was born in 1965, near Bristol, England. Her birthday, July 31, is the same as her famous hero, Harry Potter.

School days

Joanne did well in school. Her favourite subjects were English and foreign languages and she studied French at university. She graduated in 1986 and over the next few years had a variety of jobs. However, her passion was writing. She had written her first story, *Rabbit*, about a rabbit with measles, aged six.

Harry Potter is born

She started writing the first Harry Potter book in 1990. The idea for Harry – a lonely, 11-year-old orphan who is actually a wizard – came to Rowling while she was travelling by train between Manchester and London. Although she left England a short time after that to teach English in Portugal, she continued to write Harry's story.

She returned to Britain in 1993, and settled in Scotland. After a brief marriage in Portugal, she was now divorced, with a baby, Jessica. It was a difficult time – she was out of work and depressed – but finally completed her first book, *Harry Potter and the Philosopher's Stone*. It was published in Britain in 1997 and quickly became a hit with both children and adults.

JK ROWLING TODAY

JKR has been writing Harry Potter books for nearly 20 years. She writes in longhand, and each book takes one year to complete. She has now completed the series of seven Harry Potter books. The last book, *Harry Potter and the Deathly Hallows*, came out in July, 2007. Her books have won numerous awards including 'Children's Book of the Year'.

She married her second husband, Dr Neil Murray, in 2001 and has since had two more children, a boy, David, born in 2003, and a girl, Mackenzie, born in 2005.

Fans all over the world

The books have been translated into over 60 languages, and over 300 million copies have been sold worldwide. The first six books have been made into films. She has become the highest-earning woman in Britain, richer than the Queen! She has made over £600 million, more than one billion dollars. This makes her the first person ever to have become a billionaire from writing books.

GRAMMAR SPOT

1   Name the three tenses. Why are they used?

   She **lives** in Scotland.
   She **lived** in Portugal for three years.
   She**'s lived** in Scotland since 1993.
   She**'s lived** in England, Portugal and Scotland.

2   Which question asks about the activity? Which asks about the quantity?

   How long **has** she **been writing** Harry Potter books?
   How many **has** she **written**?

3   These sentences sound unnatural in the active. Make them passive. Find them in the text.

   People have translated her books into 60 languages.
   People have sold 300 million copies of her books.
   People have made six of the books into films.

▶▶ **Grammar Reference 7.1–7.6 p140–2**

---

5   **T 7.3**   Jack, aged 10, is a big fan of Harry Potter books. Listen and complete the questions he was asked. What are his answers?

1   How long _have you been_ a fan of the books?
2   How many of the books _____?
3   Which _____ like best?
4   _____ any of the Harry Potter films? _____ like them all?
5   Have you any idea how many Harry Potter books _____ in the world?
6   What _____ about the author?
7   _____ a lot of your friends _____ the books?
8   I know as well as Harry Potter you have another passion. How long _____ football?
9   What would you rather do this afternoon? Read a Harry Potter or play football?

6   What books and films are you a fan of? Talk to a partner. Ask and answer similar questions to exercise 5. Tell the class.

PRACTICE

Discussing grammar

Work with a partner.

1 Look at the pairs of sentences. Which tenses are used? Why? Discuss the differences in meaning.

1 I lived in Sydney for two years.
   I've lived in Sydney for two years.

2 I work for an international company.
   I've worked for them since 2006.

3 How long have you been working in Tokyo?
   How many countries have you worked in?

4 Have you ever met anyone famous?
   Did you meet anyone famous at the party?

5 I've already finished.
   I haven't finished yet.

6 Who's been eating my chocolates?
   Who's eaten my chocolates?

7 The President was shot in 1963.
   Have you heard? The President's been shot.

8 How long are you here for?
   How long have you been here for?

2 <u>Underline</u> the correct verb form.

1 His plane *took off / has taken off* a few minutes ago.

2 The president *has resigned / has been resigned* and a new president *has elected / has been elected*.

3 I *work / 've been working* in Dubai since last March. When *did you arrive / have you arrived*?

4 How many emails *have you sent / have you been sending*?

5 What *did you do / have you been doing* in the bathroom? You *were / 've been* in there for ages.

6 A huge snowstorm *has hit / has been hit* New York. Over 40 cms of snow *has fallen / has been falling* in the past 12 hours. People *have advised / have been advised* to stay at home.

T 7.4 Listen and check.

3 Where can the words in the box go in these sentences? Sometimes several words are possible.

just	yet	already	ever	never

1 I've read that book.
2 I've been reading an interesting book.
3 Has it been made into a film?
4 He's learned to drive.
5 The match hasn't finished.
6 Have you been to Morocco?

Compare answers with the class.

CALVIN KLEIN

4 **Calvin Klein** is a famous fashion designer. He has had a very interesting life so far. Look quickly through the chart of events in his life. What different things has he designed?

Age	Life event
0	Born on **November 19, 1942**, in the Bronx, New York
14	Developed a passion for fashion and drawing
18	Graduated from the **High School of Art and Design**
20	Studied at Manhattan's Fashion Institute of Technology where he met first wife, **Jayne Centre**
22	Married Jayne in **September 1964**
26	Launched his own clothing company with child**hood** friend Barry Schwartz. Daughter, **Marci, born**
28	Started designing **sportswear**
30	Introduced his trademark Calvin Klein **jeans**
31	Won the **Coty Award** – the youngest designer ever to win it. He won this three times from **1973–1975**.
32	Divorced Jayne
40	Started selling his own **CK brand underwear**
40–44	Won **Fashion Designers of America award** three times
44	Remarried – **Kelly Rector**, a wealthy New York socialite
45	Started making his own **perfumes**, called Obsession and Eternity. His most recent perfume, Euphoria, was introduced in **2007**.
50–now	Works with Kate Moss. Designs for Julia Roberts, Gwyneth Paltrow and Helen Hunt
51	Won **America's Best Designer award** in **1993**. Divorced Kelly
55	Launched his own CK brand **cosmetics** and **make-up**
Now	He's still designing. His company makes $6 billion every year.

a passion for fashion

5 With a partner study the chart. Ask and answer these questions about Calvin Klein's life.

1 How long has Calvin Klein been interested in fashion?
Since he was 14.

2 What different kinds of clothes has he designed in his career?

3 How many times has he been married and divorced?

4 How many children does he have?

5 How many awards has he won?

6 How long has he been making his own perfumes? What are they called?

7 Which famous people has he worked with and designed for?

8 How long has he been selling cosmetics?

T 7.5 Listen and check your answers. What extra information do you learn about Calvin Klein's life?

Time expressions

6 Complete the sentences with phrases from the box.

while he was studying at the Fashion Institute	four years after he got married
when he was 14	since the 1970s
in 1972	Between 1982 and 1986
for ten years	until he was 44

1 His interest in fashion began _____ .
2 He met his first wife, Jayne, _____ .
3 The first Calvin Klein jeans were introduced _____.
4 His daughter was born _____.
5 His marriage to Jayne lasted _____ .
6 He didn't marry again _____.
7 He's been designing sportswear _____ .
8 _____ he won the same award three times.

Roleplay

Imagine you are a journalist. You are going to interview Calvin Klein about his life. Write questions to ask him with your partner. Then roleplay the interview.

Interviewer	*Where were you born?*
CK	*In New York. In the Bronx.*
Interviewer	*Have you always been interested in fashion?*
CK	*Yes, I have. Well, most of my life, since I was 14.*

▶▶ **WRITING** DESCRIBING A PERSON *p109*

Have you ever ...?

7 Work with a partner. Choose from the list below and have conversations.

> Have you ever bought a pair of designer jeans?
>> No, I haven't. I can't afford them.
>> Yes, I have. I'm wearing them now.
>> Where did you buy them?

- buy/a pair of designer jeans?
- read/a book in English?
- drink/champagne?
- make/a cake?
- meet/someone on the Internet?
- sleep/in a tent?
- lose/your mobile phone?
- go/fancy dress party?
- ride/a motorbike?
- win/a competition?
- write/a love letter?
- be/given a present you didn't like?

Tell the class about your partner.

Maria's never bought a pair of designer jeans because ...

SPOKEN ENGLISH *How long ...?*

1 Read the two conversations. What are the two questions with *How long*?

1 **A** *How long are you here for?*
  B *Just three days. I arrived yesterday and I leave tomorrow.*

2 **A** *How long have you been here?*
  B *I've been here a week already. I arrived last Saturday.*

Which question refers to past up to the present?
Which question refers to a period around now (past and future)?

2 What is the correct question for these answers?

1 Four more days. We came two days ago.
2 Since Monday.
3 Until Friday. We're leaving Friday morning.
4 Over half an hour! Where have you been?
5 We're staying a month altogether.

T 7.6 Listen and check. Practise with a partner.

READING AND SPEAKING
Football – a global passion

1 Football – do you love it or hate it? Why? Have a class vote. How many famous footballers can you name? What teams do they play for?

2 Whether you love it or hate it, football is difficult to ignore. Read only the **introduction** and the **final part** of *The Beautiful Game*.

  1 What statistics are given? Do any of them surprise you?
  2 How did football become known as 'The Beautiful Game'?
  3 In what ways is football a 'simple' game?
  4 Which famous players are mentioned? What do they have in common?

3 Read *How football began*. Answer the questions.

  1 What was *tsu chu*?
  2 Which nationalities were the first to play a kind of football? When?
  3 What images do you have of 'mob football'? Describe a game.
  4 How was the game played at English public schools?
  5 What caused chaos when the boys tried to play football at university?
  6 How did the idea of half-time start?
  7 Why is a London pub important to football?
  8 What was the 'sticking point'? Which game was also born? Why?

4 Read *Football around the world*.

  1 Complete the sentences with the name of the continent.

   a _____ has become more enthusiastic about football since the 2006 World Cup.
   b _____ has the wealthiest football clubs in the world.
   c Not all countries in _____ have a passion for football.
   d _____ and _____ often lose their most talented players to rich European clubs.
   e In _____ football has become more popular with girls than boys.

  2 Which continents are most/least enthusiastic about football?
  3 Why is football called 'soccer' in North America?
  4 Why do some continents often lose players to European clubs?
  5 How and where has the World Cup increased interest in football?

What do you think?

- Football 'has totally changed the worlds of sport, media, and leisure'. What does this mean?
- Does football unite or divide the world? How?
- Why are some clubs so famous worldwide? Which players are superstars today?
- Do you agree with the conclusion about why football has become a global passion?

The

Over the last hundred years the game of football has totally changed the worlds of sport, media and leisure. Football is played worldwide by more than 1.5 m teams and 300,000 clubs. An amazing eight out of ten people in the world watch the World Cup. It is, as the great Brazilian footballer Pelé described it, 'the beautiful game'. *Andrew Hunt reports.*

How football began

As far back as 2500 BC the Chinese played a kicking game called *tsu chu*. Similar games were played by the Romans and North American Indians. In England in medieval times 'mob football' was wildly popular. In 1583, Philip Stubbs said of football players:

"sometimes their necks are broken, sometimes their backs, sometimes their legs, sometimes their arms."

By the mid-19th century, with the help of English public schools, the game had become less violent. Each school had different rules for playing the game. On the playing fields of Eton the ball was kicked high and long. At Rugby School the boys caught and ran with the ball. Problems arose when boys from the different schools went to the Universities of Oxford and Cambridge and wanted to continue playing. This is from the description of a match played in Cambridge in 1848:

"… The result was chaos, as every man played the rules he had been accustomed to at his school."

It became common to play half a match by one side's rules, the second half by the other's. That's how half-time came about. However, this was not good enough for the university men. They decided to sort out the rules once and for all.

On Monday October 26, 1863, they met at a pub in London. By the end of the day they had formed the Football Association and a *Book of Laws* was on its way. The sticking point was whether a player could pick up the ball and run with it or not, and this was not decided until December 8. From this decision the games of both football and rugby were born.

Beautiful Game

Football around the world

Europe is home to the world's richest professional clubs: Manchester United, AC Milan, Real Madrid, Bayern Munich. These clubs are famous in many countries far away from their home grounds. Rickshaw pullers in Mumbai, *tuk tuk* drivers in Bangkok, on discovering they have an English passenger respond with 'Ah, English, Manchester United. You know Manchester United?'

South America has produced some of the most exciting soccer on earth. Many of the world's leading players have come from poverty to play on the world stage. They have been snapped up by wealthy European teams after making their mark at home. Brazil has won the World Cup five times, Uruguay three times, and Argentina twice.

North America is the only continent where football (or soccer as it is called there to distinguish it from their homegrown game) has become more popular with females than males. In 1991, the US won the first Women's World Cup. Interest amongst American men has been growing since the World Cup in Los Angeles in 1994, and more recently since the arrival of international stars such as David Beckham.

Asia: Over the past two decades heated rivalry among Japan, China, and South Korea has increased the passion for soccer across the continent, especially after Japan and Korea co-hosted the World Cup in 2002. However, not all Asian countries share the passion: India and Pakistan prefer cricket.

The Middle East: Countries such as Saudi Arabia, Kuwait, and Qatar have lately been investing huge sums of money in football. They've hired the best players and coaches that money can buy.

Australia: Sport in Australia has long been dominated by cricket, rugby and surfing. However, since they qualified for the 2006 World Cup, Australians have become much more interested in the game.

Africa has produced a number of soccer superstars, but many of them have been lost to the rich European clubs. Africa is poor in resources but rich in talent, with thousands of gifted young players dreaming of big time football. South Africa's hosting of the 2010 World Cup is very important for African football.

A global passion

The game of football is played in every nation on earth, not only by the 120 m regular team players, but also by countless others on beaches, in playgrounds and streets. The world's love of football is simple – it's because football is simple. All that is needed is a ball, a piece of ground, and two posts. The world's greatest players, George Best, Diego Maradona, and Pelé, all learned their skills on waste grounds. These are the places where the sport is born and why football has become a global passion.

VOCABULARY AND LISTENING
Things I'm passionate about

1 Work with a partner. Look at the words and expressions in the box. Which are positive, which are negative? Which are neutral?

quite like	crazy about
adore	can't stand
loathe	don't mind
keen on	can't bear
not that keen on	fond of

2 Rewrite the sentences using the words in brackets.

1 She likes ice-cream very much. (*absolutely adore*)
   She absolutely adores ice-cream.
2 He likes all water sports. (*very keen*)
3 I hate opera. (*can't bear*)
4 My brother loves playing video games. (*crazy about*)
5 My sister doesn't really like any sports. (*not that keen*)
6 I don't like people who always talk about themselves. (*can't stand*)
7 My mum likes going to musicals. (*very fond*)
8 I quite like green tea but I prefer English breakfast tea. (*don't mind*)
9 The thing I hate most is tidying my room. (*loathe*)
10 I don't hate my job but it's time I applied for another one. (*quite like*)

3 Look at the photos of the people. Read what they say about their passion. Can you work out what their passion is?

4 **T 7.7** Listen to the people. Were you right? What are their passions?

5 Listen again. Answer the questions about each person.

1 How long have they had their passion?
2 What first created their interest?
3 Why do they like it so much?

6 Use some of the expressions from the box in exercise 1 to talk about the people.

What do you think?

- Which of the people's passions most interest you? Why? Which interest you least?
- Is there anything in your life that you feel passionate about? Tell the class about it.

1 **Julia**

'I enjoy it, I think, because it's a very psychological game, I mean, if you're playing badly, you have to push yourself to continue.'

'... there's only about 3 months that you can't play.'

Paul **2**

'They're so big and powerful but so beautiful when you see them racing round a field or on a track.'

'Of course, I have fallen off a few times, but it seems that the more you fall, the less it hurts.'

3 **Andrew**

'I felt the power of the words – the thing I like so much about it is that you can say so much with just a few words.'

'It's all about saying what often goes unsaid, and with passion.'

James **4**

'... they complain about it all the time but I love it.'

'Here, you really appreciate the sunshine, and you notice the seasons.'

5 **Harriet**

'... the thing I love best about it, is that you are away from everything and everyone up in the hills, and you work together with horses and dogs.'

'... it's a sheep farming area, so the farmers contact us if they have a problem.'

EVERYDAY ENGLISH
Making the right noises

1 Look at the words in the boxes. They are all possible responses in conversation. What do they express? Write in the correct heading.

• Agreement • Sympathy • Pleasure • Surprise

_____	_____	_____	_____
How fantastic!	Absolutely.	Did you?	What a pity!
That's great!	Definitely.	You didn't!	That's a shame.
Lovely!	Of course.	That's amazing!	Oh dear.
Congratulations!	Fair enough.	You're kidding!	That's too bad.
Brilliant!	Fine.	You did what?	How awful!
Good for you!	OK.	Really?	Bad luck.

Music of English ♫♪

1 ▮T 7.8▮ Listen and repeat these expressions with a wide voice range.

How fantastic! *Absolutely.* *Did you?* *What a pity!*

2 ▮T 7.9▮ Listen and practise.

---

2 ▮T 7.10▮ Listen and complete B's responses. Practise the conversation with a partner.

A My grandfather hasn't been too well lately.

B

A He's 79. Don't you think at his age he should slow down a bit?

B

A But he won't listen to me. He says he wants to enjoy his life to the full.

B

A Last summer he went on a two-week cycling holiday in France.

B

A We're going to give him a big party for his 80th birthday.

B

A But before that I'm going to have a word with him and tell him to take things more easy.

B

What other responses from exercise 1 are suitable in exercise 2?

3 Read the lines of conversation. Write in a suitable response. There are sometimes several possibilities.

1 **A** My boyfriend's just asked me to marry him.
   B _____ *(surprise)* _____ *(pleasure)*

2 **A** Will spaghetti bolognese be OK for dinner?
   B _____ *(agreement)* _____ *(pleasure)*

3 **A** There's a strike at the airport so my holiday's been cancelled.
   B _____ *(sympathy)* _____ *(sympathy)*

4 **A** I failed my driving test again.
   B _____ *(surprise)* _____ *(sympathy)*

5 **A** We're expecting a baby.
   B _____ *(surprise)* _____ *(pleasure)*

6 **A** So you think I should save to buy a car, not borrow the money?
   B _____ *(agreement)*

7 **A** I told him I never wanted to see him again.
   B _____ *(surprise)* _____ *(sympathy)*

▮T 7.11▮ Listen and compare. What is B's further comment?

4 Practise the conversations with a partner. Continue them if you can.

5 Work with a partner. Have a conversation about a good or bad day you have had recently. React as you listen and talk.

Last Sunday was the worst day of my life!

Well, ...

Oh dear. What happened?

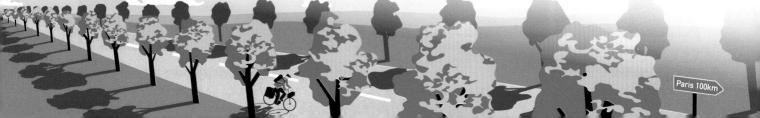

Paris 100km

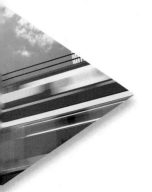

8 No fear!

Verb patterns • Body language • Travel and numbers

Match a sentence with a cartoon.

1 They stopped to talk to each other.

2 They stopped talking to each other.

What's the difference in meaning between sentences 1 and 2?

DON'T WORRY MUM!
Verb patterns

1 **T 8.1** Read and listen to the emails sent home to parents by young travellers. Where are the travellers? What has happened that gives their parents reasons to worry?

1

From: kate@oneworldmail.net
Subject: I'm fine

Hey there! Just a quick email to say Mum, please don't freak out about the photos. It looks much worse than it was!! I don't remember anyone taking the pics, and I've no idea who posted them on my Facebook website! I know you'll hate to hear this – but yes, I'd had a drink or two, but it was pitch-black dark and I was trying to climb up to the top bunk bed. Unfortunately my head hit the corner of the bed before I did (a METAL bunk bed!). Anyway, a scream of pain and lots of blood later, ooh, and I forgot to mention the ambulance ride to hospital – but now I'm fine. It's impossible to see the scar on my head!! I didn't want to say anything at the time for obvious reasons. Sorry if it shocked you!!!

Speak soon – lots of love from hot, sweaty, rainy Cairns.

miss you and love you SO MUCH
Kate x x x x x x x x

New Message   **2**

From: Dan [dantheman@fastwebmail.co.uk]
Subject: Hey Ma

Hey Ma,

Must be quick 'cos late.

Just feel I need to warn you, I met some awesome Aussies last night. They're planning to go to London next month. I said I was sure you'd like to meet them so I gave them your number. Hope you don't mind putting them up for a few nights. They're all good guys. Can't remember their names but I know you'll make them feel at home. They're looking forward to meeting you. Hope to speak to you soon.

XXX Dan

William | Reply | 3

Hello Mum, Dad and Izzy,

Had a great time yesterday. We went piranha-fishing on the Amazon in a canoe. Victor told us to throw bits of meat into the water to attract the fish but we didn't manage to catch anything. We stopped to camp on the banks in the evening and really enjoyed watching the sunset and swimming in the dark. Unfortunately, we'd forgotten to bring a torch so were lucky to escape from the crocodile.

Love to all

William

4

From: sally88@adps.mail.net
Subject: Hi from Peru!

Dear parents,

Last night we arrived at the most fantastic hotel in Arequipa, Peru. It's great to be in a room with an en-suite bathroom. We expected to have a good night's sleep but woke when an earthquake struck about 2 a.m. Panic not mother! You'll be pleased to hear that no one was hurt. We fell asleep again shortly after, and everyone felt fine in the morning despite the holes in the walls and ceilings. We're thinking of staying here two more days. I'll let you know our plans.

Lots of love, Sally x

Glossary

(to) **freak** (out) (*informal*) to have a completely shocked reaction to something

awesome (*informal*) very good; excellent

Aussies (*informal*) people from Australia

2 Read these sentences. Which verbs or phrases can fill the gaps?

1 **Kate** didn't ________ anyone taking the photos.
(a) see b ask (c) remember

2 She ________ to climb up to the top bunk bed.
a wanted b tried c remembered

3 She forgot ________ the hospital.
a mentioning b to mention c mention

4 **Dan** asked his mum ________ his Australian friends.
a put up b putting up c to put up

5 His Australian friends ________ to go to London.
a want b are hoping c are looking forward

6 He thinks his mum will make them ________ at home.
a feel b to feel c feeling

7 **William** ________ to catch piranha fish.
a didn't succeed in b didn't manage c tried

8 They stopped ________ on the river bank.
a camping b to camp c to spend the night

9 **Sally** ________ having an en-suite bathroom.
a loved b wanted c hoped

10 She is ________ staying two more days.
a planning b looking forward to c thinking of

3 **T 8.2** Listen and complete the lines. Who is speaking?

1 When we saw the photos we ________ feeling worried.
2 The photos ________ look worse than it really was.
3 Your friends must ________ keep their room tidy.
4 It's really kind of you ________ them stay.
5 Did Victor ________ escape from the crocodile?
6 He warned us not ________ swimming.
7 We couldn't ________ a bit scared.
8 Have you ________ come home yet?

GRAMMAR SPOT

1 Match a pattern in **A** with a sentence from the emails in **B**.

A	**B**
verb + *-ing*	I **need to warn** you.
verb + *to*	Victor **told us to throw** meat.
verb + sb + *to*	You'll **make them feel** at home.
verb + sb + infinitive (without *to*)	He **enjoyed swimming**.
adjective + *to*	We're **thinking of staying** two more days.
preposition + *-ing*	It's **impossible to see** the scar.

2 What is the difference in meaning between these sentences?

She remembered to email her mum. ***She remembered emailing her mum.***

▶▶ Grammar Reference 8 p142 Verb patterns p158

PRACTICE
Phoning home

1 Work with a partner. Complete Kate's phone conversation with her mother.

M Kate! It's so good __to hear__ (*hear*) from you. Are you OK?

K Oh Mum, I'm really sorry for _____ (*worry*) you so much. I really didn't mean to.

M We opened our emails and we were so delighted _____ (*see*) all your photos and then we saw that one.

K I didn't want my friends _____ (*post*) it on *Facebook*. I asked them not to.

M But Kate, all that blood, and you went to hospital. We couldn't help _____ (*feel*) worried.

K I know, but honestly Mum, my friends made me _____ (*go*) to the hospital, I really didn't need to.

M How is your head now?

K Absolutely fine. Honestly. I'll email you some more photos and you can see for yourself.

M OK. Don't forget to.

K I'll call again soon and I promise _____ (*text*) regularly. Bye.

M Bye. Take care!

2 [T 8.3] Listen and check. Practise the conversation.

SPOKEN ENGLISH *Don't forget to!* – the reduced infinitive

1 In conversation it isn't necessary to use the full infinitive if it is understood from the context.

A *I'll email some more photos.*
B *OK. Don't **forget to** ~~email~~.*
A *Can you and Mary come to lunch next Sunday?*
B *Oh yes, we'd **love to** ~~come~~.*

Find three more examples in Kate's conversation with her mother.

2 Reply to **A**, using the verb in brackets and a reduced infinitive.

1 A Did you post my letter?
  B Oh sorry, I _____. (*forget*)

2 A I can't go out with you this evening. Sorry.
  B Oh, but you _____. (*promise*)

3 A Why did you email your mother again?
  B Because she _____. (*ask me*)

4 A Do you think you'll apply for that job?
  B Yes, I've definitely _____. (*decide*)

5 A Are you taking your brother to the airport?
  B Well, I _____ (*offer*) but he said he _____ me _____. (*not want*)

[T 8.4] Listen and check your answers. Practise with a partner.

Talking about you

3 Complete the sentences so that they are true for you BUT make two of them false.

1 I really enjoy …
2 I'm no good at …
3 I mustn't forget …
4 I will always remember …
5 I've just finished …
6 I sometimes find it difficult …
7 My parents made me … when I was young.
8 I'm looking forward to …
9 I'd love …

4 Work in small groups. Read some true and some false sentences aloud to each other. Make comments and ask questions to find the false ones.

> I really enjoy cycling.

> Do you? Do you cycle to work?

> I don't believe you. You don't even have a bike!

LISTENING AND SPEAKING
Fears and phobias

1 What are typical phobias that people have? Make a list. Are you afraid of anything?

2 Work with a partner. Match the phobias in the chart with their definitions. Compare answers as a class.

> We think autophobia is fear of ...
>
> It might be ...
>
> We've no idea what ... is.

Autophobia		washing. *the colour blue.*
Ablutophobia	is a	*flying.* **birds.** feeling cold.
Aviophobia	fear of	
Frigophobia		**fridges.** *being alone.* **cars.**

3 **T 8.5** Some people have strange phobias. Listen to Jodie, Gavin, and Melissa talking about theirs. After each one discuss these questions as a class.

1 Which part of the cartoon would make them panic?
2 How did their phobia start?
3 How does it affect their lives?
4 What caused their panic attack?
5 Have they tried to cure their phobia?

4 Work in small groups to retell the stories. Use the prompts to help.

Jodie

When she was a little girl ... grandmother asked her ... opened the cupboard ... dark green cardigan ... started screaming ... her grandmother managed to ... now it's difficult to ... tries to find ... a year ago ... a colleague's jacket ... has decided to ... embarrassed ...

Gavin

His dad used to ... he didn't like watching him ... when seven started feeling ... his dad had to stop ... problem got worse ... supermarkets ... asked his wife never to ... daren't go to restaurants ... oyster ... only hamburger bars ... started to see ... hasn't succeeded in ...

Melissa

Since she was five ... trying to blow up ... popped in her face ... can remember ... her friends enjoy ... think it's fun to ... last time ... a panic attack ... they refused to ... difficulty in ... worst thing ... parties ... can't imagine ever ... even on TV ... starts to shake ...

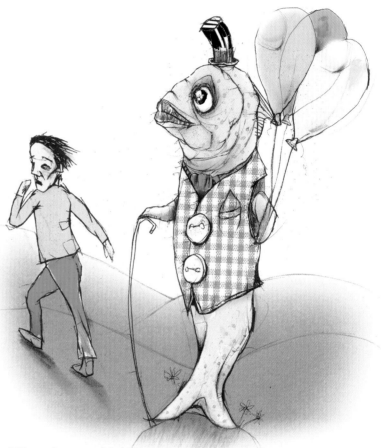

What do you think?

5 Discuss these questions in your groups.

1 Which of the three people do you think has the most difficult phobia to live with? Why?
2 Why do people get phobias?
3 Why do some people and not others get them?
4 How do you think they can be cured? Suggest ideas.

The psychologist's view

6 **T 8.6** Listen to psychologist Dr Lucy Atcheson talking about phobias. How does she answer questions 2–4 in exercise 5?

Language work

Look at T8.5 on p127. Choose a story and <u>underline</u> examples of different kinds of verb patterns.

READING AND SPEAKING
Dangerous journeys in history

1 Close your eyes. Imagine you are one of 90,000 people. You are travelling together, on foot, over mountains, rivers and plains. It's winter. What problems would you face?

2 You are going to read about two famous leaders, Hannibal Barca and Mao Zedong. They both undertook remarkable journeys with thousands of people. Look at the maps. What difficulties can you anticipate?

3 Divide into two groups.

Group A Read about HANNIBAL
Group B Read about **Mao Zedong**

First read about your leader's *Early Years*. Answer the questions with your group.

1 How did his father influence his life?
2 Who were the enemy?
3 Where did he move to?
4 Why did they set off on such a long journey?

4 Read about the journey and answer the questions.

1 When did the journey start?
2 How many began it? Who were they?
3 What kind of leader was he?
4 What problems did they face on the way?
5 How long did the journey last?
6 How did it end? How many survived?

5 Read the final part. What happened to the leader after the journey?

6 Find someone from the other group. Go through the questions again and compare the leaders and their journeys. Use the maps to help. What similarities can you find? How many years separate the two journeys?

What do you think?

• Which journey was more dangerous? Why?
• Can you imagine such a journey on foot taking place today? Where and why might it happen?

▶▶ **WRITING** TELLING A STORY (2) *p110*

HANNIBAL
CROSSES THE ALPS
247-182 BC

EARLY YEARS

Hannibal Barca was born in Carthage, North Africa, (now a suburb of Tunis, Tunisia) in 247 BC. At that time this once prosperous seaport was losing a long and exhausting war with the Romans over who should rule the western Mediterranean. His father, Hamilcar, was a general in the army, and it is said that he made his son promise to hate the Romans forever.

The 23-year-long war was finally lost in 241 BC. Hannibal and his family moved to Spain, where the Carthaginians were trying to build a new empire. Hannibal grew up to be a bold and fearless fighter like his father, and eventually became commander of the army. In 218 BC the Romans again threatened to attack. In a daring and dangerous plan Hannibal decided to march from Spain to Italy before the Romans had even declared war. This march was to be a journey of 2,415 kilometres across both the Pyrenees and the Alps.

Mao Zedong
and the Long March
1893–1976

Early years

Mao Zedong (Mao Tse Tung) was born in Hunan province in Southern China in 1893. His father was an ambitious but illiterate farmer, who wanted his son to have the education he didn't have.

At university Mao became active in revolutionary student groups and, in 1921, helped found the Chinese Communist Party. He established a base in the remote Jiangxi province, where they formed the Red Army to fight against the Nationalist Government under Chiang Kai-shek. However, in 1934, after many bloody battles, they were forced to escape from the area. They set off on a remarkable journey, which became known as the Long March.

THE JOURNEY

In May, 218 BC, Hannibal left Spain with an army of about 90,000 men and 37 elephants, which he believed were needed to get them over the mountains. In the next few months under his inspiring leadership, they marched through Spain to the Pyrenees and then to the South of France. They moved about 16 kilometres a day, and were frequently attacked by local tribesmen. They reached the River Rhone and accomplished the unbelievable task of building huge rafts to ferry the elephants across. Some fell off but managed to swim using their trunks as snorkels. It was now autumn, and snow started to fall as they approached the Alps. The army, helped by the elephants, struggled on, slipping and sliding over ice and snow, over the main pass. Finally, they were in sight of Italy. Their five-month journey at an end, Hannibal's army of 90,000 was reduced to 36,000 – over half his men had perished or deserted on the way. Winter storms now killed all but one of his elephants.

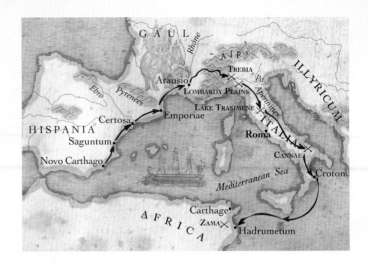

FINAL YEARS

In some ways Hannibal's march was hugely successful because he took the Romans by surprise and initially defeated them in numerous battles. However, after many years and many more battles his army failed to overcome Rome's superior resources and manpower. Hannibal, who had been 29 at the start of his journey, sailed back to North Africa aged 45. He finally committed suicide in 182 BC, aged 65. Despite his final defeat, he is still recognized as one of the greatest military leaders in history.

The Long March

The march began on October 16th. No one was sure where they were going but 86,000 men and 30 women, including Mao's wife, set out to walk from the south to the north of China. The journey took one year, ending in the northwestern Shaanxi province.

They started the march quite well, armed with 33,243 guns, but five weeks later suffered their first disastrous defeat at the Xiang River crossing. They lost 56,000 men and much of their equipment was thrown into the river.

It was at this time that Mao Zedong became leader of both the Red Army and the Communist Party. He was a tough but popular leader.

One of the worst experiences was crossing the Great Snowy Mountains, 5,000 metres high. Many men died from lack of oxygen. Exhausted, they knew that to stop to rest meant certain death. If they managed to reach the top, it was best to sit down and slide to the bottom on the ice. Many men were catapulted over cliffs.

It was now September 1935 and the army had to cross the Marshland, between the Yangtze and Yellow Rivers. It looked innocent, covered with flowers, but beneath the flowers were bogs that could swallow a man in a minute. Mao lost more men during this seven day trek than in the Snowy Mountains.

Eventually, on October 19th, after marching for 370 days and 12,500 kilometres they reached Shaanxi province. Of the 86,000 who began, only 4,000 remained.

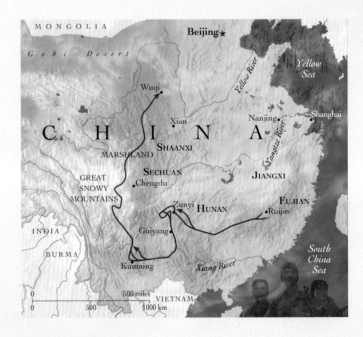

Later years

The Long March began the ascent to power of Mao Zedong. On October 1, 1949, he proclaimed the People's Republic of China and the Great Cultural Revolution followed. This radically changed every aspect of Chinese society. In October 1966, Mao's Little Red Book was published, and his ideas were taught throughout the country. Mao's image was displayed everywhere: in homes, offices, shops and streets. He finally died on September 9th, 1976, aged 82.

VOCABULARY AND IDIOM
Body language

1 As a class, brainstorm all the parts of the body. Fill the board with all that you can think of.

2 Work in small groups. Which parts of the body do you use to do the following things?

bite	blow	clap	climb	hit	hug	kick	kneel
lick	march	point	scratch	stare	whistle		

3 Which verbs in exercise 2 go with these nouns and phrases?

_____ a ladder	_____ your nails
_____ out of the window	_____ up a balloon
_____ a tune	_____ an insect bite
_____ someone tight	_____ your hands to the music
_____ a football	_____ at a place on the map
_____ an ice-cream	_____ a nail with a hammer
_____ down to pray	_____ like a soldier

T 8.7 Listen and check. What is the situation for each expression?

4 The sentences all contain idioms to do with parts of the body. Work out the meanings from context.

1 I don't get on with my brother. We don't **see eye to eye** about anything.

2 I saw a programme on TV about quantum physics but I'm afraid **it went straight over my head**.

3 **Don't waste your breath** trying to explain it to me. I'll never understand.

4 Did you hear about Millie's party? People drank too much and the whole thing **got out of hand**.

5 The house was such a mess and when her parents came back they **kicked up** such **a fuss**. I don't blame them.

6 Can you help me? I've **hit a problem** installing this program on my computer.

7 My dad keeps a stack of chocolate in his desk for while he's working. He's **got** such **a sweet tooth**.

8 I feel silly. I got so excited when he said I'd won the lottery but he was only **pulling my leg**.

5 Replace each idiom in exercise 4 with a literal meaning from the box. Read the sentences aloud with both expressions.

loves sweet things	I didn't understand a word	
agree	were furious	I'm having trouble with
got out of control	it's not worth	joking

6 Look these words up in a dictionary. Choose *one* idiomatic expression for each. Share them with the class.

heart	head	hand	foot	hair

EVERYDAY ENGLISH
Travel and numbers

1 Read aloud these numbers. When do we say *and*?

15 50 **406** 72 178 **90** 19 850 **1,520**

17.5 36 247 5,000 **180,575** 2,000,000

T 8.8 Listen and check.

Notice the way we use points and commas in English.
£6.50 (six pounds fifty)
2,500 (two thousand five hundred)
3.14 (three point one four)

2 Match a question with a number. Ask and answer them with a partner. Practise saying the numbers aloud.

Questions	Numbers
1 What time does the train leave?	07700 984 361
2 How far is it to Moscow?	27 kilos
3 How long's the flight?	1,915 km
4 How much does it cost?	13.45
5 What's your credit card number?	17.5%
6 What's the expiry date?	About 1½ hours
7 How much does it weigh?	6356 5055 5137 9904
8 What's your mobile number?	£34.99
9 What's the rate of VAT?	02/14

T 8.9 Listen and check. Practise again.

3 Work in pairs. Find the numbers in the pictures and practise saying them.

4 **T 8.10** Listen to a conversation.
1 Where is it taking place?
2 Who are the people?
3 Where does the man want to travel to?
4 What is the problem?

Listen again. Write down all the different numbers you hear. What do they refer to?

  one (bag), 30 kilos

Practise the conversation with a partner.

5 **T 8.11** Listen to another conversation and do the same again.

6 Work in groups. Write down some numbers that are important to you. Can the others guess what they refer to? Explain what they are.

> Nineteen

> Is it your age next birthday?

> No. It's the day I go on holiday. July 19th!

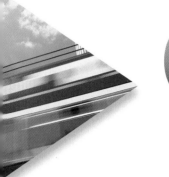

9 It depends how you look at it

Conditionals • Words with similar meaning • Dealing with money

STARTER

Ideas can be looked at in different ways.
Work in groups. Think of some pros and cons of being a teenager.

+ You aren't a kid any more.
  You are becoming more independent.

– You aren't a child, but you aren't an adult.
  You don't have any money.

Compare ideas as a class.

BILLY'S STORY
Conditionals

1 Why are some kids bullied? Why do some kids become bullies?

2 Read about Billy. What are his problems?

BILLY'S STORY

Billy enjoyed school. He tried hard, but studying wasn't easy for him.

He didn't have many friends. He felt lonely and insecure.

The other kids started bullying Billy. They called him 'Billy no mates' and stole his money.

They sent him texts. They threatened to hurt him.

He tried to talk to people, but they didn't listen.

Billy started playing truant. He felt desperate. He didn't know who to go to for help.

3 What would *you* do if you were …?

> Billy's mum Billy's sister Billy's dad
> Billy's head teacher a counsellor from Kidcare Billy

> If I were Billy's mum, I'd go to the head teacher, and explain what was happening.

> I wouldn't. I'd talk to Billy and …

4 **T 9.1** Listen. Who are the six speakers imagining they are?

I'd organize a school day which tried to educate everyone about bullying, and I'd invite social workers, police and psychologists. — The head teacher.

5 Look at the *Kidcare Report*. Read what the counsellor wrote about Billy. What *did* Billy do?
Answer the questions.

- Did people listen to Billy?
- Did he talk to Kidcare?
- Did his father stay?

Look at the sentences in **bold** in the *Kidcare Report*.
T 9.2 Listen and repeat.

Things got tough for Billy and his sister when their dad walked out.

Then the attacks started. Every day after school the bullies waited for him.

So what would you do…?

If you're being bullied, contact KIDCARE.

We're on your side. Phone 0879 364 8888.

KIDCARE REPORT

MISSING

Client: Billy Simmons
Age: 14
Counsellor: Carmen Delanie

Billy ran away from home because he was being bullied at school. He has now been missing for six months. He had tried to talk to his mother and his teachers. **If they'd listened to him, they'd have understood** how he was feeling.

Billy's father walked out on the family. **If his father had stayed, Billy might have felt happier** and less insecure.

If he'd talked to us, we could have helped him. He should have come to us a long time ago.

We are doing all we can to locate Billy. We suspect that he is somewhere in London

6 Make a sentence using *If* and the prompts.

1 People didn't understand what Billy was going through.
   understood … wouldn't … run away
   If they'd understood, he wouldn't have run away.

2 He didn't go to Kidcare.
   gone … could … talked … problems

3 His father left.
   left … Billy might … felt more secure

4 The bullies threatened him.
   threatened … he wouldn't … run away

T 9.3 Listen and check.

GRAMMAR SPOT

1 Second conditional sentences express an unreal situation about the present.

> If I **was** in trouble, I'**d** (= would) **come** to you for help.
> (*But I'm not in trouble.*)

Third conditional sentences express an unreal situation about the past.

> If you'**d** (=had) **told** me about your problems, I'**d**
> (= would) **have helped**. (*But you didn't tell me, so I didn't help.*)

How do we form second and third conditional sentences?

2 Which two of these modal verbs express a possibility?

> I **would** / **might** / **could** have helped you.

3 Look at this sentence.

> Pete **shouldn't have stolen** the money.

Is this good advice? Did Pete steal the money?

▶▶ **Grammar Reference 9.1–9.6 p142–3**

PRACTICE
It all went wrong

1 Work in pairs. Read about three robberies that went wrong. What were the robbers' mistakes?

Easy arrest

A bank robber in Marseille, France, held up a sign which said 'Give me all the money.' The cashier handed over the money, and the bank robber fled, leaving the note behind. Unfortunately, he had written the note on the back of an envelope. On the other side was his address. He was arrested later the same day.

Smile!

Car thief Lee Hoskins took pictures of himself stealing a Vauxhall Astra with a camera he found in the glove department. Lee and his girlfriend took turns posing before crashing the car and fleeing the scene, leaving the camera on the back seat of the car. 'It's amazing just how stupid some criminals can be,' said a spokesman for Somerset police.

Have a loan instead

A Finnish bank manager stopped a robbery by persuading the three criminals to take out a loan instead. The robbers burst into the bank near Helsinki, and demanded €50,000. The manager put the money on the table, but suggested that a loan would be more sensible. He offered them a €10 cash advance and told them to return in ten minutes to sign the loan papers. Police were waiting for them.

2 Rewrite the sentences about the robberies using the words in brackets.

1 It was a mistake to write his note on an envelope. *(shouldn't)*

   He shouldn't have written his note on an envelope.

2 It would have been better to take the note with him. *(should)*

   _____

3 He left his address. The police found him. *(if)*

   _____

4 It was stupid to take his photo. *(shouldn't)*

   _____

5 They crashed the car. They didn't escape. *(if, could)*

   _____

6 He left photos of himself. He could have got away with it. *(if, might)*

   _____

7 They were so stupid. They didn't escape with the money. *(if)*

   _____

8 They listened to the manager. They didn't steal the money. *(if, could)*

   _____

9 It was silly to go back to the bank. *(shouldn't)*

   _____

10 It would have been better to just run away. *(should)*

   _____

You're an idiot!

3 Your friend did some really stupid things.

> I drove home even though I was falling asleep at the wheel.

> You're an idiot! You might have had an accident! You could have killed someone!

How do you react when he tells you these things? Use *might have* or *could have*.

1 I went walking in the mountains for three days with no food or equipment.

2 I didn't feel like going to work, so I phoned in sick. I went shopping instead.

3 I had a temperature of 102, but I went out dancing all night.

4 I told Sally I couldn't see her, then went out to the pub with Danielle.

5 I used to be really good at tennis, I was an under-14 champion, but then I gave it all up.

T 9.4 Listen and compare.

Speaking

4 Think of a time in your life when things went wrong.

> I went to a party with my boyfriend.
> I kissed another boy.
> I had a row with my boyfriend.
> We broke up.

Make sentences like these.

> I shouldn't have kissed the other boy.

> If I hadn't kissed him, I wouldn't have had a row with my boyfriend.

> I should have just said sorry to my boyfriend. Then we wouldn't have broken up.

SPEAKING AND LISTENING
A social conscience

1 Work in small groups. Do you have a social conscience? Discuss the situations 1–5 and decide what you would do.

I'd . . .   I wouldn't . . .   I might . . .

Tell the class.

2 **T 9.5** Listen to five people describing a situation they were in. Answer the questions.

1 Where was he/she?
2 Who were the other people involved?
3 What was the problem?
4 Did he/she do anything? Say anything?
5 What was the other person's reaction?
6 What was the result?

Talking about you

3 What would *you* have done in the same situations? Discuss in your groups, then tell the rest of the class.

I wouldn't have done what she did.
I'd have told him . . .

SPOKEN ENGLISH *just*

1 Look at the use of *just* in these sentences.

I'd **just** reached the front of the queue . . .
I **just** need to ask a quick question.
. . . I was **just** furious!

In which sentences does *just* mean . . .?

really   a short time before   only/simply

2 Find other examples of *just* in T9.5 on p128.

3 Write the word *just* where you think it goes best in these sentences.

1 Alice isn't here. She's ⤬ gone. *(just)*
2 I'm sorry I'm in a bad mood. I'm tired, that's all.
3 I love your new coat!
4 I've finished the most wonderful book. You must read it!
5 I don't want any wine. A glass of water, please.
6 John's so generous. I think he's amazing!
7 'Who's coming tonight?' 'Me.'
8 Hold on a minute. I'm going to the loo.

T 9.6 Listen, check, and repeat.

Do you have a social conscience?
What would YOU do?

1 You are in the street. A man who says he's penniless and homeless is asking for money, so you give him some. As you're walking away, his phone starts ringing. He pulls out a really nice mobile phone and starts chatting to a friend.

2 You're in a shop. You see a woman shop-lifting some food. She's got three small children, who look hungry.

3 You're in a place where smoking is forbidden. Two men light a cigarette in front of you.

4 Your best friend is cheating on her boyfriend, Bill. She's been going out with him for ages, but she's also seeing a guy called Mark.

5 You see some kids in the street dropping litter. There is a litter bin five metres away.

READING AND SPEAKING
The victim meets the burglar

1 Have you or anyone you know ever been the victim of a crime? Discuss the questions.
  - What happened?
  - Were the police involved?
  - Was the criminal arrested?

2 There is an organization called the *Restorative Justice Consortium*. It brings together criminals and their victims.
  - What do you think it hopes to achieve by this?
  - What might the victim of a crime have to say?
  - What might the criminal learn?

3 Read the headlines and the introduction to the newspaper article. How do you think the burglar and the victim became friends?

4 Work in two groups.

  Group A Read about the victim.
  Group B Read about the robber.

  Answer the questions.
  1 What personal details do you learn? (*name, age, background …*)
  2 What was he doing in the moments before their first encounter?
  3 What was his first reaction? How did he feel? What did he think?
  4 How does he describe the act of violence?
  5 How did he feel after the crime took place?
  6 What was his reaction when asked to meet the other person?
  7 What made Will so angry?
  8 What did this outburst of anger make him realize?
  9 What does he think of the experience of restorative justice?

5 Find a partner from the other group. Compare your answers to the questions in exercise 4.

What do you think?

1 Is bringing together the criminal and the victim a good idea? Could it help with all crimes? Could it help with bullying?

2 60% of people released after serving one year in prison are convicted of another crime. What does this statistic suggest?

3 The purposes of imprisonment are …
  - to punish the criminal.
  - to protect society from the criminal.
  - to rehabilitate the criminal.

  Do you think these aims are achieved?
  What other forms of punishment might be more effective?

▶▶ **WRITING** PROS AND CONS *p112*

I'M SORRY

How a burglar and his victim became the best of friends

THE VICTIM

BUSINESSMAN Will Riley, 50, lives in Islington, north London, with his wife and daughter …

❝ I WAS getting ready to go to the gym when I walked into my hall and stopped dead. There, standing on the stairs, was a man about the same age as me, dressed in a scruffy leather jacket.

"What are you doing here?" I asked in shock. He said he was a neighbour who'd got lost. But it was obvious who he was.

I was suddenly scared. I thought, "If he's got a knife, he could kill me." We kind of fought with each other. A passer-by saw us and phoned the police. Somehow I managed to hold him until the police arrived. It was only after they arrested him and took him away that a policeman asked if I was OK. I put my hand to my head and felt blood. I hadn't realized what he'd done to me. It's incredible, but I just didn't register that he'd hit me really hard. He'd smashed a flower pot on my head, and all the bits were on the ground. I went to hospital and needed stitches.

After the burglary, my whole life changed. I've always lived in big cities, and I've never been afraid of urban crime, but suddenly I became too frightened to open my front door. All I could think was "What if my daughter had been at home? Would he have attacked her?"

PETER WOOLF, a life-long criminal, broke into Will Riley's home one March evening. Will found Peter standing in his hall, his pockets stuffed with money and jewellery.

Peter was jailed for three years for the burglary. So it's hard to think of them becoming friends.

Here, Will and Peter describe their first encounter, and why meeting each other again was the best thing for both of them …

By VICTORIA KENNEDY

CLOSE FRIENDS: Peter Woolf and Will Riley

I was asked to meet the burglar in prison. I wasn't sure what the purpose was, but I went anyway. I was curious.

We sat in the prison library, and he explained how he'd come from a dysfunctional family, was a heroin addict and spent his life in and out of jail. He spoke without any emotion. But it was when he suddenly said "Last time we met …" that I exploded.

I screamed at him, 'Why me? Why did you ruin my life?'

"We didn't meet in a bar, you little …! You broke into my house!" I was so angry. I screamed at him, "Why me? Why did you do this to me? Why did you ruin my life?"

I could see from his face that I had got through to him. He looked stunned. It was then I realized he was just an ordinary guy. And I wanted to help him …

When I got home, I felt relieved. All my fears disappeared. Because I could see Peter was just a normal human being, he became less frightening.

When he was finally released, we stayed in touch. I've met him dozens of times since and the change in him is amazing. It's hard to believe he's the same person who broke into my home. He's totally different.

I'm delighted that I've done something to help Peter get his life back. 🦵

THE ROBBER

PETER WOOLF, 50, is married to Louise, and works as a counsellor to rehabilitate criminals …

❝IT WAS easy to break into Will's house. Just one push and the lock broke. I quickly took some gold jewellery and some money from upstairs. I was feeling lucky.

But when I was coming downstairs and I bumped into Will in the hall, I suddenly felt frightened. I thought, "He's a big guy. If he wanted to, he could hurt me."

I tried to escape. I didn't want to hit him, but I did. I'm not a violent guy, but I just did what I had to do. There was a flower pot, and I smashed it on his head.

After I was arrested, all I felt was a big sense of relief. I was going back to a place I knew well. I'd been in and out of prison for 18 years, for theft, burglary, and fraud.

I started using drugs when I was 10 and became an addict at 14. I'd hit rock bottom. I stole because it was the only thing I knew how to do. I knew it would only lead me back to prison.

I was given a three-year sentence. It was while I was in jail someone mentioned Restorative Justice. I couldn't see the point, but I agreed to do it because I was bored.

It wasn't until I started walking down the corridor towards the library that I got scared.

When I got there I sat down and just looked at the floor. I said the same rubbish I always used to say to the police. But Will was furious, and I was shocked. I thought, "My God, I did all this."

I felt angry with myself, and ashamed. I was determined to make things better.

I suddenly realized that I was responsible for this man's pain. He wasn't just a faceless nobody that I'd stolen from. I felt angry with myself, and ashamed. I was determined to make things better.

I did a course of rehab to get off drugs. I also started a course to be a counsellor.

It was at the counselling class that I met Louise. I was over the moon. And my life changed completely …

I was released early after 18 months, and Louise and I got married. Life hasn't been easy, but I've worked hard to get things together.

I'm now helping others. I'm clean of drugs and haven't committed another crime. I feel proud of myself. These days, I consider myself lucky that I broke into Will's house that day. If I hadn't – and if we hadn't become friends – I don't know what I would have done. I guess I'd be dead by now. 🦵

VOCABULARY
Words with similar meaning

1 Match the words in **A** with their similar meanings in **B**. They all appeared in the newspaper article on p74–5.

A	B
prison	frightened
burglar	bump into
scared	stunned
purpose	completely
meet	furious
angry	normal
shocked	jail
ordinary	point
delighted	over the moon
totally	robber

burglar

robber

2 Complete the sentences with pairs of words from exercise 1. The first word is from **A**, the second word is from **B**.

1 'Did you _____ anyone you know in town?'
  'Yes, I _____ Alice as I was coming out of a shop.'

2 'Aren't you _____ with your exam results?'
  'You bet. I'm _____ . It's great!'

3 'The _____ of this meeting is to brainstorm ideas.'
  'Sorry, but I don't see the _____ . Why bother?'

4 'You must be _____ with Tim for crashing your car.'
  'I'm absolutely _____ with him.'

5 'I was _____ when I heard that Joe had died. Weren't you?'
  'I was _____ . He was only 48.'

6 'I'm _____ of dogs. I was bitten once.'
  'I'm not _____ of them. They're usually really friendly.'

3 These words are similar but not the same. Choose the correct word.

1 **alone / lonely**
  live _____ happily
  feel _____ and unhappy

2 **big / great**
  _____ house/mistake/feet
  _____ artist/Wall of China/party

3 **tall / high**
  _____ person/building/trees
  _____ mountain/wall/ceiling

4 **small / little**
  _____ old lady/boy/finger
  _____ room/glass of wine/dress size

5 **quick / fast**
  _____ car/train/food
  _____ drink/worker/thinking

4 Which verb goes with which phrase?

| win | Arsenal |
| beat | the championship |

| clean | my hair |
| wash | the flat |

| make | a mess |
| do | your best |

| listen | a noise |
| hear | to music |

| talk | to my mates for hours |
| speak | to my bank manager |

| rob | a bank |
| steal | some jewellery |

| buy | someone a present |
| pay | at the cash desk |

| borrow | money from someone |
| lend | money to someone |

EVERYDAY ENGLISH
Dealing with money

1 **T 9.7** Listen to the beginnings of five conversations. Match each conversation with a photo.

- Who are the people?
- What are they talking about?
- What questions are asked?

2 **T 9.8** Listen to the whole conversations. Check your answers to the questions in exercise 1.

3 Work with a partner. Look at 1–5. Try to remember the full conversations. The words in blue will help.

1 A Here's … bill.
   B Thank … Is service …?
   A No … hope … enjoyed …
   B … lovely, …
   A Can … put in … number? And then … ENTER. … card … receipt.
   B Thanks. … for you.
   A … kind. … hope … again soon.
   B Bye!

included
PIN

2 A How … standard …?
   B £55 …
   A … everything?
   B That … two people, but it … breakfast.
   A …, is it?
   B Yes, … afraid … But … £55 does … VAT.

per night
extra

3 A … tickets … MasterCard.
   B Can you … number?
   A 5484 6922 3171 2435.
   B … date?
   A 09/12.
   B And the three … security number …?
   A 721.

expiry
digit

4 A … give me … my account?
   B Sure. … number?
   A 4033 2614 7900.
   B Bear … one moment. The … cleared balance … is £542.53 …

balance
credit

5 A … gin … glasses … wine, please?
   B … £14.50.
   A Thank you.
   B And here's your change. 50p.
   A Thanks. Er …? How much …? I think … mistake!
   B Sorry?
   A I think you must … I … £20, but … given me … £15.
   B No, I …
   A Well, I … pretty … I gave you …
   B Oh, …? Er … Here …
   A Thanks.

change
made a mistake

4 **T 9.8** Listen again to the conversations. Check your answers in T9.8 on p128.

5 Discuss the questions.

- What's the exchange rate between your currency and the US dollar? Between your currency and sterling?
- Are you overdrawn at the end of the month? Can you economize if you have to?
- What credit cards do you have? Do you have any store cards? Do you keep within your credit limit?

10 All things high tech

STARTER

1 <u>Underline</u> the nouns in these sentences.

My brother has the best computer in the world. Mine is just an old laptop.

Find . . . a definite article an indefinite article
a possessive adjective a possessive pronoun

2 <u>Underline</u> the reflexive pronouns in these sentences.

Mike programs his computer himself.
I live by myself, which suits me fine.

CHIPS WITH EVERYTHING
Noun phrases

1 Work with a partner. Read the text about microprocessors. Answer the questions.

1 Do you agree with these statements? Why/Why not?

Microchips are huge. Microchips are tiny.

2 What things in our daily lives have microchips in them?
3 In what way are computers very simple?
4 How long does it take to make microprocessors?
5 Why do designers put pictures on the chips?
6 In what ways is the future exciting?

Microprocessors
The biggest thing since the invention of the wheel

What are they?

A microprocessor (also known as a microchip, or just a chip) is a small, thin piece of silicon that has been printed with transistors. One chip can contain hundreds of millions of transistors, performing billions (yes, billions) of calculations each second. The smallest are just a few mm². It is the most complex product that has ever been made.

What do they do?

Microprocessors are the brains of your personal computer. They control everything in our lives. They are used in all digital devices – calculators, cameras, radios, ovens, fridges, washing machines, DVDs, and watches. Without microprocessors, modern cars wouldn't start or stop (there are about 60 per car), TV remotes wouldn't switch channels, and we couldn't text each other on our mobiles. Doctors and surgeons wouldn't be able to diagnose, treat, or operate. Nearly all of their equipment contains microchips.

How do they work?

Transistors are microscopic electronic switches that turn on and off billions of times a second. It's hard to believe that basically that is all a computer does – it either says *Yes* or *No*.

To process the words, images and sounds we use every day, computers and other devices (such as CD players) transform these communications into a simple code that uses the numerals 0 and 1 to represent the on and off states of a transistor. This language of 0s and 1s is known as digital information.

How are they made?

It takes months to make a microprocessor, and involves over 250 manufacturing steps, but it can take years to design them. Sometimes the engineers put pictures on the surface of the chip because they want to show it's theirs. The pictures are incredibly tiny, and can only be seen with a microscope. They are like the designers' signature.

What about the future?

The digital world is only a few decades old. There are still countless more things we could do with microprocessors. Soon they'll be able to fix themselves and even make themselves. No one knows what will happen. The future hasn't happened yet.

2 Look back at the text on p78. Find and complete these sentences.

Microprocessors are the biggest thing since …
A microchip is a …
The smallest … mm².
… most complex product …
Microprocessors control …
They are used in all …
We couldn't text …
Doctors and surgeons … Nearly all …
It takes months …
Microprocessors will be able to … and even …

GRAMMAR SPOT

Noun phrases can consist of:

Articles

A chip is **a** small piece of silicon.
It is **the** biggest thing since **the** invention of **the** wheel.

Possessives

All of **their** equipment contains microchips.
They want to show it's **theirs**.
The pictures are like the designer**s'** signature.

all / everything

Microchips control **everything** in our lives.
They are used in **all** digital devices.

Pronouns

Microchips will be able to fix **themselves**.
We couldn't text **each other**.

▶▶ Grammar Reference 10.1–10.5 p143–5

---

3 Read these facts. Which surprise you most?

Did you know ...?

There are **20 billion** microchips in use in the world today. Every year another **5 billion** are produced.

Every **18** months, the technology develops to allow **twice** as many transistors to fit on a chip, **doubling** its speed and capacity.

The smallest wire on a chip is less than **0.1 microns** wide. A human hair is **100 microns** thick.

PRACTICE

Articles – *a/an/the*/no article/*one*

1 Discuss the use of articles in these sentences.

I bought **a** laptop and **a** printer on Saturday.
The laptop has **an** *Intel* microprocessor.
Intel is **the** largest manufacturer of computer chips in **the** world.
One chip contains millions of transistors.
I don't understand **(-)** computers.

2 Complete the text with *a/an/the*, or no article.

THE FIRST COMPUTER

Charles Babbage (1791–1871) was (1) _____ scientist and (2) _____ engineer. He had the idea for (3) _____ first programmable computer. He wanted to build (4) _____ machine that could do (5) _____ calculations without making the mistakes that human 'computers' made.

He designed a machine called the Difference Engine, and (6) _____ British Government provided funds. (7) _____ machine was never completed because Babbage ran out of (8) _____ money.

In 1991, (9) _____ team of engineers from (10) _____ Science Museum in London built one of Babbage's machines, using his original designs, and it worked perfectly.

T 10.1 Listen and check.

3 Complete the sentences with *a/an/the*/no article, or *one*.

1 'Where's Jane?' 'In _____ kitchen cooking _____ lunch.'
2 Washington, D.C. is _____ capital of _____ United States.
3 We had _____ dinner in _____ best restaurant in _____ world.
4 _____ day I'm going to be _____ rich man.
5 Jake's in _____ hospital. He's had _____ operation.
6 Certainly _____ computers have changed _____ modern life.
7 'How do you like your coffee?' 'Black with _____ sugar, please.'
8 I have two daughters. _____ daughter is _____ teacher, _____ other works in _____ advertising.
9 Today is _____ first day of _____ rest of your life. Enjoy it.

Speaking

T 10.2 Work in small groups. Listen to and then answer the questions. Be careful with articles.

Where did you have lunch today?   I had lunch in a café/in the school canteen.

Possessives

4 In these sentences, which word is a possessive adjective? Which are possessive pronouns?

> I'm very proud of **my** children.
> Don't touch that! It's **mine!**
> James is an old friend of **ours**.

Don't touch that! It's mine!

Underline the correct word.

1 'Is that *her / hers* book?' 'Well, it isn't *my / mine*.'
2 '*Who's / Whose* is that car?' 'It's *our / ours*. Nice, huh?'
3 Microsoft owes *it's / its* success to Windows. That's why *it's / its* the biggest software company in the world.
4 Those aren't *your / yours* socks. These blue ones are *your / yours*.
5 Mary, this is Pete. Pete's an old friend of *me / mine*.
6 My sisters borrow *my / mine* clothes, and I borrow *their / theirs*.

5 In these sentences when does the apostrophe come before *s*? When does it come after?

> My wife**'s** family live in the north-east.
> I went to a boys**'** school.

Put the apostrophe in the correct place in these sentences.

1 I've borrowed my dads car.
2 My parents new house is great.
3 I like Alices boyfriend.
4 The childrens room is upstairs.
5 I really like my brothers girlfriends.

its or *it's*

6 **T 10.3** Listen to the sentences. Underline the words you hear.

| 1 its | it's | 3 there | their | 5 they're | their |
| 2 theirs | there's | 4 it's | its | 6 there's | theirs |

all and *every* . . .

7 Correct the mistakes in these sentences.
1 I buy ~~my all~~ ^all my^ clothes in the market.
2 All was stolen in the burglary.
3 'Did they take any of your CDs?' 'All.'
4 In my family we like all football.
5 All enjoyed the party.
6 All of employees in my company work hard.

8 Complete the sentences with *all/everything/everybody/ everyone*.

1 Two plus two is four. _Everybody_ knows that.
2 _____ I want is you.
3 I'm having a terrible day. _____ is going wrong.
4 My girlfriend gets at me _____ the time.
5 My sister is really popular. She knows _____ , and _____ knows her.

Reflexive pronouns and *each other*

9 Look at the sentences.

> I cut **myself** shaving.
> They send **each other** Christmas cards.

Which sentence expresses the idea: ⇆ ?
Which sentence expresses the idea: ↻ ?

Complete the sentences with *myself/yourself,* … or *each other*.

1 We love _____ and we're going to get married.
2 He's crazy! He could have killed _____ !
3 Do you like the cake? I made it _____ .
4 'Can you make me a cup of tea?' 'No. Do it _____ .'
5 My kids get on well with _____ .
6 Please make _____ at home.
7 We're very different, but we understand _____ .
8 Her kids are good. They know how to behave _____ .
9 The food's all ready, so help _____ to whatever you want.

mime

With a partner or on your own, mime these to the class. The others must say what you're doing.

• look at yourself in the mirror
  You're looking at yourself in the mirror.
• talk to yourself
• hate each other
• help yourself to a drink
• enjoy yourself
• help each other with homework
• shout at each other
• not speak to each other

LISTENING AND SPEAKING
What do you do on the Net?

1 Work in small groups. Do you think these statements are true or false?

> 1 billion searches are made on *Google* search engine every day.

> Over half of young people in Britain have their own web page on social networking sites such as *Facebook* and *MySpace*.

> In 2005, the original Hollywood sign was sold on *eBay* for $450,400.

> 86 per cent of the web pages on the Net are in English.

> 1 out of 8 couples who marry in the US met on an online dating site.

> 88% of websites are never visited.

> There is a web that no one knows about. It is called the deep web, and is 500 times bigger than the surface web we all know about.

2 Put the words into the correct order to make sentences about using the Internet.
1 websites / onto / go / sport / I / about
2 Net / mainly / *Facebook* / use / I / the / for
3 log / bank / onto / my / I / and / 'Pay Now' / click / on
4 shopping / do / my / nearly / online / I / all
5 player / onto / download / MP3 / I / music / my

3 **T 10.4** Listen to five people talking about what they do on the Net. <u>Underline</u> what they say they do.

1 Tom
1 <u>watch videos</u> 3 learn languages
2 talk to friends 4 buy and sell things

2 Monica
1 watch films 3 look for work
2 do social networking 4 see what's on

3 Justin
1 pay bills 3 book and buy things
2 watch sport 4 make friends

4 Daisy
1 watch DVDs 3 do shopping
2 send emails 4 get news and weather

5 David
1 make friends 3 practise languages
2 research family history 4 download music

4 Work in pairs. Choose one of the people and listen in more detail.
Tell the rest of the class about the person you chose.

> **SPOKEN ENGLISH** *also*, *as well*, and *too*
>
> **1** Look at the position of the expressions *also*, *as well*, and *too* in these lines from T10.4.
> *I'm **also** selling some of my old stuff.*
> *...I update my Sat Nav system **as well**.*
> *I get traffic reports, **too**.*
>
> **2** Put the three expressions in these sentences.
> I go onto social networking sites.
> I download music and videos.
> I go onto websites to get the weather.
>
> **3** Only two of the expressions sound right in these sentences.
> 'Dave's nice.' 'His sister is _____.'
> 'I'm going home now.' 'I am _____.'
> Don't forget your coat. And take your umbrella _____.
> Buy some bread. And some coffee _____.
>
> **4** Only *one* of the expressions sounds right in these sentences.
> 'I like Harry.' 'Me _____.'
> 'I'm thirsty.' 'Me _____.'

Talking about you

• What do *you* do on the Net?
What are your favourite websites?

• Do you use websites like *Facebook* and *eBay*?

• The Internet represents the democracy of ideas. Is it right that it has no censorship? What are the dangers of this?

Architecture old and new

1 What do *you* want from an airport or railway station? Put these features in order for you. (1 = the most important)

- ☐ a beautiful building
- ☐ a convenient situation near the city centre
- ☐ good shops and restaurants
- ☐ modern and efficient service
- ☐ a wide variety of destinations

Compare your answers with a partner, then with the class.

2 Look at the photos of St Pancras International Station. Describe what you can see.

3 Read the first two parts of the article on this page. Find the answers to these questions.

1 When did the new station open?
2 Where can you travel to from St Pancras?
3 When was the original station built?
4 What was special about the glass roof?

4 Read the rest of the article carefully. Complete the chart.

Original station	New station
Cost $436,000	
	Took three years to restore
Basement used for storage	
	Fifteen platforms

St Pancras Station, London, 1958

Meet me at St Pancras

Technologies old and new come together under one roof. It's the new age of the train.
JENNIE HISLOP reports.

London now has a railway station that is the equal of New York's Grand Central and the Paris Gare du Nord. St Pancras International is the UK home of Eurostar. It is a stunning Victorian station in the heart of London, with connections that spread out across the country, linking the UK with the rest of Europe.

The new station opened in 2007, and handles 50 million passengers a year. It provides access to the northern European cities of Paris, Brussels and Lille. From there you can travel to Spain, the French Alps, the south of France, and Germany. Eurostar flashes along the railway line, known as High Speed 1 (HS1), at 300 km per hour (186 mph), just as the TGV has done in France for many years. The whole area around St Pancras and King's Cross has had a major regeneration. It is now a thriving, inner-city district, home to multinational businesses, art galleries, bars, and restaurants.

THE ORIGINAL STATION

When St Pancras Station was built in Victorian times, it took 6,000 men and 1,000 horses five years to complete, and cost £436,000. It opened in 1868, a masterpiece in iron and glass, designed by the great engineer W.H. Barlow. He created a cathedral on two floors. Below, there was an enormous basement, used as a storage area for beer coming south from breweries in the Midlands. Above this floor, he built a vast crystal palace, the tallest and widest of its day, and one of the great feats of Victorian engineering. The glass roof, all 240 feet (75 metres) wide, appeared to float unsupported. It crossed the five platforms in a single, undivided span.

THE NEW STATION

The 21st century St Pancras International was restored over a three-year period at a cost of £800 million. The basement area is now the check-in and departure lounge. Escalators lead to the platforms on the floor above. The glass roof has been carefully restored, and the iron arches painted the original sky blue. An 18-car Eurostar train is about a quarter of a mile long, so the roof was extended. There are now fifteen platforms.

The restoration of this building is a triumph of great tradition, high technology, and style. There is a 300ft (92m) champagne bar. A farmers' market is supplied with fresh produce brought in from Europe daily. There are boutiques, patisseries, delicatessens, chocolatiers, and a whole range of places to eat, from brasseries to organic home-made burger bars.

THE STATION HOTEL

The large Gothic building in front of St Pancras is not, in fact, the station but the Midland Grand Hotel. When it opened its doors in 1873, it was one of the most advanced hotels in the world. It was the first building in London to have a 'rising room', or lift, and the first to have revolving doors. It had a Ladies' Smoking Room, which was quite shocking in its day. There were laundry lifts, coal lifts, and speaking tubes to send instructions to the staff. The Victorian decoration was rich and expensive, but the hotel was built with old-fashioned plumbing. There were 300 bedrooms but only nine bathrooms. People took a bath in a tub in their bedroom. The hotel closed in 1935. Its facilities were outdated, and it was too expensive to run.

It is now known as St Pancras Chambers. There is a 245-bedroom, five-star luxury hotel, with every comfort and modern amenity, and 68 private apartments and penthouses on the upper floors.

THE PLACE TO MEET

When someone says 'Meet me at St Pancras', everyone knows what they mean. There is a 9-metre tall, 20-ton bronze statue called 'The Meeting', which depicts a couple caught in a deep embrace. It is THE place to meet, under the great glass roof, where Eurostars glide to a halt, beneath the famous station clock. See you there!

The Station Hotel

5 Work with a partner. Are these statements about the station and the hotel true (✔) or false (✗)? Correct the false ones.

1 The escalators lead up to the departure lounge.
2 The glass roof has been replaced.
3 The iron arches have been painted the same colour as the original.
4 Farmers bring in fresh produce from all over England.
5 The building in front of St Pancras International is a hotel.
6 The hotel was advanced for its time because it had so many bathrooms.
7 The hotel has now been restored with over 300 bedrooms and apartments.
8 The best place to meet at St Pancras is the Champagne Bar.

6 Here are some numbers from the article. What do they refer to? Practise saying them.

1	50m	6	¼ mile
2	300kph	7	300ft
3	6,000	8	1873
4	240ft	9	1935
5	21st	10	9/20

T10.5 Listen and check.

What do you think?

- How does St Pancras International rate according to the features in exercise 1?
- What buildings is your town or capital city famous for? When were they built? Why are they famous?
- What's your favourite building? What building would you like to knock down?

▶▶ **WRITING** A FAMOUS TOWN OR CITY *p114*

VOCABULARY AND SPEAKING
Compound nouns

1 Nouns can be combined to make a new word.
Here are some examples from the text on p82–83.

| railway station | art gallery | masterpiece | departure lounge |

Where is the stress on these compound nouns?

2 Look at the dictionary entries. Practise saying the words.

3 Answer the questions.
1 Why do people take aspirin?
2 Where do you find the words *Here lies James Barlow – RIP*?
3 What can you do if you want to listen to music without disturbing other people?
4 What are the different lights on a car?
5 What's the first thing you read in a newspaper?
6 Where are the headquarters of the United Nations?
7 Are *you* making headway in English?

4 In these lists, one compound noun doesn't exist. Which one is it?

sun	sunglasses	**sunpool**	suncream	**sunset**
card	credit card	**parking card**	birthday card	**business card**
tea	**tea bag**	teacup	**teatime**	tea table
case	money case	**briefcase**	suitcase	**bookcase**

T10.6 Listen and repeat.

5 Put one word in each box to form three compound nouns.

1	dining waiting [ ] changing
2	lights [ ] warden jam
3	antique second-hand [ ] shoe
4	Spider- post [ ] chair
5	brush [ ] dresser cut
6	news travel [ ] estate
7	way [ ] bike racing
8	wrapping toilet [ ] wall

headache /ˈhedeɪk/ *noun* [C] **1** a pain in your head: *I've got a splitting (= very bad) headache.* ◆ note at **ache 2** a person or thing that causes worry or difficulty: *Paying the bills is a constant headache.*

headlight /ˈhedlaɪt/ (also **headlamp**) *noun* [C] one of the two large bright lights at the front of a vehicle ◆ picture on **page P9**

headline /ˈhedlaɪn/ *noun* **1** [C] the title of a newspaper article printed in large letters above the story **2 the headlines** [pl] the main items of news read on TV or radio

headphones /ˈhedfəʊnz/ *noun* [pl] a piece of equipment worn over or in the ears that makes it possible to listen to music, the radio, etc. without other people hearing it ◆ note at **listen**

headquarters /ˌhedˈkwɔːtəz/ *noun* [pl, with sing or pl verb] (*abbr* **HQ**) the place from where an organization is controlled; the people who work there: *Where is/are the firm's headquarters?*

headstone /ˈhedstəʊn/ *noun* [C] a large stone with writing on, used to mark where a dead person is buried ◆ look at **gravestone**, **tombstone**

headway /ˈhedweɪ/ *noun*
IDM **make headway** to go forward or make progress in a difficult situation

Oxford Wordpower Dictionary (third edition) © Oxford University Press 2006

6 Work with a partner. Use your dictionary to find some compound nouns made with one of these words.

| hand | foot | finger | fire | air | water |

Describe them for the other students to guess.

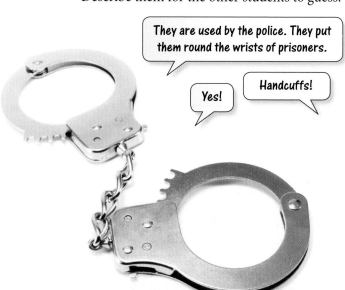

They are used by the police. They put them round the wrists of prisoners.

Yes!

Handcuffs!

EVERYDAY ENGLISH
I need one of those things . . .

1 **T10.7** Listen to five students each describing one of the things in the pictures, but they don't know the word in English. Which object are they describing?

2 Listen again and complete the lines.
   1 'I need _____ when you want to open a bottle of wine.'
   2 'I'm looking for _____ when you want to clean between your teeth. It's _____ . It's white.'
   3 'They're _____ , and the Chinese _____ to pick up food.'
   4 'It's _____ , and it's used _____ flies.'
   5 'They're _____ you're cooking and you want to pick up something that's hot.'

Music of English 🎵

1 **T10.8** Listen to the stress patterns in these sentences. Practise them.

I need one of those things you use to open a bottle of wine.
I'm looking for some of that stuff you use when you want to clean between your teeth.
They're long and thin, and the Chinese use them to pick up food.

2 Practise the other sentences in exercise 2.

---

3 Work in groups. Describe the other things in the pictures.

4 **T10.9** Listen to the descriptions. What objects do you think are being described? Turn to p151. Listen again. Which objects are they?

5 Look at the language the people used in the descriptions in exercise 4:
   • It's one of those things you . . .
   • It's long and thin and . . .
   • It looks like . . .
   • It's the stuff you . . .
   • It's used for . . .
   • They're made of . . .
   • It's a kind of . . .
   • It's something you use when . . .
   • You know! It's got a . . .

T10.10 Listen and complete these lines. Practise saying them.

6 Work with a partner. Turn to p151. Take turns describing some of the other objects.

7 **T10.11** Listen to two conversations in a shop. What does each person want to buy?

8 In pairs, write a similar conversation in a shop. Act it out to the class.

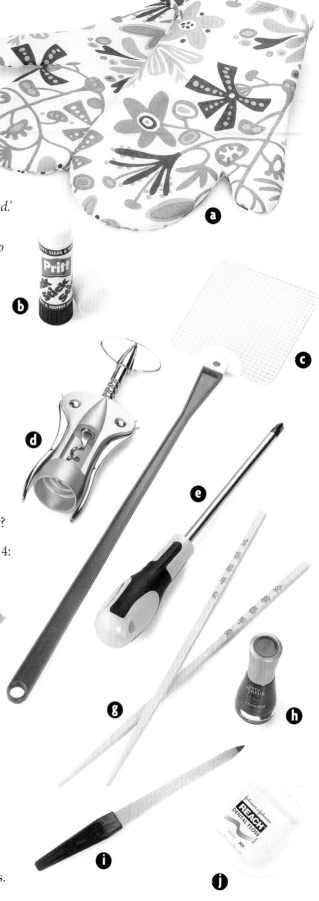

11 Seeing is believing

Modals of probability • Phrasal verbs (2) • Expressing attitude

STARTER

Work with a partner. Look at the optical illusions. Can you find . . . ?

eight people   three animals   an old lady   five young ladies
a word   the colour red   parallel lines   a musical instrument

1

2

3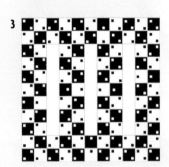

4

5

6

7

8

9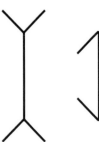

OPTICAL ILLUSIONS
must be/can't be/looks like

1 Two people are discussing the optical illusions on this page. Here are some lines from their conversation. Which optical illusion does each line refer to?

a It **looks like** a man playing the saxophone.
b That **must be** a candlestick in front of her face.
c They **can't be** the same colour.
d She **might be wearing** a feather in her hat.
e It **can't have** five legs.
f It **could be** a duck or a rabbit.
g The one on the left **must be** longer.
h It **looks like** someone wearing glasses.
i It **looks wobbly, like** a jelly.
j The dots **must be creating** the illusion.

2 **T 11.1** Listen to the full conversation. As you listen, point to the picture they are talking about.

• What is the truth about each one?
• Which *two* optical illusions can the woman *not* see?

GRAMMAR SPOT

1 Which of these sentences is the most sure?
   Which two sentences are less sure?

   It **must be** a duck.
   It **could be** a duck.
   It **might be** a duck.

2 The above sentences all mean *I think it's possible that it is a duck.*
   What does *It can't be a duck* mean?

3 Compare the sentences. When do we use *like*?

   It **looks like a man** playing the saxophone.
   It **looks red** to me.
   You **look like your mother**.
   You **look hot and tired**.

4 Look at the example of the continuous infinitive (*be + -ing*).

   She **might be wearing** a feather.

   Find another example in exercise 1.

   ▶▶ **Grammar Reference 11.1–11.2 p145**

PRACTICE
Fact or fiction?

1 Work with a partner. Do you believe these statements are true or false? Use modal verbs in your comments. Discuss ideas as a class.

1 Lightning never strikes in the same place twice.

> That must be true. I've often heard this.

> It could be true but I'm not so sure.

2 Hurricanes always have ladies' names.
3 Women have a higher pain threshold than men.
4 The sea is blue because it reflects the sky.
5 A penny dropped from a skyscraper can kill a person.
6 Hair and nails continue to grow after death.
7 Birds are bird-brained and stupid.
8 No two snowflakes are the same.
9 Bats are blind.

2 **T 11.2** Listen and check your ideas. Do you learn anything that surprises you?

Grammar and speaking

3 Work with a partner. Take turns to read aloud the statements and respond using the words in brackets.

1 I think I've lost my passport (*must, worried*)
   You must be very worried.
2 Your phone's ringing! (*might, Jane*)
3 Paul's taking his umbrella. (*must, rain*)
4 Harry and Sally never go on holiday.
   (*can't, much money*)
5 Hannah's not in class. (*could, coffee bar*)
6 Look! Three fire engines! (*must, somewhere*)
7 Tom hasn't seen Zoë for ages.
   (*can't, go out together any more*)
8 Whose jacket is this? (*might, John's*)
9 You got top marks in the test! (*must, joke!*)

T 11.3 Listen and check your answers.
Practise again.

What are they talking about?

4 **T 11.4** Listen to five short conversations. With a partner, guess the answer to the questions. Give reasons for your conclusions.

1 **A** A glass of white wine and a mineral water, please.
  B Still or sparkling?
  A Sparkling, please.
  B Do you want ice and lemon with that?
  A Just ice, thanks. How much is that?

  Where do you think the people are? *At home? In a restaurant? In a pub?*

  They can't be at home because they're paying for the drink. They could be in a restaurant but... They must be in ...

2 What are they talking about? *A TV? A mobile phone? A computer?*

3 What do you think she's talking about? *An exam? A job interview? Her driving test?*

4 Who are the people? *Two friends? Husband and wife? Brother and sister?*
  What are they talking about? *A birthday present? A wedding present? An anniversary present?*

5 What do you think they are doing? *Watching a film? Drinking at a bar? Dancing?*

WHAT ON EARTH HAS HAPPENED?

must have been/can't have been

1 **T 11.5** Christina is calling Rachel. Read and listen to Rachel's side of the conversation. What do you think has happened?

R Hello.

C …

R Hi, Christina, what on earth's wrong? Tell me.

C …

R Oh, no! That's terrible. When?

C …

R They must have known no one was at home. What did they take?

C …

R Had you saved everything?

C …

R Thank goodness. What else is missing?

C …

R Not your camera! Well at least you still have your photos. Oh, and Ella's expensive leather jacket! Does she know?

C …

R She's going to get such a shock when she gets back – and she's got her final exams soon.

C …

R Yeah, that's good. I know she always takes it with her to lectures. Have you called the police?

C …

R Good. Have they any idea who might have done it?

C …

R So it wasn't just *your* flat then? Is there much mess? Did they ransack the place?

C …

R Oh, how awful! Your lovely clothes. Did they take any of them?

C …

R Yes, of course, and anyway, it must be really difficult to see exactly what's missing.

C …

R Look, Christina you're obviously really upset. I'm coming round. I'll help you tidy up. I'll be there in 15 minutes.

C …

2 What can you work out from Rachel's side of the conversation? Read the questions. Discuss and tick (✓) the most likely answer.

1 What is the relationship between Rachel and Christina?

☐ They must be friends.

☐ They could be sisters.

2 What do you think has happened?

☐ Christina's flat must have been burgled.

☐ Christina's flat might have been burgled.

3 When did it happen?

☐ It could have happened during the night.

☐ It may have happened while she was at work.

4 Who is Ella?

☐ She must be Christina's flatmate.

☐ She can't be a student.

5 What was taken from the flat?

☐ Christina's laptop computer could have been taken.

☐ Ella's laptop may have been taken.

6 Has Christina told Ella about her jacket?

☐ She might have told her.

☐ She can't have told her.

7 Has she called the police?

☐ She can't have done.

☐ She must have done.

8 What happened to Christina's clothes?

☐ They can't have been stolen.

☐ They must have been thrown onto the floor.

What do you think?

3 Go through the questions in exercise 2 and tell the class what you think.

> We think Rachel and Christina must be friends and that Christina's flat ...

4 **T 11.6** Listen to the full conversation and check your answers.

SPOKEN ENGLISH *What on earth ...?*

1 Questions with *... on earth ...?* are often used in spoken English to express disbelief.

> *What on earth* has happened?
> *Where on earth* have you been?
> *Who on earth* left the window open?

T 11.7 Listen and repeat. Pay attention to the stress and intonation.

2 Work with a partner. Read the statements aloud and respond with disbelief.

1 I can't carry all these shopping bags. *What ...?*
2 Tom's broken his arm in three places. *How...?*
3 There's someone at the door! *Who ...?*
4 My aunt left all her money to a cats' home. *What ... for?*
5 I can't find my car keys. *Where ...?*

T 11.8 Listen and compare your answers. Practise them.

GRAMMAR SPOT

1 These sentences all express **past** probability. What is the present?

> They **must have been** friends.
> They **might have caught** the burglar.
> It **can't have been** my jacket.

2 What is the past of these sentences?

> He **must love** her very much.
> She **can't be** at home.

3 Remember *must* also expresses obligation. What is the past of this sentence?

> I **must call** the police.

▶▶ **Grammar Reference: 11.3 p145**

PRACTICE
Grammar and pronunciation

1 Match the phonemic script with the words.

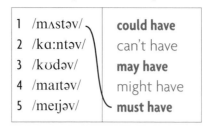

1 /mʌstəv/	**could have**
2 /kɑːntəv/	can't have
3 /kʊdəv/	**may have**
4 /maɪtəv/	might have
5 /meɪjəv/	**must have**

T 11.9 Listen and repeat.

2 **T 11.10** Listen and chorus these lines as a class.

1 It must have been stolen.
2 I can't have lost it.
3 He could have taken it.
4 I might have dropped it.
5 She may have found it.

3 Work with a partner. Read aloud the following situations. Take it in turns to respond using the words in brackets.

1 I can't find my ticket. (*must, drop*)

>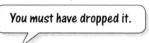
> You must have dropped it.

2 John didn't come to school yesterday. (*must, ill*)
3 Why is Isabel late for class? (*might, oversleep*)
4 I can't find my notebook. (*must, leave at home*)
5 The teacher's checking Maria's exercise. (*can't, finish already*)
6 Why is Carl looking so happy? (*may, do well in the test*)

T 11.11 Listen and check. Practise again with your partner.

Discussing grammar

4 How many of these modal verbs can you fit naturally into each sentence? Discuss as a class. What are the different meanings?

can	can't	could	must	might	shall	should

1 He _____ have been born in the 1960s.
2 _____ you help me with the washing-up, please?
3 You _____ see the doctor immediately.
4 _____ we go out for a meal tonight?
5 I _____ stop smoking.
6 I _____ learn to speak English.

READING AND LISTENING
The Adventures of Sherlock Holmes

1 Sherlock Holmes is probably the most famous detective in the world of English literature. What do you know about him?

1 Sherlock Holmes lived in *Chicago / London / Edinburgh.*

2 Stories about him first appeared in the *19th / 20th / 21st* century.

3 He was helped in all his adventures by *Dr Krippen / Dr Jones / Dr Watson.*

2 You are going to read a Sherlock Holmes story called *The Three Students.* Look at the picture and headings. What can you guess about the story?

3 Read **Part 1** and answer the questions.

1 Where was Sherlock Holmes staying? Why?

2 Who is Hilton Soames?

3 What did Mr Soames receive that afternoon?

4 What was lying on the floor when he returned to his room after tea?

5 Why did Mr Soames refuse to call the police?

6 Who is Bannister?

7 What clues did Mr Soames find?

8 What does he think has happened?

4 Read **Part 2**. Who and what can you see in the picture? Are these sentences true (✔) or false (✗)? Correct the false ones.

1 The tutor's room was on the same floor as the three students'.

2 Holmes couldn't see into the room through the window.

3 He found a clue on the carpet.

4 The papers were next to the window because it was easier to read them in the light.

5 Holmes found another clue in the bedroom.

6 The intruder saw Mr Soames returning.

7 He escaped through the study window.

5 Read **Part 3**. What motives did each of the students have? Who do you think copied the papers? Why? Discuss with a partner and then the class.

I think it could have been . . .   No, it can't have been . . .

THE THREE

PART 1 ❖ *Who copied the exam questions?*

Sherlock Holmes and Dr Watson were in one of England's most famous university towns doing some research. One evening, Holmes received a visit from an old acquaintance, Mr Hilton Soames, a tutor at one of the colleges. Mr Soames looked very nervous and agitated.

'I hope you can spare me some of your valuable time, Mr Holmes. Something very serious has happened at my college.'

Holmes was very busy. 'Why don't you call the police?' he said irritably.

'No, no that's impossible. We can't have a scandal at the college. I must explain. You see, tomorrow is the first day of the university examinations, and this afternoon I received the Greek translation papers. I put them on the desk in my room while I went to have tea with a friend. When I returned, I saw immediately that the papers had been disturbed. Indeed some were lying on the floor by the window.'

'I see,' said Holmes. 'Please continue.'

'Well, at first I thought that perhaps my servant, Bannister, was responsible because he'd been in the room after I left, but he denied touching the papers and I believe him. He is a good and honest man. I examined the room very carefully.'

'And what did you find?' asked Holmes impatiently.

'On the table by the window I found a broken pencil. Also, there was a cut, about three inches long, in the red leather top of my desk and next to it, a small lump of black mud. There were no signs of entry at the window. Please help me, Mr Holmes. Someone must have copied the exam questions. If I don't find who did it, I will have to cancel the exam and there will be a scandal.'

'We need to visit your room,' said Holmes. 'Come on, Watson.'

STUDENTS

They walked towards the tutor's room, which was on the ground floor. Holmes tried to look in through the window but he wasn't tall enough. He had to stop and stand on tiptoe. Above lived three students, one on each floor. Holmes entered the room and examined the carpet.

'Nothing,' he said. 'Let me look at the table by the window. Ah, yes, I see what might have happened. Someone took the papers from your desk over to the window table to copy them, because from there he could see when you were returning.'

'Actually, Holmes, nobody could see me. I came back through the side door.'

'Ah, so you may have surprised him and he had to leave hurriedly. Did you hear someone running away as you entered?'

'No, I didn't.'

'Interesting. So, our only clues are the cut in the leather and one small lump of black mud. Now tell me, where does that door go to?'

'My bedroom.'

'Can I examine it?'

'Yes, of course.'

Holmes followed Soames into his bedroom.

'Hello,' said Holmes,' What's this? Another small lump of black mud, exactly like the one on the desk. Clearly your visitor came into the bedroom.'

'I don't understand. Why did he do that?'

'Well, when you came back so suddenly, he must have run into your bedroom to hide. Look at the bedroom window, it's open. That must be how he escaped.'

PART 3 ❖ *The three suspects*

'Now,' said Holmes, 'The three students who live above you. Are they all taking this examination?'

'Yes.'

'Tell me about them.'

'Well, on the first floor is Gilchrist, an excellent student and an athlete, he plays rugby and cricket and is particularly good at the long jump. He's hard-working but poor. His father gambled away all the family money.'

'And the second floor?'

'Daulat Ras lives there. He is from India, very quiet and hard-working, but Greek translation is his weakest subject. And finally there's Miles McLaren on the top floor. A very intelligent student, one of the best when he chooses to work – but he's been very lazy this term, he's been playing cards until late at night and I think he must be worried about this exam.'

'Now tell me,' said Holmes, 'how tall are these young men?'

'How tall? What a strange question. Erm … I think Miles is taller than the Indian, but Gilchrist is the tallest, over six feet.'

'Ah, that's important. Now, Mr Soames. I wish you goodnight. I'll return tomorrow.'

Next morning Sherlock Holmes left his house at 6 a.m. He returned at 8 a.m. to pick up Watson and they made their way to the tutor's rooms. Mr Soames was waiting nervously for them.

Listening

6 **T 11.12** Listen to **Part 4**. Whose ideas in exercise 5 were correct? Did you guess who copied the papers? Now answer these questions.

1 What was it about the culprit that made Holmes suspicious?
2 Where did Holmes go to solve the mystery? What did he discover there?
3 What was Holmes' explanation? Describe what happened.
4 What does Watson say to congratulate his friend? How does Holmes reply?
5 Why does Bannister apologize?
6 Why can the examinations take place?

What do you think?

• What were the cleverest parts of Holmes' investigation?
• How might the mystery be solved by detectives today?
• What methods of detection are used now which were not available 100 years ago?

Language work

1 Work out the meanings of the highlighted words from their contexts.

2 Here are some things that Sherlock Holmes could have said while he was working out who did it. Rewrite the sentences using the words in brackets.

1 One of the students is undoubtedly the culprit. (*must*)
2 I don't think Bannister did it. (*can't have*)
3 The lump of mud is possibly a clue. (*could*)
4 Perhaps the leather was cut by a knife. (*might have*)
5 I don't think he escaped through the study window. (*can't have*)
6 Perhaps the culprit is still hiding in the bedroom. (*may*)
7 Maybe he jumped out of the bedroom window. (*could have*)
8 I'm pretty sure that Gilchrist did it. (*must have*)

Telling the story

Tell the story round the class in your own words. Begin:

Student 1   *Sherlock Holmes was working in a university town, probably Oxford.*

Student 2   *His friend Mr Soames, who was a tutor, asked Holmes to help him because …*

Student 3   *…*

VOCABULARY
Phrasal verbs (2) with *out* and *up*

1 Read the dictionary entries for two phrasal verbs. Answer the questions.

  1 What are the verbs?
  2 What do *sth* and *sb* stand for?
  3 Which groups of phrasal verbs are separable? Which are inseparable?

> **PHR V work sth out 1** to find the answer; to solve sth: *I can't work out how to do this.* **2** to calculate sth: *I worked out the total cost.*
>
> **work out 1** to progress in a good way: *I hope things work out for you.* **2** to do physical exercise to keep your body fit: *We work out to music at my exercise class.*

> **PHR V make sth up 1** to invent sth, often sth that is not true: *to make up an excuse.* **2** to form sth: *the different groups that make up society.*
>
> **make up (with sb)** to become friends again after an argument: *Has she made up with him yet?*

2 Complete the sentences with the correct form of one of the phrasal verbs in exercise 1.

  1 Sherlock Holmes _____ who commited the crime.
  2 That's a lie. You _____ that _____, didn't you?
  3 I know we argue a lot, but we always kiss and _____ afterwards.
  4 Don't worry, things will _____ in the end. They always do.
  5 He's determined to lose weight. He _____ at the gym every day.
  6 Women _____ 56 per cent of the students in this university.
  7 Can you _____ this bill for me? I don't understand all those figures.
  8 You must have _____ the answers by now.

Archimedes works it out.

3 Many more phrasal verbs are formed with *out* and *up*. Match a verb in **A** with a line in **B**.

A	B
1 find out	all my CDs
2 break up	in a Chinese restaurant
3 break out of	golf
4 eat up	with a boyfriend/girlfriend
5 eat out	all your greens and you'll be healthy
6 save up	what time the train leaves
7 sort out	with a friend after a row about money
8 take up	a good idea
9 fall out	to buy a new car
10 come up with	jail

4 Replace the words in *italics* with one of the phrasal verbs from exercise 3 in the correct form.

  1 You need to learn to relax. Why don't you *start doing* yoga?
  2 He's just *thought of* a brilliant plan to save the business.
  3 There's no dessert until you've *finished* all your meat and vegetables.
  4 Anne and Tony aren't talking to each other. They must have *had an argument.* They may even have *ended their relationship.*
  5 Did you hear the news? Three dangerous prisoners have *escaped from* the local prison.
  6 You must learn to *organize* your washing into coloureds and whites.
  7 We *aren't spending much money* so we can buy a house.
  8 Have you *discovered* why you didn't get the job?

T 11.13 Listen and check.

5 Work with a partner. Complete these sentences in any suitable way. Read them aloud to the class and compare ideas.

  1 I've just found out …
  2 I never eat out …
  3 I don't ever fall out with …
  4 I can't work out …
  5 I'm saving up …
  6 I need to sort out …
  7 I've just come up with …
  8 It's important to make up …

T 11.14 Listen and compare. What are the responses?

EVERYDAY ENGLISH
Expressing attitude

1 **T 11.15** Read and listen to the conversation. Who are they talking about? What has happened?

A Have you heard about Sam?

B No, I haven't.

A Well, I haven't spoken to him myself but, **apparently**, he was caught cheating in his Maths exam.

B **No kidding!** I can't believe that. Does he have a problem with Maths?

A No. **Actually,** Maths is his best subject.

B **Really?** So why would he cheat? He doesn't need to.

A **Exactly.** And **anyway**, Sam's not the type to cheat.

B He must be very upset. **Presumably,** he's going to complain.

A Yeah, he's seeing the principal this afternoon. **Obviously,** he's going to deny it completely.

B Well, **hopefully,** the principal will believe him. Let me know what happens.

A I will. **Personally,** I think he'll be OK.

B I hope you're right. Cheers. See you later.

A Yeah. Fingers crossed for Sam. Bye.

2 **T 11.16** Read and listen to the conversation again. The words in **bold** express the attitude of the speaker.

3 Choose the correct word or phrase to complete the lines.

Did you hear about Marcus? You know, the guy who works in my office. Well **apparently / obviously**, he's going to be promoted. **Of course / To be honest**, I don't understand why. **Exactly / Personally**, I think he's hopeless at his job. He never does any work. **In fact / Naturally**, all he does all day is chat to his friends on the phone and drink coffee. **Unfortunately / Really**, his desk is next to mine. **Generally / Presumably**, he'll move to another office now, so **hopefully / really** I won't have to work with him any more. **Anyway / Apparently**, enough about me. How's your work going? Are you still enjoying it?

T 11.16 Listen and check. Read the lines aloud with a partner.

4 Complete the sentences with your own ideas.

1 **A** Hi! You're Pete, aren't you?
   B **Actually,** _____ .

2 **A** What did you think of the film? Great wasn't it?
   B **Personally,** _____ .

3 **A** What's the latest gossip about Clara and her boyfriend?
   B **Apparently,** _____ .

4 **A** What's the weather like in spring?
   B **Generally,** _____ .

5 **A** What time will we arrive?
   B **Hopefully,** _____ .

6 **A** I've phoned and left messages for them but no reply.
   B **Presumably,** _____ .

7 **A** What did you do when you saw the accident?
   B **Obviously,** _____ .

8 **A** How did you feel when they offered you the job?
   B **To be honest,** _____ .

T 11.17 Listen and compare your answers. Practise with your partner and continue the conversations.

▶▶ **WRITING** EXPRESSING ATTITUDE *p116*

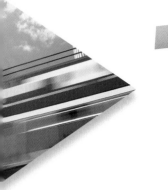

12 Telling it how it is

Reported speech • Ways of speaking • *You know what they say*

 STARTER

1 Look at the reported speech. What were the girl's words?

She said she was a student.
She asked me what I was doing in London.
She told me she'd arrived on Monday.

2 Here are some reported thoughts. What were my thoughts?

I thought she worked in an office.
I knew I'd seen her somewhere before.
I wondered if she'd phone me.

I READ IT IN THE PAPERS ...
Reported speech

1 Read the newspaper article. Who is Jack Neal? What did he do? What happened in the end?

2 Work with a partner. Complete the article by reporting the words and thoughts 1–10.

T 12.1 Listen and check.

Look, Mum! I've bought a car on eBay for £9,000

By a Daily Telegraph Correspondent

A three-year-old boy used his mother's computer to buy a £9,000 car on the Internet auction site *eBay*.

Jack Neal's parents only discovered their son's successful bid when they received a message from the website.

> **1** You have bought a pink Nissan Figaro.

The message said they (1) **had bought** a pink Nissan Figaro.

> **2** We can't understand it.

Mrs Neal, 36, said that they (2) _____ it. She explained that she (3) _____ on the Net the day before, but she (4) _____ anything.

> **3** I was on the Net yesterday.

> **5** I'm so happy!

> **4** I didn't buy anything.

'Jack kept telling us that he (5) _____ so happy, and that we (6) _____ soon get a big surprise.'

> **6** You'll soon get a big surprise!

> **7** He's joking.

Mrs Neal, from Sleaford, Lincs, thought Jack (7) _____. He often used the computer, and she was pretty sure that he (8) _____ her password .

> **8** I'm pretty sure he knows my password.

> **9** There has been a mistake.

Her husband, John, 37, phoned the seller of the car, and explained that there (9) _____ a mistake.

'Fortunately he saw the funny side and said he (10) _____ the car again.'

> **10** I'll advertise the car again.

Mr Neal has told Jack to be more careful, and he has asked his wife to change her password.

3 Here are Mr Neal's words to Jack and his wife.

> *You've got to be more careful, son.*
> *Do you think you could change your password, dear?*

How are these words reported in the article?

4 Report these sentences.

1 'My Jack is very clever,' his mother said.
   Mrs Neal said her son was very clever.
2 'He usually plays computer games,' she told me.
3 'I bought the computer for my work,' his father explained.
4 'I won't use *eBay* anymore,' Mrs Neal decided.
5 'I don't know how it happened,' said Jack.
6 'I've always liked computers,' he told reporters.
7 'Please tidy your room,' his mother asked Jack.
8 'Go and play football,' his father told him.

T 12.2 Listen and check.

Reported questions

5 Read the newspaper article below. Match the direct questions and thoughts to numbers 1–7 in the article, then report them.

Has there been a road accident?

Why did you do it?

Are you going to arrest me?

What's happening?

Where did the money come from?

Why are you giving away all your money?

Do you know the man?

T 12.3 Listen and check. Repeat the reported questions.

GRAMMAR SPOT

1 When we report words or thoughts, we usually move the tense back.

> 'I**'m** tired.' She said she **was** tired.

Complete the reported speech.

> 'I've seen the film before.' She told me _____.
> 'You'll like it.' She was sure I _____.

2 What does *tell* mean in these two sentences?

> She **told me that** she loved me.
> She **told me to** go away.

3 When we report questions, there is no inversion, and no *do/does/did*.

> 'Where do you live?' **He asked me where I lived.**

Report these questions.

> 'How long are you staying?' **She asked me . . .**
> 'Do you know Mike?' **She wanted to know if . . .**

▶▶ Grammar Reference 12.1–12.3 p146

---

6 Imagine you were stopped by the police and asked these questions. Report them.

> 'Where are you going?' (*ask*)
> **They asked me where I was going.**
> 'Where have you been?' (*ask*)
> 'Do you live in the area?' (*want to know*)
> 'How old are you?' (*wonder*)
> 'Were you with friends?' (*want to know*)
> 'Have you been drinking?' (*demand to know*)
> 'What time did you leave home?' (*ask if I could remember*)

T 12.4 Listen and compare. Look at T12.4 on p131 and practise the conversation with a partner.

Man throws away £20,000 in town centre

Daily Mail Reporter

A mystery man started a riot in a busy town centre yesterday by hurling £20,000 in banknotes into the air.

Traffic was stopped at 11.00 a.m. in Alexandra Road, Aberystwyth, mid-Wales, as money rained down from the sky.

Local shopkeeper Anthony Jones, 55, said 'I couldn't understand it, so I asked my neighbour (1) **what was happening** .' They saw people on their hands and knees grabbing money. 'No one knew (2)_____,' he said. 'They were just stuffing it in their pockets.'

Passer-by Eleanor Morris said, 'I wondered (3)_____, because the traffic was at a complete standstill.'

Flower seller Cadwyn Thomas saw the man, who was wearing a red Welsh rugby shirt. 'I asked him (4)_____ all his money, but he didn't answer. He just laughed.'

Police asked Cadwyn if she (5)_____. 'I told them I'd never seen him before. He certainly wasn't from around here.'

Dyfed-Powys police later confirmed that a forty-year-old man from Aberystwyth had been questioned. 'He refused to tell us (6)_____,' a spokesman said, 'so it's a complete mystery. He wanted to know if we (7)_____ arrest him, but giving away money isn't against the law.'

PRACTICE

But you said . . . !

1 Complete the conversations with an idea of your own.

1 **A** Bill's coming to the party tonight.
  B Really? I thought you said <u>he wasn't feeling well</u>.

2 **A** Have you got a cigarette?
  B I didn't know you _____!

3 **A** Oh, no! I've spilt tomato ketchup on my white shirt!
  B I told you to be careful. I knew _____.

4 **A** Did you get me a drink?
  B Sorry. I didn't realize _____. What would you like?

5 **A** I'm 25 today!
  B Are you? I didn't know _____. Many happy returns!

6 **A** Oh, no! It's raining!
  B Really? But the weather forecast said _____.

7 **A** You left the doors and windows of the flat open this morning.
  B I'm sorry. I was pretty sure I _____ everything.

8 **A** Where did Tom go last night?
  B I've no idea _____.

T 12.5 Listen and compare. Practise the conversations.

The interview

2 Work with a partner. Think of questions you are asked when you have a job interview.

How old are you?
Where have you worked before?
Do you like working in a team?

> Full-time RECEPTIONIST
> required in ★★★★ London Hotel
> Experience and
> foreign language preferred
> Annual salary £19k
> Please send CVs to:
> info@hotelcharlesIII.com

3 Julia has just been for a job interview as a receptionist. She's telling her friend about it.

They asked me why I wanted the job.
They asked me if I had any experience.
They wanted to know if I could do word processing.

What other questions do you think they asked?
Use ideas from exercise 2.

T 12.6 Listen and compare.

Reporting verbs

4 Match the reporting verbs in the box with the direct speech.

a invite	b persuade	c explain	d promise
e ask	f remind	g offer	h encourage

1 _e_ 'Can you help me?' she said to me.
2 __ 'Don't forget to post the letter,' he said to her.
3 __ 'I really will work hard for my exams,' she said.
4 __ 'Come to my party,' he said to me.
5 __ 'You really must go travelling. You'd love it,' she said to me.
6 __ 'I'll give you a lift to the airport,' he said to me.
7 __ 'I'm not sure about this job.' 'Go on! Apply for it! You'd be good at it,' he said. 'OK, I will,' I replied.
8 __ 'I've been very busy,' she said.

5 Report the sentences using the reporting verbs.

She asked me to help her.

T 12.7 Listen and check.

She didn't say that!

6 **T 12.8** Listen to the conversations. What mistakes do the people make when they report the conversations?

1
> Merinda rang from work. She said she'd phone you again later.

She didn't say she'd phone later. She asked Jenny to phone her.

2
> I've got a job as manager! I'm going to earn £30,000 a year!

3
> My mum said you couldn't have a turn.

4
> James - Sally rang. Meet her outside the cinema at 6.45.

5
> Tom offered to mend my computer. He said he was sure he could do it. He wanted £75!

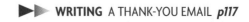

▶▶ **WRITING** A THANK-YOU EMAIL *p117*

VOCABULARY AND SPEAKING
Ways of speaking

1 There are many verbs that describe ways of speaking.

to discuss   to promise   to agree

Add two more verbs from the box to each category in red on the diagram.

advise	chat	scream	row	accuse
recommend	whisper	criticize		gossip
order	quarrel	demand	protest	deny

2 Write in a verb from the diagram. Sometimes there is more than one possibility.

1 _____ to a mate in the pub about football
2 _____ with your parents about staying out late
3 _____ at the kids because they're annoying you
4 _____ that you made a mistake
5 _____ to the waiter about the cold soup
6 _____ if you see blood/your favourite pop star/a rat
7 _____ against the war/about pay and conditions
8 _____ that your friend should see a doctor

3 Complete the sentences with the correct preposition (or no preposition).

1 I talk _____ my kids _____ everything.
2 My boss criticizes _____ me _____ my work.
3 I agree _____ you _____ most things, but not politics.
4 I discuss _____ everything _____ my wife.
5 People love gossiping _____ celebrities.
6 The teacher accused me _____ cheating in the exam.

4 Work with a partner. Think of a sentence to complete these ways of speaking.

My mother told me to tidy my room.

1 My mother The teacher My doctor	advised told persuaded	me the students …	to . . .

2 My friends I My brother	suggested admitted complained	that	we . . . the teacher . . . …

5 With your partner, write a conversation that illustrates some of the verbs on this page. Act it out to the class.

A Have you been out spending money again? We just can't afford it!

B Don't be so mean! It's only a few pounds!

The others must say who the people are and what they're talking about.

It's a husband and wife. They're arguing. He's complaining that she spends too much money. She accuses him of being mean.

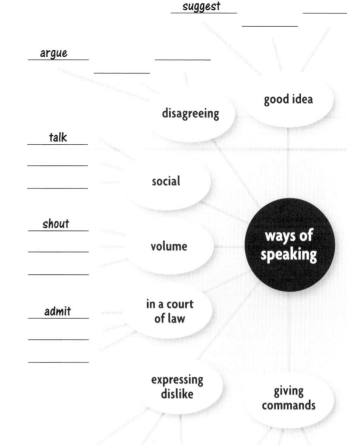

argue _____ _____
talk _____ _____
shout _____ _____
admit _____ _____
complain _____ _____
tell _____ _____
suggest _____ _____

disagreeing
good idea
social
volume
in a court of law
expressing dislike
giving commands

ways of speaking

READING AND SPEAKING
People who changed the world

1 Do you have a hero or heroine? Is he/she in the world of …?

art	politics	entertainment
style	science	sport

Tell the class.

2 Read the introduction to *Movers and shakers*. Look at the pictures of the five people. Write down what you know about each person.

Compare your lists as a class.

3 Work with a partner. Discuss these questions. How many can you answer?

1 Who is known simply as 'The King'?
2 Who is seen as 'the principal fighter for women's equality in the UK'?
3 Who is referred to as the 'father of modern science'?
4 Whose book has been called 'the book that shook the world'?
5 Who is referred to as 'the father of psychoanalysis'?

Read about the five people *quickly* to check.

4 With a partner, choose one of the people and answer the questions.

1 What was their area of activity (politics, science …)?
2 What was an important year for them? Why?
3 Why were their ideas opposed?
4 What did they say themselves? What did other people say?

Compare and exchange information with other students.

5 Discuss the questions.

1 How did each of the people change the world?
2 What prevailing ideas did they challenge?
3 What happened as a result?

What do you think?

• Think of someone from your country who changed people's ideas.
• What did he/she do?
• How did other people react?

Movers and shakers

It's hard to imagine that what we now believe to be true wasn't always so. There was a time when people believed the earth was flat . . .

Every now and again, someone comes along and breathes new ideas. ANN WILSON profiles five people who left the world a different place.

Charles Darwin 1809–82

His book, *On the Origin of Species by Means of Natural Selection*, published in 1859, has been called 'the book that shook the world'.

Today, most scientists and ordinary people, with the exception of creationists, accept the theories put forward in this book. Darwin believed that all species (plants, animals, and human beings) were not created individually, but evolved over millions of years through a process of natural selection. The struggle for existence meant that the species that could adapt best were those that survived.

These ideas contradicted religious beliefs. People thought that God had created Adam and Eve and all the animals as they were then. It was also believed that the Earth was just 4,000 years old.

HE SAID

'The mystery of the beginning of all things is insoluble by us; and I for one must be content to remain an agnostic.'

THEY SAID

'Mankind is not descended from monkeys. There is no point in a world without God.'

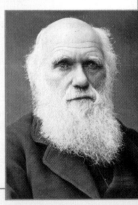

GALILEO GALILEI 1564–1642

Galileo was born in Pisa, Italy. He spent years observing the movements of the planets through a telescope. At the time it was generally thought that the earth was the centre of the universe. Galileo believed, as Copernicus had done seventy years before, that the earth rotated on its axis once daily and travelled round the sun once every year. At the time, this was a fantastic concept, and considered dangerous by the Church.

In 1633 he was found guilty of heresy, and spent the final years of his life imprisoned in his own home.

Galileo is referred to as the 'father of modern science'. He paved the way for the separation of science and religion.

HE SAID

'All truths are easy to understand once they are discovered; the point is to discover them.'

THEY SAID

'The proposition that the sun is in the centre of the world is absurd, philosophically false, and heretical; it is contrary to Holy Scriptures.'

Sigmund Freud 1856–1939

Sigmund Freud was born in Austria. He developed the technique of psychoanalysis in his treatment of patients with mental disorders. His most famous book, *The Interpretation of Dreams*, was published in 1900.

Freud argued that we all have an unconscious mind as well as a conscious one. The unconscious is where our motivations originate and our fears are buried. Memories, especially from childhood, have a huge influence on the way we are now, but we are largely unaware of their significance. We deny or resist becoming conscious of these motives.

Freud's proposals came at a time when strict scientific methods were seen as the only way to discover truth. By introducing the notion of the unconscious, Freud undermined the belief that we are in control of our actions, thoughts, and behaviours at all times.

He is commonly referred to as 'the father of psychoanalysis' and his work has been highly influential.

HE SAID

'The mind is like an iceberg, it floats with one-seventh of its bulk above water.'

THEY SAID

'His ideas are unverifiable. His attitude to scientific research is irresponsible.'

Emmeline Pankhurst 1858–1928

Emmeline Pankhurst is seen as 'the principal fighter for women's equality in the UK'. Women were not given the vote because they were considered to be incapable of rational thought. Their place was in the home.

In her twenties Emmeline Pankhurst belonged to the suffragists, who wanted to achieve equal voting rights for women by peaceful means. She later led the suffragettes, who had a more militant approach. Their tactics for attracting attention included smashing shop windows, burning down buildings, slashing paintings in art galleries, organizing marches, and chaining themselves to railings.

In 1908–09 Pankhurst was sent to prison three times. She experienced force-feeding after going on hunger strike.

The British government changed the law on voting rights for women in 1918. In 1928, women finally achieved equal voting rights to men.

SHE SAID

'We are here, not because we are law-breakers; we are here in our efforts to become law-makers.'

THEY SAID

'These women are hysterical and unreasonable. Heaven help us if they had the vote. They have abandoned their duties as wives and mothers.'

Elvis Presley 1935–77

Elvis Presley is known simply as 'The King'. When he arrived on the pop scene in 1956, he introduced a new rhythm to music, sex, language and fashion. Before his arrival, adolescent kids dressed like their parents. Then Elvis shook his hips and changed everything. This new sex symbol mesmerized one generation, and at the same time alienated another. Boys wanted to be him, girls fell instantly in love with him and – most importantly – their parents all hated him. The teenager was born.

He did more than anyone else to invent youth culture, and as such he was considered a dangerous threat to society.

John Lennon said, 'Nothing really affected me until I heard Elvis. If there hadn't been an Elvis, there wouldn't have been a Beatles.'

HE SAID

'If you like rock 'n' roll, if you feel it, you can't help but move to it. That's what happens to me. I can't help it.'

THEY SAID

'He was an indifferent singer, a mediocre musician, and a totally uninteresting person. In five years' time, he will be totally forgotten.'
(Obituary 1977)

LISTENING AND SPEAKING
What the papers say

1 Which newspaper in your country …?
- has the best reputation
- is the most popular
- is the best for sport
- is the best for scandal

2 Do you believe everything you read in the newspapers? Do you think some stories are made more sensational?

3 **T 12.9** Listen to an interview with the singer, Jamie Seabrook. Answer the questions after each part.

Part 1
1 What are some of the highs and lows of Jamie's career?
2 What was he doing in Texas?
3 What does he like about all the press attention? What doesn't he like about it?
4 What does he think of reporters?

Part 2
5 Complete the chart.

	What did they say about him?	What did *he* say?
reporters		
ex-friends		
people in clubs		
police officers		
Barbara James		

6 Why did he go into the clinic?

Part 3
7 How has Jamie's life changed?
8 Why has he changed his attitude to life?
9 What did the news presenter refuse to do? Why?
10 How does he reply? What does he say about himself?

BOY SUES BURGER CHAIN
'Eating burgers made me fat'

ALIENS EXIST SAYS POPE

DOG WITH TWO HEADS BITES POSTMAN – TWICE!

Football boss leaves wife for bimbo

JAMIE CHECKS INTO PRIVATE CLINIC
Last chance to save my marriage, says pop star Jamie Seabrook

---

SPOKEN ENGLISH *don't mind / don't care*

1 Look at these sentences from the interview.

> **I don't mind** the press attention.
> **I don't care** what people think.

I don't mind = I'm easy. I have no strong opinions.
I don't care = Other people's opinions aren't important to me. (Careful! This can sound rude.)

2 Reply to these sentences with *I don't mind* or *I don't care*.
1 'Tea or coffee?' '_____. Whatever you're making.'
2 'I hate your tattoo!' '_____. *I* like it.'
3 'What shall we do today?'
   '_____. I'm happy whatever.'
4 She's so upset!' '_____. That's *her* problem.'

What do you think?

- Who do you believe – Jamie, or all the other people in his life?
- When you read a story in the news, how do you know whether to believe it?
- What are the big stories (political, environmental, sports, scandal) in the news at the moment?
   What are the different angles on the story?
   Do people agree on the basic facts, or are there different opinions?

EVERYDAY ENGLISH
You know what they say . . .

1 Some people like to bring a conversation to an end with a cliché. Nothing else needs to be said, the cliché says it all! <u>Underline</u> the clichés in these conversations.

'I didn't get that job I applied for. They said I need more experience.'
'Oh, well! You win some, you lose some.'

'Did you know 25% of the world speaks English?'
'Well I never! You learn something new every day!'

2 Match the lines in **A** with the clichés in **B**.

	A	B
1	I'm so fed up! I lost my mobile yesterday! I got the time wrong, and I missed my plane.	Never mind. We all make mistakes. Cheer up! It's not the end of the world.
2	I forgot her birthday, so I sent her a text. So you like Russian novels, do you? So do I!	Well done. Better late than never. Great minds think alike.
3	Tim's strange. He's not like me at all. I worked so hard for that exam, and I still failed.	You did your best. You can't do any more. It takes all sorts to make a world.
4	I've got ten exams in the next two weeks. I've got three months' holiday!	Rather you than me. It's all right for some.
5	I'm going to pack some anti-malaria tablets. I haven't heard from my kids for weeks!	No news is good news. Good idea. Better safe than sorry.
6	That party was awful. I hated it. I reversed into a wall and broke a tail light.	It could be worse. You could have hurt someone. You can say that again. I couldn't stand it.
7	She's been so sad since her husband died. I wonder if their marriage will last.	I'm sure it's tough, but time's a great healer. Only time will tell.
8	Our neighbours are extreme right-wing. I trusted Peter, and he stole all my money!	Oh, well. You live and learn. Live and let live. That's what I say.

3 **T 12.10** Listen and check.

And finally . . .

In the words of William Shakespeare …

All's well that ends well.

Writing

REFERENCE

1 It is important to try to correct your own mistakes when you write. Look at the symbols in the box. What kind of mistakes to they signify?

2 Read the letter that Kati, a Hungarian student, has written to her English friend, Stephanie. Use the symbols to help you correct her mistakes.

T Tense	*WW* Wrong word
Prep Preposition	*P* Punctuation
Gr Grammar	*Sp* Spelling
WO Word order	*λ* Word missing

23 St. Mary's Road,
Dublin 4, Ireland
Tuesday, 10 May

Dear Stephanie

   How are you? I'm very well. I came <u>in</u> [Prep] Dublin two weeks ago <u>for to</u> [Gr] study at a language school. I want λ[P] learn <u>e</u>[P]nglish because λ[Gr] is a very important language. I'm <u>stay</u>[Gr] with <u>a</u>[Gr] Irish family. They've got two so<u>n</u>[Gr] and a <u>dauhgter</u>[Sp]. Mr Kendall is λ[Gr] teacher and Mrs Kendall wor<u>k</u>[Gr] in a hospital. The Irish <u>is</u>[Gr] very kind, but they speak very quickly!

   I study in the morning. My teacher<u>s</u>[P] name is Ann. She <u>said</u>[WW] me that my English is OK, but I <u>do</u>[WW] a lot of mistakes. Ann <u>don't</u>[Gr] give us too much homework, so in the afternoons I <u>go always</u>[WO] sightseeing. Dublin is much <u>more big</u>[Gr] than my town. I like <u>very much painting</u>[WO] and I'm very interest<u>ing</u>[Gr] <u>for</u>[Prep] modern art, so I visit galleries and museums. I've met a girl named Martina. She <u>came</u>[T] from Spain and <u>go</u>[Gr] to Trinity College. Last night we <u>go</u>[T] to the cinema, but the film wasn't very <u>exiting</u>[Sp].

   <u>Do</u>[WW] you like to visit me? Why don't you come for a weekend?

I'd love to see you.

Write to me soon.

Love, **Kati**

P.S. Here's my new email address:
Katik@intermail.hu

3 Answer the questions.
  1 Where is Kati? Where is she staying?
  2 Why is she there?
  3 What does she do each day?
  4 What does she do in her free time?
  5 Who has she met?

4 Imagine that you are a student in another town. Answer the questions in exercise 3 about *you*.

5 Write a similar letter to an English friend. Swap letters with a partner. Try to correct your partner's letter using the symbols.

1 Read the lines 1–10 from some letters and emails. Which are formal, which are informal? Which are beginnings? Which are endings?

1 *Great to hear from you again.*

2 *I am writing in response to your advertisement in today's Guardian for an IT consultant.*

3 *Give my regards to Robert and all the family.*

4 *I'm sorry I haven't been in touch for so long but you know how it is.*

5 *Thank you for your invoice of April 16th. Please find enclosed a cheque for the full amount.*

6 *Write or, better still, email me soon.*

7 *We trust this arrangement meets with your satisfaction.*

8 *Just a note to say thank you so much for having me to stay last weekend.*

9 *Take care. I can't wait to see you next week.*

10 *I look forward to hearing from you at your earliest convenience.*

2 Read the **beginnings** of these letters and emails. Match them with their *next line* and *ending*.

Beginnings	Next lines	Endings
1 Dear Jane, thanks for your email. It's great to hear from you after so long.	**a** We had no idea John was such a good cook!	**e** Let me know asap. All the best, Danny
2 Dear Mr Smith, We have received your order and payment for the Children's Encyclopaedia CD-ROM.	**b** It's good to catch up on all your news. I've been pretty busy lately too. I've just started a new job.	**f** We apologize for the inconvenience. Your order will be processed as soon as we receive the additional amount. Yours sincerely, Pigeon Publishing
3 Hi Pete, Any chance you're free next Saturday evening?	**c** Unfortunately your cheque for £90 did not include postage of £7.50.	**g** Let's meet soon. Give my love to Alan and the boys. Yours, Julie
4 Dear John and Liz, Thank you so much for a great evening and meal.	**d** Chris and Nick are coming over and we wondered if you'd like to join us.	**h** Thanks again. We hope to see you both soon. Love Vicky and Jamie

3 Which letter or email in exercise 2 is …?

- an invitation
- a formal request
- exchanging news
- saying thank you

<u>Underline</u> the words or phrases which helped you decide.

4 You have just found the email address of an old friend. Write to him/her. Give news about your personal life and work. Ask about his/her news.

1 Read the story. Look at the picture. Who are the people?

The Farmer and his Sons

There was once an old, dying farmer **(1)** _____. Before he died he wanted to teach his three sons how to be good farmers. So he called them to his bedside and said, 'My boys, I have an important secret to tell you: there is a great treasure buried in the vineyard. Promise me that you will look for it when I am dead.'

The sons gave their promise and **(2)** _____ they began looking for the treasure. They worked very hard in the hot sun **(3)** _____. They pictured boxes of gold coins, diamond necklaces, and other such things. **(4)** _____ but they found not a single penny. They were very upset **(5)** _____. However, a few months later the grapes started to appear on the vines. Their grapes were the biggest and best in the neighbourhood and they sold them for a lot of money. Now the sons understood **(6)** _____ and they lived happily ever after.

2 Where do clauses a–f go in the story?

a ☐ as soon as their father had died
b ☐ who had worked hard in his vineyard all his life
c ☐ what their father had meant by the great treasure
d ☐ and while they were working they thought about what their father had said
e ☐ because they felt that all their hard work had been for nothing
f ☐ Soon they had dug up every inch of the vineyard

3 Read the lines from another story. Who are the people in the picture?

The Emperor and his Daughters

There was once an emperor **(1)**_____ lived in a palace.
He had three daughters **(2)**_____ no sons.
He wanted his daughters to marry **(3)**_____ he died.
He found three princes. **(4)**_____ his daughters didn't like them.
They refused to marry the princes, **(5)**_____ the emperor became very angry.
He said they must get married **(6)**_____ they were sixteen years old.
The three daughters ran away **(7)**_____ the night and found work on a farm.
They fell in love with the farmer's sons **(8)**_____ they were working there.
They married the sons **(9)**_____ they were sixteen.

4 Complete the lines using a linking word from the box.

before	as soon as	while	during
when	but	However,	so	who

5 In what ways are the lines below different from the ones in exercise 3?

There was once an old emperor who lived in an enormous, golden palace in the middle of the city Ping Chong. He had three beautiful daughters, but unfortunately no sons …

Continue rewriting the story, adding more detail to make it more interesting.

6 Write a folk tale or fairy story that you know. Write about 200 words.

Begin: *There was/were once …*

End: *… and they lived happily ever after.*

Mother Teresa of Calcutta (1910–1997)

1 What do you know about Mother Teresa? Share ideas as a class.

2 Work with a partner. Look at the information about Mother Teresa's *Early years*. Compare the sentences in **A** with the paragraph in **B**. Note the different ways the sentences combine.

A Early years	B
Mother Teresa was a missionary. She worked among the poor people of Calcutta, India. She was born Agnes Gonxha Bojaxhiu. She was born in Skopje, Macedonia. She was born on 26 August, 1910. Her father was Albanian. He died when she was eight years old. Her mother was left to bring up the family.	Mother Teresa was a missionary who worked among the poor people of Calcutta, India. She was born Agnes Gonxha Bojaxhiu, in Skopje, Macedonia on 26 August 1910. Her father, who was Albanian, died when she was just eight years old, leaving her mother to bring up the family.

3 Read the sentences in *Working as a teacher*. Work with your partner and use the information in **A** to complete the paragraph in **B**.

A Working as a teacher	B
Agnes was very young. She wanted to become a missionary. She left home in September 1928. She joined a convent in Ireland. She was given the name Teresa. She was sent to India in January 1929. She taught in St. Mary's High School Convent. St Mary's was in Calcutta. She worked in St Mary's for over 20 years. At first she was called Sister Teresa. She was called Mother Teresa in 1937.	From a very young age Agnes had wanted …, so in September 1928 she … to join … in Ireland, where she was given … . A few months later, in …, she was sent to … to teach in … in Calcutta. Here she worked for …, first as Sister … and finally, in 1937, as Mother Teresa.

4 Do the same with the information in *Working with the poor*. Read your completed paragraph aloud to the class.

A Working with the poor	B
In 1946 Mother Teresa felt called by God. She was called to help the poorest of the poor. She left St. Mary's convent on August 17, 1948. She started visiting families in the slums of Calcutta. She looked after sick and dying children. She started a religious community in 1950. It was called the Missionaries of Charity. The communities spread all over the world in the 1960s and 70s. Mother Teresa was awarded the Nobel Peace Prize in 1979. She developed severe health problems. She continued to work amongst the poor. She died on September 5, 1997. Thousands of people from all over the world came to her funeral.	Mother Teresa finally left … on August 17, 1948. Two years earlier, in …, she had felt called by … to help…, so she started visiting …, looking … sick …. In 1950, she started … called the Missionaries of Charity, which by the 1960s and 70s had spread …. In 1979 Mother Teresa …. She continued to work … despite developing …. When she finally … on September 5, 1997, thousands of people ….

5 Research some facts about a famous man or woman, dead or alive, that you admire. Write a short biography.

1 What topics are in the news at the moment? Are they national or international? Are they to do with the environment, politics, crime, sport…? Discuss any that concern you with the class.

2 **T 5.9** Read and listen to a girl talking about a topic that concerns her.

1 What is her cause for concern?
2 Why does she have a personal interest?
3 How did Craig use to be?
4 What does research tell us about the addiction?
5 Do most children become addicts?
6 What concerns Dr Griffiths?
7 What other concerns does the girl have?

3 Now read the talk carefully and answer the questions.

1 Underline the phrases that introduce each paragraph. Why are these words used?
2 Find examples of the speaker talking from her own experience.
3 Find examples where she quotes research.
4 How does the girl conclude her talk?
5 Read the paragraph beginning 'Research shows …' aloud to a partner.

Preparing your talk

4 Choose a cause for concern from the topics you discussed. Make notes. Say why it concerns you.

5 Write a talk to give to your class, of 200–300 words. Use your notes and these guidelines to help.

1 Introduce your topic
   My cause for concern is …
   I want to talk about X because …
2 Give the reason why
   Let me explain why.
   Two years ago …
   I've always been interested in …
3 List your research
   Research shows that…
   A recent study found that …
   I read in the newspaper/heard in the news that …
4 Introduce new points
   I have two more concerns .
   Firstly, … secondly, …
   Another thing is …
5 Conclude
   Finally, I'd like to say …
   Thank you all very much for listening to me.
   Are there any questions?

My cause for concern

The thing I'm concerned about at the moment is the influence that video games may have on children.

Let me explain why. I've been reading lots of newspaper articles on the subject, and I also have a personal interest. You see, I have a younger brother, Craig, he's 13 years old, and I'm afraid he's becoming a video game addict. Just a few years ago, Craig had many interests, he played football, he was learning judo, he went out on his bike with his friends. He was a happy, fun-loving boy. Now he spends hours every day in front of a screen, in a virtual world, playing virtual games, usually violent ones, and he becomes really angry if our parents tell him to stop.

Research shows that today 40% of family homes have computers, so there is plenty of opportunity for very young children to start using them, and by the age of seven many have developed an interest in video games. This is not a problem for most of them. However, by their early teens, a small minority have become addicts, playing for at least 30 hours a week. Dr Mark Griffiths of Nottingham Trent University, an expert in video addiction, finds this figure very worrying. He says that children may become so addicted that they stop doing homework, start playing truant, and even steal money in order to buy the games.

I have two more concerns. Firstly, I worry that the violence in the games could cause children to become more violent. My brother isn't violent but he is certainly bad-tempered if he is stopped from playing. Secondly, I worry that sitting without exercise for so long is bad for the health. Craig often plays five hours a day, and some days his thumbs are really painful and he can't sleep because he is over-excited. His schoolwork is going from bad to worse.

Finally, Dr Griffiths says that more research is needed but I don't need to read more research to conclude that video games cause problems. He should come and meet my brother. That's all the evidence he needs.

6 Practise reading your talk aloud first to yourself, then to a partner. Give your talk to the class. Answer any questions.

1 Think of your favourite room. Draw a plan of it on a piece of paper. Write down why you like it and some adjectives to describe it.

My favourite room is . . .   I like it because . . .

Show a partner your plan and talk about your room.

2 Read the description *My favourite room*. Why is this kitchen more than just a room where you cook and eat?

3 Complete the description using the relative clauses below:

… which tells the story
… that we're going to next Saturday
… where we cook and eat
… whose family have all emigrated
… which is the focal point of the room
… which means
… we haven't seen
… I like best
… who are cross and sleepy
… where family and friends come together

GRAMMAR SPOT

1 Underline the relative pronouns in exercise 3. What do they refer to? When do we use *which, who, that, where*, and *whose*?

2 Look at the these sentences. We can omit the relative pronoun from one in each pair. Which one? Why?

This is the room **which** I like best.
This is the room **which** has the best view.

He's a friend **who** we haven't seen for years
He's a friend **who** lives in London.

3 Look at these examples of participles. Rewrite them with relative pronouns.

I have so many happy memories of times spent there.

There is a large window looking out onto two apple trees in the garden.

▶▶ **Grammar Reference 6.3 and 6.4 p140**

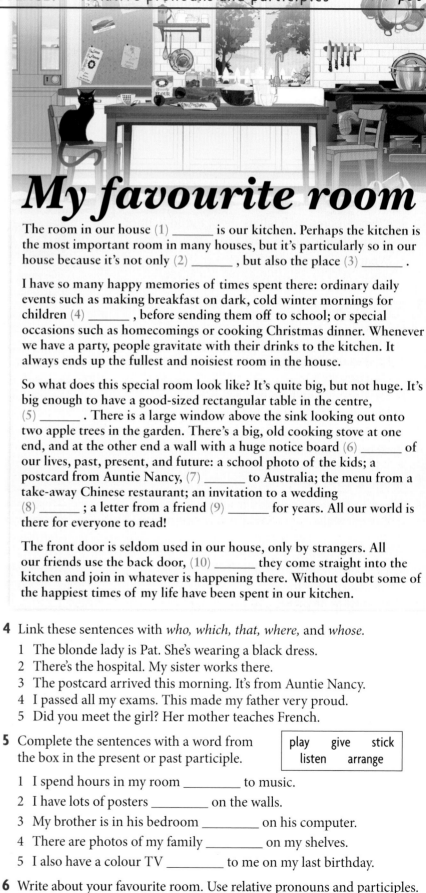

My favourite room

The room in our house (1) _____ is our kitchen. Perhaps the kitchen is the most important room in many houses, but it's particularly so in our house because it's not only (2) _____ , but also the place (3) _____ .

I have so many happy memories of times spent there: ordinary daily events such as making breakfast on dark, cold winter mornings for children (4) _____ , before sending them off to school; or special occasions such as homecomings or cooking Christmas dinner. Whenever we have a party, people gravitate with their drinks to the kitchen. It always ends up the fullest and noisiest room in the house.

So what does this special room look like? It's quite big, but not huge. It's big enough to have a good-sized rectangular table in the centre, (5) _____ . There is a large window above the sink looking out onto two apple trees in the garden. There's a big, old cooking stove at one end, and at the other end a wall with a huge notice board (6) _____ of our lives, past, present, and future: a school photo of the kids; a postcard from Auntie Nancy, (7) _____ to Australia; the menu from a take-away Chinese restaurant; an invitation to a wedding (8) _____ ; a letter from a friend (9) _____ for years. All our world is there for everyone to read!

The front door is seldom used in our house, only by strangers. All our friends use the back door, (10) _____ they come straight into the kitchen and join in whatever is happening there. Without doubt some of the happiest times of my life have been spent in our kitchen.

4 Link these sentences with *who, which, that, where*, and *whose*.
  1 The blonde lady is Pat. She's wearing a black dress.
  2 There's the hospital. My sister works there.
  3 The postcard arrived this morning. It's from Auntie Nancy.
  4 I passed all my exams. This made my father very proud.
  5 Did you meet the girl? Her mother teaches French.

5 Complete the sentences with a word from the box in the present or past participle.

play	give	stick
listen	arrange	

  1 I spend hours in my room _____ to music.
  2 I have lots of posters _____ on the walls.
  3 My brother is in his bedroom _____ on his computer.
  4 There are photos of my family _____ on my shelves.
  5 I also have a colour TV _____ to me on my last birthday.

6 Write about your favourite room. Use relative pronouns and participles.

1 Think of someone in your family and write three sentences about them. Read your sentences aloud to the rest of the class.

2 Which relative did you choose? Why? Did you write about their character, their appearance, or both?

3 Read the description of crazy Uncle Joe. Which sentence below accurately describes the writer's opinion of him?

– *The writer likes Uncle Joe but is critical of his way of life.*

– *The writer admires everything about Uncle Joe.*

4 The text consists of *factual description* and *personal opinions*. Work with a partner and read through the text again. Underline like this _____ what is factual, and like this _ _ _ _ what is personal opinion.

5 Find words and lines which describe:
- his physical appearance
- his character
- his past life
- his current lifestyle

6 Find the following words:

much (line 2)	**really** (line 13)
such (line 4)	**quite** (line 13)
completely (line 10)	**particularly** (line 15)
absolutely (line 11)	**extremely** (line 18)

How do they change the meaning of the adjectives which follow them?

7 Write a similar description of a member of your family in about 200 words. Include your sentences from exercise 1 and the following:
- your relation to him/her
- your opinion of him/her
- a little about his/her past life
- his/her physical appearance
- his/her character
- his/her current lifestyle

MY CRAZY UNCLE JOE

1 Of all my relatives, I like my Uncle Joe the best. He's my mother's much younger brother. He was only nine when I was born, so he's been more like a big brother to me than an uncle. He is in his mid-20s now and he is always such good fun to be with.

5 He studied at a drama school in Liverpool, and then he moved to London a year ago to try his luck in the theatre. He shares a flat with three other would-be actors, and he works as a waiter and a part-time DJ. He's passionate about his music, it's called House Music, and it's a kind of electronic dance music. When he 'deejays'
10 he goes completely wild, waving his arms and yelling at the crowds. His enthusiasm is infectious. He's absolutely brilliant, I'm proud that he's my uncle.

Also, I think he is really good-looking. He's quite tall with sandy-coloured hair, and twinkly, dark brown eyes. He's had lots
15 of girlfriends, but I don't think there is anyone particularly special at the moment. He has a great relationship with his flatmates, they are always laughing and joking together. He knows how to have fun but he's also an extremely caring person. I can talk to him about all kinds of problems that I could not discuss with my
20 parents. He's very understanding of someone my age.

He works hard, and he plays hard. He's had lots of auditions for various theatrical roles. He hasn't had much luck yet, but I'm sure that one day he'll be a highly successful actor. I think he's really talented but he says he doesn't want to be rich or famous, he just
25 wants to prove to himself that he's a good actor.

1 What do you know about the sinking of the *Titanic*?

It happened at the beginning of the twentieth century.
There was a film about it starring Leonardo DiCaprio.

2 Work with a partner. Look at the pictures and tell the story in your own words. Then read **Text A** and match the lines with the pictures.

| Text A | **The Unsinkable *Titanic*, 1912** |

On April 10, 1912, the *Titanic* left Southampton on her way to New York. There were many rich passengers on board. Everyone believed the ship was unsinkable so she didn't have many lifeboats.

On the night of April 14, the passengers were having dinner and listening to the band. The *Titanic* was travelling fast because the owner wanted his ship to beat the record for crossing the Atlantic. Some ships nearby warned of icebergs but the messages were not delivered. A look-out sounded the alarm but it was too late. The *Titanic* hit an iceberg and the ship sank quickly. The band played until it sank. The lifeboats only saved some of the people. Most of them died in the sea.

People today are still interested in the *Titanic*. The film, '*Titanic*', was very popular.

3 Now read **Text B**. Compare it with **Text A**. Which is the more interesting text? Why? Give some examples.

| Text B | **The Unsinkable *Titanic*, 1912** |

On April 10, 1912, the liner *Titanic*, the luxurious ship they called unsinkable, left Southampton on her maiden voyage to New York. Her passengers were a mixture of the world's wealthiest in their magnificent first class accommodation, and immigrants packed into steerage. The ship was believed to be so safe that she carried only 20 lifeboats, enough for only half her 2,235 passengers and crew.

On the evening of April 14 there was no wind and the sea was calm. The band were playing as the rich enjoyed their evening meal in the sumptuous dining room. At 9.40 p.m. nearby ships warned of icebergs. However, the messages were not delivered. The *Titanic* was travelling at 22 knots. The owner of the ship was on board, encouraging the captain to go faster to beat the record for crossing the Atlantic. Finally, a look-out on the bridge sounded the alarm but it was too late. At 11.40 p.m. the *Titanic* struck an iceberg. Passengers felt only a slight bump and carried on dancing and dining. After all, this ship was unsinkable. In fact, the ship was sinking fast, but it was not until nearly 12.45 that an SOS signal was sent and the first lifeboat was lowered. The last one was lowered at 2.05 a.m., and at 2.20 a.m. the ship sank, just two hours and forty minutes after hitting the iceberg. 713 people were saved. The remaining 1,522 all met their death in the dark waters of the Atlantic Ocean. These included most of the men and third class passengers, the crew, and all of the band. Amazingly, they had kept playing until the ship disappeared beneath the waves.

The ship sank almost 100 years ago but interest in the *Titanic* continues. Books and films have kept its memory alive. '*Titanic*' is the most watched film in movie history. Incredibly, in 1985, the wreck itself was discovered and photographed on the sea bed.

4 Go through the *Titanic* texts again with your partner. Discuss the differences. Consider the following questions.

The general organization
How is the scene set?
What forms the main part?
How is the story concluded?

Telling the story
What information is given?
How is interest created?
What is the order of events?

The language
Which adjectives and adverbs are used?
How are the sentences constructed?

5 With your partner discuss what you know about the story of *The Trojan Horse*. Look at the pictures and prompts to help.

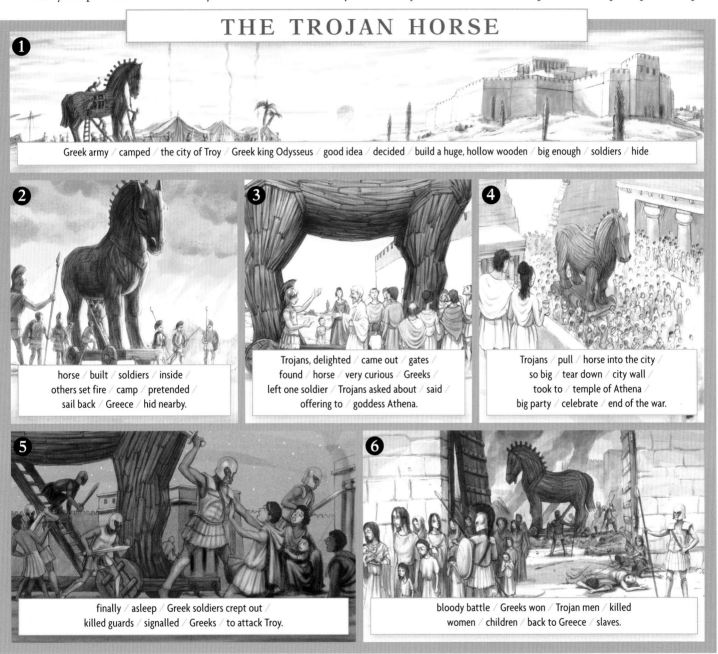

THE TROJAN HORSE

1 Greek army / camped / the city of Troy / Greek king Odysseus / good idea / decided / build a huge, hollow wooden / big enough / soldiers / hide

2 horse / built / soldiers / inside / others set fire / camp / pretended / sail back / Greece / hid nearby.

3 Trojans, delighted / came out / gates / found / horse / very curious / Greeks / left one soldier / Trojans asked about / said / offering to / goddess Athena.

4 Trojans / pull / horse into the city / so big / tear down / city wall / took to / temple of Athena / big party / celebrate / end of the war.

5 finally / asleep / Greek soldiers crept out / killed guards / signalled / Greeks / to attack Troy.

6 bloody battle / Greeks won / Trojan men / killed women / children / back to Greece / slaves.

6 Work together to write the story. Remember to set the scene, create interest, and use adverbs and adjectives.
Begin like this: **The Greeks and the Trojans had been at war for ten years.**

7 Read some of the stories aloud to the class. Compare with the story on p150–51.

1 Do you think childhood is the best time of your life? Discuss as a class.

2 Read the text about the pros and cons of childhood. Replace the underlined words and phrases in the text with those in the box.

> For instance
> One advantage is that
> pros and cons
> One disadvantage is that
> Finally,
> All things considered
> in my opinion,
> In conclusion
> In fact,
> Another point is that
> Moreover,

3 There are four paragraphs. What is the purpose of each one?

Pros and

Childhood – the best time of your life?

1 **Some people say that childhood is the best time of your life. However, being a child has both <u>advantages and disadvantages.</u>**

2 <u>On the plus side</u>, you have very few responsibilities. <u>For example</u>, you don't have to go to work, pay bills, or do the shopping, cooking, or cleaning. This means you have plenty of free time to do whatever you want – watch TV, play on the computer, go out with friends, play sports, or pursue other hobbies. <u>On top of that</u>, public transport, cinema, and sports centres cost much less for children. <u>All in all</u>, being a child is an exciting, action-packed time in life.

3 However, for every plus there is a minus. <u>For one thing</u>, you have to spend all day, Monday to Friday, at school. Studying usually means you have to do homework, and you have to take exams. <u>What is more</u>, you may have a lot of free time, but you are rarely allowed to do whatever you want. You usually have to ask your parents if you can do things, from going shopping in town to staying out late or going to a party. <u>Last of all</u>, although there are often cheaper prices for children, things are still expensive – and parents are not always generous with pocket money. There's never enough to do everything you want. <u>The reality is that</u> sometimes there's not enough to do anything at all!

4 <u>To sum up</u>, although some people see childhood as the best time in life, <u>I think that</u> children have no real choice, independence, or money. Nevertheless, it is true that choice, money, and independence all bring responsibilities and restrictions – which increase with age.

4 Match the pros with the cons.

	pros	cons
1	don't have to go to work	are never given enough pocket money
2	can go out to parties with friends	have to do homework and take exams
3	don't have to cook and clean	have to go to school Monday to Friday
4	pay less for things	need to ask your parents' permission

5 Work with a partner. Choose one of these subjects and briefly discuss the pros and cons.

1 Restorative justice (where criminals meet their victims to talk about the effect of their crimes)
2 Getting older
3 Having children while young

6 Work together to complete these phrases with your ideas from exercise 5.

On the plus side …
For example, …
Another point is that …
However, there are also disadvantages …
For instance …
What is more, …
Last of all, …
In my opinion, …
In conclusion, …

7 Use the ideas from exercises 5 and 6 to write four paragraphs on your chosen subject. Read your essay aloud to the class. Do they agree with your conclusion?

1 Write down everything you know about New York City. Collect all your ideas as a class.

2 Work with a partner and study the diagram about New York. Compare the information with your ideas.

Geography
- **Hudson River**
- **same latitude as Naples and Madrid**

History
- **Dutch 1614 / New Amsterdam**
- **British 1664 / New York**
- **19th c./ immigration**
- **20th c./ economic boom**
- **Sept. 11th 2001**

Its people
- **densely populated / 8,214,246**
- **36% foreign born**
- **170 languages**

'The Big Apple'

NEW YORK CITY

'The city that never sleeps'

Transport
- **12,000 taxis**
- **3 airports**
- **Grand Central Station**
- **subway / 1.4 billion passengers**

Sport
- **baseball**
- **marathon / 37,000 runners**

Tourism
- **Shopping / 5th Ave.**
- **Empire State Building, etc.**
- **40 million visitors**

Food
- **variety**
- **haute cuisine / hotdogs**

NEW YORK CITY

Although New York City is not the capital of the United States, its influence is seen throughout the world. Its nickname, (1) "_____", was given to it by early immigrants because the city seemed so huge and full of promise.

Geography

It is located at the mouth of the (2) _____ and lies on the same latitude as the European cities of (3) _____.

History

The Dutch founded the city in 1614, calling it (4) _____. However, in (5) _____ it was captured by the British and renamed New York. The city grew in importance and was the US capital until 1790. During the 19th century it was transformed by (6) _____and from the early 20th century became a world centre for industry, commerce, and communication. With the economic (7) _____ came the construction of its distinctive skyline of skyscrapers, two of which, the Twin Towers of the World Trade Center, were destroyed in the attacks of (8) _____, when nearly 3,000 people died.

Its people

New York is the most **(9)** _____ and cosmopolitan city in the United States with 8,214,246 inhabitants speaking **(10)** _____ languages. 36% of the city's population is **(11)** _____ . Five of the largest ethnic groups are: Puerto Ricans, Italians, West Indians, Chinese, and Irish.

Transport

One in three New Yorkers uses public transport to get to work, whereas in the rest of the US 90% of commuters go by car. The New York City Subway, which is open 24/7, is used by **(12)** _____ a year. New York is also home to the famous Grand Central Station, three major airports, and **(13)** _____ distinctive, yellow taxi cabs.

Sport

The New York Marathon, held annually on the first Sunday of November, is the largest marathon in the world. It attracts **(14)** _____ . However, many New Yorkers prefer a less energetic jog round Central Park. New Yorkers are also keen **(15)** _____ fans. The two most popular teams are the New York Yankees and the New York Mets.

Tourism

About **(16)** _____ tourists visit New York City each year. Major attractions include the Empire State Building, the Metropolitan Museum of Art, Times Square, Central Park, and, of course, the luxury **(17)** _____ along Fifth Avenue. Tourists are also attracted by the incredible **(18)** _____ of places to eat, from diners, with their burgers, bagels, and pizza, to many of the finest haute cuisine restaurants in the US, and not forgetting the Grand Central Oyster Bar, and the steaming **(19)** _____ sold on every street corner.

Finally

With so much to do and see it is no surprise that New York is often called **(20)** "_____".

3 Read and complete the text using the information from the diagram in exercise 2.

4 Read the text again. What extra information to the diagram can you find? Give some examples.

5 Find these words and expressions in the text and discuss why they are used.

although	its	However	distinctive
two of which	whereas	is home to	with (so much to do)

6 Complete these sentences with the words or expressions from exercise 5.

1 Tokyo is the biggest city in the world. _____ population is over 28 million.
2 Britain has many big cities, _____ are Birmingham and Manchester.
3 Manchester _____ one of the most famous football teams in the world, Manchester United.
4 The temperature in Canada can be as low as -25ºC in winter. _____, in summer it is often over 30ºC.
5 _____ most people in Canada speak English, French is also an official language.
6 It is easy to recognise pictures of Sydney harbour because of its _____ bridge and the Opera House.
7 Madrid is located in the centre of Spain, _____ Barcelona is on the coast.
8 _____ so much to see, it is impossible to do a tour of Europe in two weeks.

7 Choose a famous town or city. Research it, make notes (you could draw a diagram), and then write about it. Use the headings about New York, or choose headings of your own.

1 Join the sentences in different ways using the words in brackets.

  1 George was rich. He wasn't a happy man. (*but / although / however*)
  2 Jo rang me from a phone box. She's lost her mobile. (*because / so*)

2 Look at these words and expressions. They prepare people for what you are going to write or say next. Read and complete the sentences with your own ideas.

  1 **In fact/Actually** (*I'm going to add more information to support this statement.*)
    Peter doesn't like working in London. **In fact**, he's thinking of changing jobs.
    Peter and I are in love. **Actually**, we _____.

  2 **Of course/Naturally** (*What I am going to say is obvious.*)
    Of course, having a baby has totally changed our lives.
    Naturally, when I was a child I didn't _____.

  3 **Fortunately/Unfortunately** (*What I am going to say is/is not good news.*)
    She tried really hard, and **fortunately**, she passed the exam.
    She stood and waited for over an hour, but **unfortunately**, _____.

  4 **Nevertheless** (*I am going to tell you about a result or effect which is unexpected.*)
    The accident wasn't her fault. **Nevertheless**, she felt terrible.
    My father didn't do very well at school. **Nevertheless**, _____.

  5 **Anyway** (*I am going to finish talking about the subject and move on to something new.*)
    What traffic! I thought I'd never get here. **Anyway**, now let's get on with the meeting.
    Anyway, you've heard enough about me. What _____ ?

in fact
actually
of course
naturally
fortunately
unfortunately
nevertheless
anyway

3 Read the letter and write the word or words that fit best.

Hi Melody,   *August 15th*

   I hope you're all well. Things are busy here. Maya moved out last week. She found a small apartment not far from here, (1) _____ (so / anyway) we still see her all the time. She also got a new job at a radio station. (2) _____ , (Unfortunately / Because) it doesn't pay very well, (3) _____ (of course / but) at least she likes it. Now that Maya has moved out, it's only Joe and me at home. After 24 years of having kids around the house, it's a little strange to have the place all to ourselves. (4) _____ , (However / In fact) it's nice to come home to a clean house at the end of the day.

   Samantha is going to graduate from Oberlin College this year. We're all very proud and, (5) _____ , (however / of course) we're going to have a party for her. (6) _____ , (So / Actually) it's going to be a surprise party! So, shhh! Samantha says she wants to travel somewhere interesting in the autumn, (7) _____ (but / because) she hasn't decided where to go yet. Joe's fine, (8) _____ (although / so) he's been in a bad mood lately. He hasn't been able to do much in the garden (9) _____ (because / actually) it's rained every day for the last two weeks! (10) _____ , (In fact / Nevertheless) it's been the rainiest summer for 20 years. (11) _____ , (Anyway / Of course) that's enough of our news. How are you all? What are you up to?

Write back and tell me everything!
Love, Jackie

1 Kati was a student of English in Dublin, where she stayed with the Kendall family. She has now returned home. Read the email she has written to Mr and Mrs Kendall. Her English has improved, but there are still over 25 mistakes. How many can you find?

To:	GillandBobKendall@lightspeed.net	Attachment:	GoodbyeDublin.jpg
Subject:	**Hello from Kati**		

Dear Mr and Mrs Kendall

I am home now since two weeks, but I have to start work immediately, so this is the first time is possible for me to write. How are you all? Are you busy as usual? Does Tim still work hard for his exam next month? I am miss you a lot and also all my friends from Dublin. :-)

Yesterday I've received an email from my Spain friend, Martina, and she told me about some of the other people I met. She say that Atsuko and Yuki will write me from Japan. I am lucky because I made so many good friend during I was in Ireland. It was really interesting for me to meet people from so many different countries. I think that we not only improved our English (I hope this!) but we also knew people from all over the world and this is important.

My family are fine. They had a good summer holiday by the lake. We are all very exciting because my brother will get married just before Christmas and we like very much his girlfriend. They have looked for a flat near the city centre but it is no easy to find one. If they won't find one soon, they will have to stay here with us.

Please can you check something for me? I can't find my red scarf. I think maybe I have forgotten it in the cuboard in my bedroom.

Please write soon. My family send best wishes to you all. I hope I can come back next year. Stay with you was a very wonderful experience for me. Thank you for all things and excuse my mistakes. I already forget much words.

Love and best wishes to you all,

Kati x x

P.S. I hope you like the attached photo. It's nice, isn't it?
It's the one you took when I was leaving!

---

2 Compare the mistakes you have found with a partner.
Correct the email.

3 Write a thank-you email to someone you have stayed with.

Tapescripts

UNIT 1

T 1.1 One World Quiz

1 In which country do men and women live the longest?
Women and men live longest in Japan. Women live on average 86 years and men 79. The average life expectancy in Japan is 81.25. In the USA it's 77.8 and in Germany 78.8.

2 In which year did the world population reach 6 billion?
The world population reached 6 billion in 1999. There are now over 6.8 billion people in the world.

3 If you are standing on the equator, how many hours of daylight do you have?
If you are standing on the equator you have 12 hours of daylight every day of the year. You also experience the fastest sunrise and sunset in the world, between128 and 142 seconds depending on the time of year.

4 Where does most of the world's oil come from?
Most of the world's oil comes from Saudi Arabia. It produces 10.9 million barrels per day. Russia produces 9.4 million, and Iran 4.3 million.

5 Which of these seven wonders of the world is still standing?
Of the seven wonders of the ancient world only the pyramids of Egypt are still standing. The Colossus of Rhodes and the Lighthouse of Alexandria were destroyed by earthquakes hundreds of years ago.

6 Why didn't dinosaurs attack humans?
Dinosaurs didn't attack humans because they became extinct 65 million years ago. Human beings didn't appear on earth until 130,000 years ago.

7 Where was the Titanic sailing to when it sank?
The Titanic was sailing to New York from Southampton when it hit an iceberg on April 14th, 1912.

8 How long has Elizabeth II been Queen of England?
Elizabeth II has been Queen of England since 1952. She was on holiday in Kenya when her father, King George VI, died.

9 How many people have won the Nobel Peace prize since it started in 1901?
94 people have won the Nobel Peace prize since it started in 1901. These include Nelson Mandela, in 1993, and Mother Teresa, in 1979.

10 How long have people been using the Internet?
People have been using the Internet since 1969. It was invented by the US Department of Defense as a means of communication. It first went live in October 1969, with communications between the University of California and the Stanford Research Institute.

11 How many languages are spoken in Switzerland?
4 languages are spoken in Switzerland: German, French, Italian and Romansch. German is the most widely spoken. 63.7% speak German, 19.2% French, 7.6% Italian, and 0.6% Romansch.

12 In which country were women first given the vote?
New Zealand was the first country in the world to give women the vote in 1893. Canadian women were given the vote in 1917, but women in Liechtenstein weren't allowed to vote until 1984.

T 1.2 You're so wrong!

1 A The Pope lives in Madrid.
   B He doesn't live in Madrid! He lives in Rome. In the Vatican!
2 A Shakespeare didn't write poems.
   B You're wrong. He wrote hundreds of poems, not just plays.
3 A Vegetarians eat meat.
   B Of course they don't eat meat. They only eat vegetables and sometimes fish.
4 A The Internet doesn't provide much information.
   B Rubbish! It provides lots. Sometimes I think that it provides too much!
5 A The world is getting colder.
   B It isn't getting colder, it's getting hotter. Haven't you heard of global warming?
6 A Princess Diana was travelling by plane when she was killed.
   B No, you're wrong. She wasn't travelling by plane. She was travelling by car, in Paris.
7 A England has never won the World Cup.
   B England *has* won it, just once. I think it was in 1966. My dad goes on about it all the time.
8 A The 2008 Olympics were held in Tokyo.
   B No, they weren't held in Tokyo. They were held in China, in Beijing.

T 1.3 is or has?

1 My brother's just got a new job.
2 He's working in South America.
3 He's been there 3 months.
4 He's having a great time.
5 He's never worked overseas before.
6 His company's called Intext Worldwide.

T 1.4 Making conversation

R = Ruth (mother)   N = Nick (son)
L = Lily (daughter)
R So kids, did you have a good day at school?
N No.
L Yes, I did. We were practising for the school concert.
R Oh, lovely. Do you have much homework?
L Ugh! Yes, I do. Loads. I've got Geography, French, and Maths! Have you got a lot Nick?
N Yeah.
R Nick, have you remembered your football kit?
N Er …
L No, he hasn't. He's forgotten it again.
R Oh, Nick you know it needs washing. Are you playing football tomorrow?
N No.
R Lily, do you need *your* sports kit tomorrow?
L Yes, I do. I've got a hockey match after school. We're playing the High School.
R Didn't they beat you last time?
L Yes, they did. But we'll beat them tomorrow.
N No, you won't! Your team's rubbish.
R OK, that's enough children. Do up your seatbelts! Let's go!

T 1.5

R So kids, did you have a good day at school?
N No, I didn't. Not really. We didn't have *any* of my favourite subjects.
L *I* did. I had a brilliant day. We were practising for the school concert.
R Oh, lovely. Do you have much homework?
L Ugh! Yes, I do. Loads. I've got Geography, French and Maths! Have you got a lot Nick?
N Yes, I have. Loads of it, I have to write a Geography essay on Antarctica. 1,500 words!
R Oh Nick, have you remembered your football kit?
N Oh no, I haven't – sorry mum.
R Oh, Nick you know it needs washing. Are you playing football tomorrow?
N No, I'm not, thank goodness. The match was cancelled.
R Lily, do you need *your* sports kit tomorrow?
L Yes, I do. I've got a hockey match after school. We're playing the High School.
R Didn't they beat you last time?
L Yes, they did. But we'll beat them tomorrow.
N Mmmm – I'm not so sure about that.
R OK, that's enough children. Do up your seatbelts! Let's go!

T 1.6 see p9

T 1.7 A world in one family

An interview with Xabier
I = Interviewer   X = Xabier
I So, Xabier – how old are you?
X I'm 21.
I And I know you have an interesting background, what nationality are you?
X Well, I've got a British passport …
I … so you're British, but your parents – what nationality are your parents?
X Well, my dad's Bolivian, he was born in Bolivia, in South America, but he's had a British passport for the last 20 years. My mum was born in Spain, in the Basque country, and she still has her Spanish passport.
I So how did they meet and end up having children in England?
X Erm … they met when they were both studying English in England erm … and er … about 3 years after that they got married and here I am, and then my brother.
I And what was it like growing up in England with a Spanish mother and a Bolivian father?
X I don't think I actually noticed nationality for years –erm … probably the first time I really noticed a difference was at secondary school, England were playing Spain in Euro '96 and my classmates made me choose which country to support.
I So which country did you support?
X I stayed neutral. Actually I didn't mind which team won.
I And which nationality do you feel now?
X I'd say I was English, rather than British –erm … but I'm also very proud of my parents' heritage, half Basque and half Bolivian. I like that.
I What contact have you had with your family abroad?
X Well, I've only actually been to Bolivia once –er … when I was a baby. I've had more contact on my mum's side. My Spanish grandparents visit us in England and when I was growing up we always went to Spain in the summer, and …
I Very nice!
X … and if I'm at home I speak to them –er … to my grandparents, on the phone –er … maybe once a week,
I And do you think that your Spanish heritage has influenced you at all?
X Well, yes, I think so. I think it influenced my degree choice. I'm studying modern languages at Durham University, Spanish and French. I'm in my 3rd year, I have one more year to do.
I And what are you hoping to do in the future?
X Erm–. That's a very good question. Erm … hopefully a job that offers some kind of opportunity to travel but ultimately I want to settle down for good in England. I've always been interested in my background but I think that I

realize England is my home and it's where I see myself living.
I Thank you very much Xabier.
X You're welcome.

T 1.8 I = Interviewer   A = Ana

An interview with Ana
I Ana, you're Spanish, aren't you?
A Yes, I am. I'm from Bilbao, in the Basque country.
I And how long have you lived here in Oxford?
A –er … 23 years.
I And how did that happen?
A Well, I wanted to improve my English so I came to England, to study. Originally, I came for 6 months but –er … I met my husband –er … we met at the college – actually we met on the way to the college, in the street.
I You met in the street?
A Yes, it was my first day and I was walking up the hill to the college and Teo, that's my husband, was driving up the hill and he stopped and offered me a lift, which I refused.
I You refused?
A Yes, but we ended up in the same class. I went into the class and there he was.
I And your husband's from Bolivia, isn't he?
A Yes, he is.
I So that means you speak the same language.
A Yes, Spanish.
I So why did you decide to live in England?
A Well, mainly because my husband had a job here and erm– we kind of decided we wanted a place in the middle, between Spain and Bolivia.
I A nice idea. And you have two sons.
A Yes, I do. Er … Xabier is 21, nearly 22, and James is 19.
I So, what's it been like for them growing up in England with parents of different nationality?
A Well, I think because we live in Oxford, a cosmopolitan city, they didn't notice it too much.
I They are both bilingual presumably?
A No, not really …
I Oh.
A … because, when they were children, even though we spoke to them in Spanish they always replied in English.
I Erm, interesting. Tell me, how much contact has your family here had with the families in Spain and Bolivia?
A I think more with my family in Spain because it's closer. We always spent summer there –er– 2 or 3 weeks usually.
I And the Bolivian side?
A Well, my husband keeps in touch all the time but his family have never been here.
I Never?
A Never. We went to Bolivia once when Xabier was 18 months old. James has never been.
I So what are the children doing now?
A Xabier's at university and James has just finished school. He's been working in a restaurant saving money to travel.
I And what do they want to do in the future?
A Well, James. He's going to travel to Bolivia, at last! Then he's going to university to study Biology.
I And Xabier?
A I think he wants to work in the Foreign Office.
I Ana, is it possible to sum up the pros and cons of bringing up a family in another country to your own?
A Well, I think in a way it's good because you can take the best things from both cultures, but I don't think my sons will ever feel 100% English because their parents aren't English. It's quite tricky.

T 1.9 **Pronunciation**
1 rose   goes   does   toes
2 meat   beat   great   street
3 paid   made   played   said
4 done   phone   son   won

T 1.10
mother   enjoy   apartment   holiday   population

T 1.11 **Everyday situations**
1 **A** I need to make an appointment. It's quite urgent. I've lost a filling.
B We have a cancellation this afternoon. 2.45 if that's OK?
A That's great. I'll be there.
2 **A** A medium latte and a muffin, please.
B Have here or take away?
A Here, please.
B That'll be £3.90 please.
3 **A** I can't make the meeting. I'm stuck in traffic.
B Never mind. We'll start without you and brief you later.
A Oh, hang on! We're moving again. I should be there in about an hour.
4 **A** Can you put in your PIN number and press 'Enter'?
B Oh no! I can't remember my number for this card. Oh, what is it?
A Have you got another card you could use?
5 **A** Sparkling or still? And do you want ice and lemon in it?
B Sparkling, please. Ice but no lemon.
A No problem. Is that all?
6 **A** I don't think you've met Greg. He's joining us from our New York office.
B Hello. Good to meet you. I've heard a lot about you.
A Yeah, at last we meet. I'm looking forward to working together.
7 **A** How many bags are you checking in?
B Just the one.
A And did you pack it yourself?
B Yes, I did.
8 **A** The lift's on your right. Would you like someone to help you with your luggage?
B No thank you. I'll manage.
A OK. If you're sure. Here's your key. Enjoy your stay.
9 **A** Please hold. Your call *is* important to us. All our operators are busy at the moment, but one of them will be with you shortly.
B If I have to listen to that again, I'll go mad!
C Can I help you?
B At last a real person! Do you know how long I've been waiting?
10 **A** There are still tickets for the 5.45 performance but the 8.45 performance is sold out, I'm afraid.
B That's fine. We'll have two, please, one adult and one child.
A Right. Two for 5.45. The doors open at 5.

T 1.12 **Roleplay**
1 **A** Maria, this is my friend Peter. We came to England together. We come from the same town in Germany.
B Hello, Peter. Nice to meet you. I hope you're having a good time.
2 **A** Excuse me. I don't think this is mine. I ordered a medium latte and a muffin.
B Oh sorry. My mistake. This is for the next table.
3 **A** Good evening. Reception? I'm in room 216. My TV isn't working. Can you send someone to fix it?
B Of course, sir. I'll send someone immediately.
4 **A** Excuse me. Can you tell me which is the check-in desk for Prague? I can't see my flight on the screen.
B Oh dear. You're at the wrong terminal. Flights to Prague go from Terminal 5. You can get a bus to the terminal over there.
5 **A** OK everyone. The meal's ready! Can you all come to the table? Bring your drinks and just help yourselves to the food.
B+C+D Mmmm. It smells good. Can we sit where we like?

UNIT 2

T 2.1 **Blue Monday, by Fats Domino**
Blue Monday, how I hate Blue Monday
Got to work like a slave all day
Here come(s) Tuesday, oh hard Tuesday
I'm so tired (I've) got no time to play

On Wednesday, (I) work twelve hours, then
Go home, fall into bed at ten,
'Cause Thursday is a hard working day
And Friday I get my pay

Saturday morning, oh Saturday morning
All my tiredness has gone away
Got my money and my honey
And I'm out on the town to play

Sunday morning my head is bad
But it's worth it for the fun that I had
Sunday evening it's goodnight and amen
'Cos on Monday I start again.

T 2.2 **My favourite day of the week**
Vicky
I go to a boarding school, so I don't live with my parents during term-time. Erm …,what I like is being with my friends all the time. Whether we're working or just chatting, it's great to know that there's always someone there. There's also a lot of freedom. I don't have to tell my parents where I'm going, who I'm going with, you know … Normally Monday is my favourite day because I only have two lessons on a Monday, but I'm having a very bad day today because I have homework from every one of my teachers, and I have to do it now!

Terry
I work in a restaurant in Manchester. I have two days off a week, usually Monday and Wednesday, but my favourite day of the week is, in fact, Friday, even though I work that day. It's the best night because all my mates come into the restaurant and we have a great laugh. There's a real buzz to the place, and it doesn't feel like work at all. Time just flies by. The restaurant's being redecorated at the moment, so everything's a bit crazy.

Dave
I'm a police officer. I like my job because it's challenging, but I live for surfing. I go as often as I can. I'm opening two shops that sell surfboards in the next few months. The boards are made in South Africa. Sunday is my favourite day of the week. I get up as early as I can, and spend the day on the beach.

Jenny
Mike and I live on a farm in beautiful countryside. I know we're very lucky, but it's hard work. We rarely have a day off at the weekend or Christmas Day, or any day of the year. We have to feed the sheep. Now we're lambing, so we aren't getting any sleep, either. But I suppose our favourite day is Wednesday because that's the day we generally go hunting. We go on the moors with about twenty friends.

T 2.3 **Dave Telford, police officer and surfer**
D = Dave
What's your background?
D I'm 46, and I'm divorced. I have two kids, who I see once a fortnight. I live in Devon, in the south-west of England. I'm a police officer. I've been in the police force for over twenty years. I love my job, but my passion is surfing.
What hours do you work?
D I work different shifts. The morning shift starts at 5.00, and I can't stand that because I have to get up at 4.30. My favourite shift is 2.00 in the afternoon till midnight because I get home about 12.30. What's good is that I work ten hours a day for four days, then have three days off.

What do you think of your job?

D My job is extremely busy and very hard. But I like it because it's challenging, and I never know what's going to happen. I like working in a team. We look after each other and work together.

Why do you like surfing?

D My work is very stressful, so I surf to get away from it all. It's just me and the sea, and my mind switches off. I concentrate so hard on what I'm doing that I don't think about anything else.

How often do you go surfing?

D I go surfing whenever I'm not working. Sometimes I'm on the beach before 7.00 in the morning. I go all over the world surfing. Next month I'm going to Costa Rica, and in the autumn I'm going to Thailand.

Do you have a business?

D I've got a surf school. I teach all ages, from kids to pensioners. The business is doing well. I'm also opening two shops that sell surfboards. The boards are made in South Africa. They're the best.

What's your favourite day of the week?

D I like Sundays best of all. I work as a lifeguard all day, then around 6.00 me and my mates barbecue some fish and have a few beers. Fantastic! I've been all round the world, but when I look around me, I think there's nowhere else I'd rather be.

T 2.4 **Questions and answers**

1 A Has he got any children?
  B Yes, two.
2 A How often does he see them?
  B Once a fortnight.
3 A Why doesn't he like the morning shift?
  B Because he has to get up at 4.30.
4 A How many hours a day does he work?
  B Ten.
5 A What does he like about his job?
  B He likes it because it's challenging, and he likes working in a team.
6 A What does he think about while he's surfing?
  B He only thinks about surfing, nothing else.
7 A Where's he going next month?
  B Costa Rica.
8 A Is his business doing well?
  B Yes, it is. He's opening two shops.
9 A What do he and his friends do on Sunday evenings?
  B They eat barbecued fish and drink beer.

T 2.5 **The office**

A = new employee   B = established employee

A Gosh! I don't know anybody! Can you help me? Who *are* all these people?
B Uh, well, that's Simon. He's sitting at the top of the table reading something.
A He's the one with glasses wearing a jumper, right?
B Yeah, that's it.
A And what does he do?
B He's the Managing Director. He's the man in charge.
A The boss, in other words.
B Uh huh. He shouts a lot, but he listens as well. Then there's Edward. He's wearing a suit. He's standing up talking to Anna. Edward's the Sales Director. He's charming. He always has a nice word to say to everyone. Anna's standing next to him. She's drinking a coffee. She's wearing a jacket and she's got a scarf round her neck.
A And Anna is the …?
B Anna's the Accountant. Money, money, money. Very bright, very quick.
A Ah, OK. And who's that talking on her phone?
B In the white blouse and blue skirt? That's Jenny; she's the Human Resources Manager, HR Manager. She looks after all the personnel. She's a sweetheart. Everyone loves her. Then there's Matthew. He's the IT Manager. He's only working here for a few months. He's from our New York office. I don't really know him very well.

A He's the guy working on his laptop?
B That's him. Wearing a shirt, no tie. He knows everything about technology. And finally that's Christina talking to Simon. She's his PA. She's …
A Sorry. What was that?
B She's Simon's PA, Personal Assistant. She organizes his diary, but she helps all of us, really. We couldn't cope without her. She runs the whole place, actually. She's wearing a black suit and has fabulous earrings. Very smart.
A Right. I think I've got that …

Song: Teacher's Book p147

T 2.6 **Who earns how much?**

Part 1

A Well, I reckon that doctors earn quite a lot.
B Yeah. I think so, too. They have a lot of responsibility and a lot of training. I'd say that doctors get about … £105,000? What do you think?
A Could be … or it could be even more, £120,000.
B One of those two, anyway. Shall we look at the high earners first?
A Uh huh. £750,000 …
B There's one higher …
A Oh, is there? Oh, yeah. A million. Mmm.
B I'd say … that has to be the footballer.
A Yes, definitely. They do earn ridiculous amounts of money, don't they? So what about £750,000? Who earns three quarters of a million?
B Erm … I think that's the lawyer.
A As much as that? What about the senior director? Do lawyers earn more than them?
B Maybe, maybe not. I suppose the lawyer could be £105,000, and the Senior Director £750,000. Senior Directors are in charge of huge companies.
A OK. Now … the pilot. Pilots earn quite a lot, don't they? They need a lot of experience, they have people's lives in their hands … I think they get … oh, at least a hundred, a hundred and fifty.
B Mmm. I know what you mean, but I don't think they get as much as that.
A Don't they? Oh. Anyway, there isn't 150 on this list, so …
B I reckon pilots get about £65,000 …
A OK. I'd say that's about right …

T 2.7

Part 2

B Let's go on down to the bottom. What's the lowest salary?
A £11,000. I guess that's the nurse. They don't get paid much, nurses.
B I thought they earned more than that, actually. I know they don't get much, but even so …
A Then there's £12,500, and the next up is £22,500.
B Oh, look! Supermarket cashier. I don't suppose they get much. £12,500, I'd say.
A OK. That seems about right. What about farmers? How much do they get?
B I don't know. It depends what sort of farmer. They can earn a fortune, can't they?
A I suppose so, yes … But they're always complaining that supermarkets don't pay them enough for what they produce.
B I still reckon they get a decent salary. They own so much land! I bet they get 50 or 60 thousand.
A No, I think it's much lower. I'd say £22,500.
B Hmm. Not so sure. Then we've got … teachers. What do they earn?
A I reckon they get … um … £32,000?
B But it all depends how many years they've worked and how many qualifications they've got.
A Yeah, I know, but we're talking about the average.
B Don't teachers and police officers earn about the same?
A Do they? I'm not so sure. I'd say that police officers get more. What have we got? £32,000 … £36,000.
B I think 32 for the police officer and 36 for the teacher.

A Um, well, actually I'd say the other way round. 36 for the police officer and 32 for the teacher. My mother's a teacher, and she doesn't earn anything like that!
B What does that leave? We haven't decided about the farmer or the nurse yet.
A I think the nurse gets less than the farmer. She gets the least.
B Why she? Nurses can be men, you know.
A True. Sorry. Nurses – men and women – earn less than farmers.
B Men *and* women.
A Absolutely.

T 2.8 **Free time activities**

John

My favourite hobby is cooking, and that's a thing you do at home, obviously. I cook most days, though not every day. We also like eating out, you see. What clothes and equipment do I need? Uh, well, I always wear a chef's apron to protect my clothes, because you can make a mess when you're cooking, and tomatoes and spices change the colour of your clothes forever! The most important piece of equipment is knives. I'm very fussy about my knives. They're German, and very sharp, and I really look after them. Obviously in the kitchen you need all sorts of things like pots and pans and casserole dishes and chopping boards and food mixers, but I don't really have a lot of gadgets. I like to keep things simple. What I like about cooking is the fact that it's creative and it's real. We have to eat, and what we eat is really important, so I like to know that what I'm eating, and what my family is eating, is good. I actually like all the preparation. Going out shopping, seeing the food, feeling it, smelling it, talking to the people who are selling it, is half the fun. People often ask me what I like cooking, and I don't really have an answer. Whatever looks good, and whatever I feel like cooking that day. The best bit is of course seeing people enjoy my food, but what's also very important to me is seeing everyone happy, and enjoying being at the table. It's about the occasion as much as the food.

T 2.9 **Making small talk**

A = Ann   L = Lars

A So what do you think of Liverpool, Lars?
L It's really interesting. Liverpool's such an old city, isn't it? There are some lovely buildings, and the people are so friendly!
A Yes, they are, aren't they? When did you get here?
L Two days ago. I got the plane from Oslo. We were a bit late landing, but it didn't matter.
A Oh, good. Where are you staying in Liverpool?
L At the Grand Hotel. It's very convenient for the office. My room isn't very big, but it's OK.
A What a pity! Never mind. Where are you from?
L Well, from Norway. I was born in Bergen, but I live in a suburb of Oslo. It's very pretty, and it's not far from the sea.
A Really? It sounds beautiful. Your English is very good. Where did you learn it?
L That's very kind of you, but I know I make a lot of mistakes. I learned it at school for years, and I've been to England quite a few times.
A Oh, have you? How interesting! And what are you doing here in Liverpool, Lars?
L I'm attending a conference. I'm here for five days, and I'm going home on the 17th.
A Oh, so soon! And have you managed to get around our city yet?
L I haven't seen very much. I've been for a walk along the riverside and I've taken a ferry across the Mersey, but I haven't seen the Beatles' Exhibition yet.
A Well, I hope you enjoy it. Don't work too hard!
L I'll try to enjoy myself! Bye. It was nice to talk to you.

T 2.10

1 Who do you work for?
2 Do you enjoy your job?
3 Where do you come from?
4 Have you been to New York?
5 What do you do when you're not working?
6 The weather's amazing at the moment, isn't it?
7 Are you having a holiday this year?
8 This city's very exciting, isn't it?
9 What's your favourite programme on television?

T 2.11

1 A Who do you work for?
   B Siemens. I've been with them for four years. They're a good company. How about you?
2 A Do you enjoy your job?
   B Yes, I do. It's quite hard, but I enjoy the challenge. I don't earn very much. What about you? Do you like your job?
3 A Where do you come from?
   B I was born in Montreal, and I've lived there all my life with my parents. I'd like to live abroad some time.
4 A Have you been to New York?
   B No, I haven't, but I'd love to. I've heard it's one of the most amazing cities in the world. Have you been there?
5 A What do you do when you're not working?
   B Well, I like horse-riding, and I play golf. And I love music, so I often go to concerts. Do you?
6 A The weather's amazing at the moment, isn't it?
   B Yes, it's so mild. We haven't had any really cold weather at all! Have you heard a weather forecast for the weekend? It's supposed to be good, isn't it?
7 A Are you having a holiday this year?
   B Yes, I'm going to Mexico with some friends. I haven't been there before, so I'm really looking forward to it. What about you?
8 A This city's very exciting, isn't it?
   B Really? Do you think so? There isn't very much to do. I get so bored here. What *do* you find to do?
9 A What's your favourite programme on television?
   B I haven't got a favourite, but I like soaps and documentaries. And quiz shows. And the news. I suppose I like everything. What about you?

UNIT 3

T 3.1   Vincent Van Gogh

1 Where was he born?
2 What was his job?
3 Why was he dismissed?
4 Why did he try to commit suicide?
5 Which artists did he meet?
6 What was he doing when he met them?
7 Who came to live with him?
8 Where did they first meet?
9 What was he carrying?
10 Why did he cut off part of his ear?
11 Which paintings were completed there?
12 What was he doing when he shot himself?
13 Why did he shoot himself?
14 Where was he buried?
15 Why didn't he have any money?

T 3.2

1 Where was he born?
   In Brabant in the Netherlands.
2 What was his job?
   He worked as an art dealer.
3 Why was he dismissed?
   Because he'd had an argument with customers.
4 Why did he try to commit suicide?
   Because he'd fallen in love with his cousin and she'd rejected him.
5 Which artists did he meet?
   Degas, Pissarro, Seurat, Toulouse-Lautrec, Monet, and Renoir.
6 What was he doing when he met them?
   He was studying art.
7 Who came to live with him?
   Gauguin.
8 Where did they first meet?
   In Paris.
9 What was he carrying?
   A razor blade.
10 Why did he cut off part of his ear?
   Because he'd been drinking, and he'd had an argument with Gauguin.
11 Which paintings were completed there?
   Starry Night, Irises and Self-Portrait without a Beard.
12 What was he doing when he shot himself?
   He was painting outside.
13 Why did he shoot himself?
   Because he was depressed.
14 Where was he buried?
   In Auvers.
15 Why didn't he have any money?
   Because he'd sold only one of his paintings.

T 3.3   see p23

T 3.4

/t/ worked   dismissed   published

/d/ tried   quarrelled   moved   continued   died   recognized

/ɪd/ rejected   completed

T 3.5   I didn't do much

1 I didn't do much. I just had something to eat, watched telly for a while, and then had an early night. I was in bed by ten.

2 I went to my yoga class, then went for a drink with a couple of friends. I got home about nine and did a bit of housework, and that was it.

3 I went out with some people from work, so I didn't get home till about midnight. Well, after midnight, actually. Quite a late night for me!

4 I met some friends in town for a coffee, and we talked for a bit. Then I went home and did some stuff on the computer, you know, *Facebook*, then went to bed about eleven thirty.

T 3.6   Smash! Clumsy visitor destroys priceless vases, by Tom Ball

A clumsy visitor to a British museum has destroyed a set of priceless 300-year-old Chinese vases after slipping on the stairs.

The three vases, which were produced during the Qing dynasty in the 17th century, had stood on a windowsill at the Fitzwilliam Museum in Cambridge for forty years. Last Thursday they were smashed into a million pieces. The vases, which had been donated in 1948, were the museum's best-known pieces.

The Fitzwilliam decided not to identify the man who had caused the disaster. 'It was a most unfortunate and regrettable accident,' museum director Duncan Robinson said, 'but we are glad that the visitor wasn't seriously injured.'

The photograph of the accident was taken by another visitor, Steve Baxter. 'We watched the man fall as if in slow motion. He was flying through the air. The vases exploded as though they'd been hit by a bomb. The man was sitting there stunned in the middle of a pile of porcelain when the staff arrived.'

The museum declined to say what the vases were worth.

T 3.7   I = Interviewer   NF = Nick Flynn

I It's 7.45, and you're listening to the *Today* programme. The man who broke Chinese vases worth £100,000 when he fell downstairs at a museum has been named by a daily newspaper. He's Nick Flynn, and he's with us now. Are you all right, Mr Flynn? You didn't hurt yourself falling downstairs, did you?
NF I'm on the mend, which is more than I can say for the vases!
I Too true! How did it happen?
NF I was coming down the stairs, looking at the pictures, and I slipped. The stairs are very shiny, and it had been raining, so I guess my shoes were a bit wet. And I just went head over heels.
I It must have been a strange feeling, lying in the middle of all that priceless porcelain?
NF I was surprised that these incredibly valuable vases were left just standing on a windowsill. I'd seen them lots of times before, but I hadn't really paid them any attention.
I And I hear you've been banned from the museum? Is that right?
NF Yes, I got a letter from the director of the museum asking me not to go back. It's a shame, because I used to go twice a week. So now I've got to find somewhere else to go.
I Well, thank you, Mr Flynn, and good luck.

T 3.8   Dictation

The man who broke Chinese vases worth £100,000 when he fell downstairs at a museum has been named as Nick Flynn.
He was coming down the stairs, looking at the pictures on the wall, when he slipped. The stairs were shiny, and it had been raining.
He'd seen the vases lots of times before, but hadn't paid them any attention.
The museum has asked him not to go back. He's disappointed because he used to go there twice a week.

T 3.9   see p25

T 3.10   Words that sound the same

knew/new   read/red   wore/war   threw/through   flew/'flu

T 3.11   see p25

T 3.12   see p25

T 3.13   see p25

T 3.14   see p26

T 3.15   The first time I fell in love

Sarah
The first time I fell in love was when I was 13. It was with a boy called Max. We were on a school trip, a geography trip, so a whole group of us were living together for a week. I'd never really noticed this boy before, because we used to go around with different people, but I suddenly started looking at him, and I remember thinking, 'Hmm! You're nice!', and I couldn't understand why I hadn't looked at him before. He was very quiet, and he had dark eyes that seemed to see everything, and he made me go all weak at the knees. We kind of started going out. When we held hands, it was electric! And the first time we kissed, I'd never felt anything like it in my life! Wow! I don't think he felt the same passion as me. He was very cool about everything. It only lasted a few months. Then he went back to his friends, and I went back to mine.

Tommy
T = Tommy   I = Interviewer
T Well, I fell in love with a girl called Emma, but it didn't last very long.
I How long did it last?

T Well … about two weeks. It all ended last Friday.
I Oh, dear! What happened last Friday?
T I decided that I'd had enough of being in love. I didn't like the feeling.
I Was Emma upset?
T Not really. She didn't know anything about it.
I What?
T No. I hadn't told her that I was in love with her, so she didn't know that it had ended.
I Was it so bad?
T Oh, yes. I couldn't sleep, I used to get this funny feeling here in my tummy when I saw her coming, and my heart went bang, bang, bang. It was horrible!
I So how did you manage to stop loving her?
T Well, I'm only 9, and I figured that I'm too young to only love one person for the rest of my life.
I Fair enough. I'm glad you didn't hurt her feelings.
T I'm glad it's all over.

James
Well, I've only been in love once in my life, and that was when I was 22. I'd had other girlfriends, of course, but it was never more than that. Just a girlfriend. And then I met this other girl, Ruth, and my whole life just turned upside down. I remember thinking at the time that I'd never felt anything like it. Nothing looked the same, felt the same, life had never been so amazing, so colourful. I wanted to do everything – climb mountains, fly like a bird, stay up all night – life was far too amazing to sleep. It's funny, I never used to care what I looked like, but suddenly I started to care. I wanted to look good for this girl in my life. I felt that I hadn't really lived until that moment, until I'd met her and fallen in love. Thank goodness she felt the same! We're still together. Thirty years and four kids later. Amazing, huh?

T 3.16 **see p29**

T 3.17
1 We had a great time in Paris, didn't we?
2 The weather was lovely, wasn't it?
3 The French really love their food, don't they?
4 It's a lovely day today, isn't it?
5 Alice and Tom are a really lovely couple, aren't they?
6 Tom earns so much money, doesn't he?
7 They want to get married, don't they?

T 3.18
1 **A** She's quite nice.
  B She's absolutely wonderful!
2 **A** The film was good.
  B The film was just brilliant!
3 **A** The hotel's all right.
  B The hotel's really fabulous!
4 **A** I like dark chocolate.
  B I absolutely adore dark chocolate.
5 **A** I quite like Peter.
  B I really love Peter.
6 **A** The book wasn't very good.
  B The book was absolutely awful!
7 **A** I don't like noisy bars.
  B I just can't stand noisy bars!

 # UNIT 4

T 4.1 **Discussing grammar**
1 I don't get on with my boss. Do you think I should look for another job?
2 We're giving Tom a surprise birthday party. You mustn't tell him about it.
3 Please Dad, can I go to Tom's party? It'll be great.
4 You have to drive on the left in Britain.
5 Do you have to wear a uniform in your job?
6 Are you allowed to take mobile phones to school?
7 I had to go to bed early when I was a child.

8 You don't have to go to England to learn English, but it's a good idea.

T 4.2 **Giving advice**
Conversation 1
A Are you going to Charlotte's party?
B I don't know if I should go or not.
A What do you mean?
B Well, her parents are abroad and they told her she wasn't allowed to have friends over while they were away.
A Oh, come on! You must come. It's a party. Everyone has parties when their parents are away.
B Yeah, but her mum and dad are best friends with mine.
A Look. You don't have to tell your mum and dad. Just go to the party and help to clear up after.
B I'm not sure.

Conversation 2
A Do you see that woman over there?
B Yeah, what about her?
A She's smoking!
B So?
A You're not allowed to smoke in here.
B Well …
A Do you think I should tell her to stop?
B No, no, you mustn't say anything. It's embarrassing. The waiter will tell her.
A No! I can't just sit here. I must say something. Er – excuse me …

Conversation 3
A I'm so mad!
B Why?
A I've got a parking ticket. I had to go to the shops for my dad and when I got back to the car there was a ticket on the windscreen.
B Oh, that's bad luck!
A I think *he* should pay the fine.
B Who? Your dad? Why? He wasn't driving.
A Yeah, but I was doing *his* shopping.
B But he didn't tell you to park illegally.
A OK, OK, so it's my fault. Er – I still think he should pay it.

T 4.3 **Great-grandma Alice**
This is a story that my great-grandma Alice loved telling about her school days. She started school when she was 5 and, apparently, she was very bright. Anyway, that's what she told us. And when she was 11 the teacher, Miss Fox, came to her and said: 'Alice, you've learnt everything that I know. I can't teach you any more now. But you're not allowed to leave school until you're 12 years old, so you'll just have to sit at the back of the class.' So that's what Great-grandma Alice did. She sat at the back for a whole year and her dad, my great-great grandpa, was really angry 'cos he wanted her to be out earning money for the family. She was a domestic servant.

T 4.4 **Rules for life**
1 Millie
Well, so many teenagers seem to think life is about just one thing, you know – money and fame, they think it will bring them happiness. Honestly, I would hate to be famous. When I read the magazines, and see all the photos of these rich, famous film stars, footballers and the like, it frightens me. They can't move without being followed and photographed. Often they've got to employ bodyguards. When I grow up I just want to enjoy my work, if I earn lots of money, fair enough, but if I don't I'll still be happy. I never want to be famous. That's scary stuff.

2 Richard
My rule for life is that you only get out of life what you put in. I mean, you should never ask that question people always ask 'Why are we here? What is the meaning of life?' – you'll never find the answer. You've got to *give* meaning to your life by what you *do* with your life –er … and I think you can do this in all kinds of ways. It doesn't matter

if you are president of your country or a rubbish collector – you have a place in the world, you have a part to play.

3 Frank
I believe you've got to look for the good in people and things. So many people of my age do nothing but complain about today's world – oh, on and on they go about –ooh, how bad the traffic is, or how mobile phones are such a menace. Oh, and most of all they complain – about young people – they're loud, they're impolite, not like in the 'good old days'. Well, I say 'rubbish' to all that. There's always been good and bad in the world and I think we should look for the good. The rule I try to live by is find three things every day to be happy about.

T 4.5 **Spoken English**
1 **A** 'Isn't your mum away at the moment?'
  B 'Uh, yeah, so Dad's got to do all the cooking and I've got to do all the ironing.'
2 **A** 'Where's my briefcase? I've got to go to work'
  B 'It's where you left it when you came home. In the hall by the front door.'
3 **A** 'Mum, why can't I go out now?'
  B 'You've got to tidy your room first. Your friends will just have to wait.'
4 **A** 'Won't you be late for work?'
  B 'Oh, goodness. Look at the time I've got to go now. I mustn't stay here chatting. We'll catch up later. Bye!'

T 4.6 *I Believe*
I believe in bottle banks.
And beauty from within
I believe in saying thanks
And fresh air on the skin

I believe in healthy walks
As tonic for the feet
I believe in serious talks
And just enough to eat

Chorus
That's what I believe
Surprising as it seems
I believe that happiness
Is well within our dreams

I believe in being nice
In spite of what you think
I believe in good advice
And not too much to drink

I believe in being true
In everything you try to do
I believe in me and you
I hope you share my point of view

Chorus (repeat)
I believe in being kind
Especially when it's hard
I believe an open mind
Can show a fine regard

I believe that manners make
A person good to know
I believe in birthday cake
And going with the flow

Chorus (repeat)
That's what I believe
Although it seems naïve
I believe that peace and love
Are there to be achieved

That's what I believe…

Song: Teacher's Book p150

T 4.7 **Phrasal verbs**
1 **A** Who do you take after in your family?
  B Mmm … I don't think I take after anyone in particular. Mind you the older I get, the more I think I'm like my mother. Humh …!

2 **A** Do you get on well with both your parents?
  B Yes, I do. Most of the time. I do a lot of stuff with my dad. Football and things.

3 A Have you recently taken up any new sports or hobbies?
  B Me? No! My life's too busy already!
4 A Do you often look up words in your dictionary?
  B Sometimes, if I'm really stuck.
5 A Are you looking forward to going on holiday soon?
  B I wish! I've just been on holiday so I've got to wait till Christmas now.
6 A Do you pick up foreign languages easily?
  B Well, I picked up Italian quite easily when I was living in Milan but I already knew French, so I think that helped a bit.
7 A Have you got any bad habits that you want to give up?
  B Yes, I bite my nails. I just can't stop and I'm a teacher so I have to hide my hands from the kids 'cos I don't want to set a bad example.

T 4.8 see p37

T 4.9 see p37

T 4.10

Conversation 1
A Hello, it's me again. I've just remembered that I have a doctor's appointment in the morning. Could we possibly make it lunch instead of coffee?
B Erm …, no problem. I can do lunch too. How about 12.30 in the usual restaurant?

Conversation 2
A Would you mind if we didn't go out for a drink after work? I want to watch the match on TV.
B Hey, we could have a drink at Bar Metro. They have a huge screen. We could both watch the match there.
A You're on. A great idea.

Conversation 3
A So, anyway, there I was just finishing my report, when suddenly the boss calls me into his office and he starts …
B Sorry darling, I really do want to hear all about it, but the baby's crying. Do you think you could go and check him? He might need changing.

Conversation 4
A Help! Urgh … I don't know what's gone wrong with my computer. The screen's frozen again.
B I'll try and fix it if you like. I'm quite good with computers.
A Oh, go ahead. Be my guest. I've had it with this machine!

UNIT 5

T 5.1   **Things our grandchildren may never see**

H = Hannah   D = Dan
H Do you ever worry about what the world will be like when our grandchildren grow up?
D Hang on! We haven't had our baby yet. I'm not thinking about grandchildren!
H I know, but having a baby makes me wonder – what will the world be like when he or she grows up? Look at these pictures. Don't they make you worry about what could happen in the future?
D Mmm – OK, of course things are going to change a lot in the next hundred years, even in the next fifty but …
H I know and I'm getting worried. Everyone says global warming is a fact nowadays. No one says it *may* get warmer or it *might* get warmer any more. Scientists say that it definitely *will* get warmer. It's going to be a very different world for our children and grandchildren.

D Look, Hannah, it's no good worrying. Not *all* scientists think the same …
H Yes, I know but *most* do! Look, it says here over 2,500 climate scientists agree. They say temperatures might rise by up to 4°C before the end of the century. Dan, this is the world our son or daughter is going to grow up in.
D Hannah, you've got to take it easy, you're having a baby soon and I don't …
H I can't help being worried. If the Arctic ice melts there'll be floods and the polar bears will have nowhere to live. Oh, look at this …
D Come on, Hannah. Look here, it also says humans are clever enough to find solutions. We'll do our bit and we'll bring up our baby to do the same. Every little helps. …
H OK, but maybe it won't help. It may be too late already.

T 5.2   **What do you think will happen?**

1 A Do you think the earth will continue to get warmer?
  B Yes, I do. The more I read about it, the more I think it will. A few years ago I wasn't so sure.
2 A Do you think all the ice will melt at the Poles?
  B Well, I don't think *all* the ice will melt, but a lot has melted already. Do you know a new island near Greenland has just appeared? They thought it was part of the mainland but it was just an ice bridge and it melted. It's called *Warming Island*. A good name, don't you think?
3 A Do you think polar bears will become extinct?
  B I think they might. They only live in the Arctic and I read that the ice there has decreased by 14% since the 1970s.
4 A Do you think more people will travel by train?
  B Definitely. I think lots more people will choose train travel when they can, especially across Europe. Of course it won't always be possible to.
5 A Do you think that air travel will be banned to reduce CO$_2$ emissions?
  B Well, I think it could become much more expensive to travel by air but I don't think it'll be banned.
6 A Do you think new sources of energy will be found?
  B I hope so. Some people say nuclear energy is the only answer but I think this could cause more problems. Actually, I like wind farms, they look amazing. But I know some people hate them.
7 A Do you think there'll be more droughts or more floods in the world?
  B I don't really know. There might be both droughts and floods. I think parts of London may be flooded – there's already a barrier across the River Thames to stop flooding.
8 A Do you think our lifestyles will have to change?
  B Definitely. They're already changing. We're told all the time to do things like drive smaller cars, use cleaner petrol, and recycle our rubbish. That worries me a lot – the amount of rubbish we make.

T 5.3   **Discussing grammar**

1 A Have you decided about your holiday yet?
  B No, not yet. We've never been to Prague so we might go there.
2 A Are you going to take an umbrella?
  B No, I'm not. The forecast says it'll be fine all day.
3 A Why are you making a list?
  B Because I'm going shopping. Is there anything you want?
4 A Would you like to go out for a drink tonight?
  B Sorry, I'm working late. Um, how about tomorrow night? I'll call you.
5 A What are you doing Saturday night?
  B I'm not sure yet. I may go to friends' or they may come to me.

6 A Are you enjoying your job more now?
  B No, I'm not. I'm going to look for another one.
7 A Your team's rubbish! It's 2-0 to United!
  B Come on. It's only half-time. I think they could still win.
8 A You won't pass your exams next month if you go out every night.
  B I know, I'll work harder nearer the time. I promise.

T 5.4   **World weather warnings**

1   The British Isles
A prolonged period of heavy rain and thunderstorms will affect parts of the country on Friday and into Saturday. Rainfall could total 20-30mm in the south but there may be up to 60-90mm in the north and Scotland. The heavy rain might lead to flooding in some areas.

2   Canada
High winds following in the path of Hurricane Gloria will head north from the US overnight. They could reach up to 160 kilometres per hour and may cause damage to buildings across north-west Ontario. These winds are going to bring with them high temperatures across the country and thunderstorms in many areas.

3   Hungary
The country's heatwave is going to continue. Temperatures could rise to more than 40 degrees Celsius by midday tomorrow. Budapest's city council are going to send out teams of workers to distribute 22,000 bottles of drinking water to local people. Meteorologists say that temperatures will continue to rise until the end of the week.

4   Mexico
Tropical storm Barbara is forming rapidly over the coast and will move towards land. Winds of 110 kilometres an hour are expected and they could reach the popular tourist destination of Acapulco over the next few days. Hotels and houses may have to be evacuated. Meteorologists say that the winds might even reach hurricane status.

5   South Africa
For the first time in 25 years forecasters in Johannesburg are predicting snow. Up to 10 centimetres could fall during the night and this is causing much excitement throughout the city. SABC News is reporting that some parents are going to take their children to the local parks after midnight to play in the snow. Tambo International airport may be affected.

T 5.5

1 I think it'll be a cold night tonight. Wrap up warm if you go out.
2 I think I'll get a new computer. I want a laptop this time.
3 I think I'll do a cookery course. I can't even boil an egg.
4 I think you'll like the film. It's a great story, and really well cast.
5 I think we'll get to the airport in time. But we'd better get a move on.
6 I think you'll get the job. You've got all the right qualifications.

T 5.6

1 I don't think it'll be a cold night tonight. You won't need to take a jacket.
2 I don't think I'll get a new computer. It may seem old-fashioned to you but it's OK for me.
3 I don't think I'll do a cookery course. I'll get lessons from my mum.
4 I don't think you'll like the film. It's not really your kind of thing.
5 I don't think we'll get to the airport in time. There's too much traffic.
6 I don't think you'll get the job. You're too young, and you've got no experience.

T 5.7 **Rocket man**

I = Interviewer (Fi Glover, *Saturday Live*, BBC)
S = Steve Bennett

I Steve Bennett's ambition was to be a rocket scientist. A few years ago he almost won a £10 million prize, the X prize. Now Steve is building a rocket that will take him and 2 passengers up into space. He believes that space tourism is not really that far away.

S Space tourism is just about to happen, There are quite a lot of people around the world actually putting a lot of money into space tourism. So it's simply a question of *when* not *if*. You know, just as the Internet made billionaires, well, space tourism is going to make trillionaires. And all the big names are at it – you've got Jeff Bezos, he did Amazon.com, he's building his own spaceship; you've got Richard Branson, even he's commissioning someone to build a spaceship for him. So it really is going to happen.

I And what are you intending to take people into space in? What is your rocket?

S A rocket that can carry 3 people into space. We're not going into orbit. It's going straight up, straight down, but it will go into space, it'll give you about 3 or 4 minutes of weightlessness, you'll see the blackness of space, the curvature of the earth and you really will truly become an astronaut just like the early American astronauts.

I And you're going to be one of the people who goes up, so it's going to be you and two space tourists. Have you been up in this exact rocket before Steve?

S No, we're still working on this one. We've launched 16 big rockets to date, but this actual space tourism rocket, called 'Thunderstar', we're still working on it, we're still building it. I was influenced as a small child watching too many episodes of *Thunderbirds*, I think.

I Were you very much struck by the first moon landings as well?

S Yup. I was about 5 years old when they landed on the moon. Erm, my parents wouldn't let me stay up to watch the actual landing which was a bit of a shame.

I How mean!

S Yeah … Yeah. Well, they just didn't get it. 'Oh it's marvellous, but they should spend the money on something better' kind of attitude

I Lots of young boys will have had exactly that kind of experience themselves but very few of them will now have a business that is making rockets. Did you always feel that eventually you would get to do it professionally?

S I kept it pretty quiet. 10, 15 years ago you start talking about space tourism and people, they think you're nuts, so you keep that kind of thing to yourself.

I Why do we really need to do that, though? I mean, is there actually any necessity to have more humans in space?

S Well, that's pretty much where the human race needs to be, you know, in terms of expansion. You know there's enough resources in space to allow the human race to continue to grow and expand for the next 10 thousand years.

I What kind of training do you have to do in order to go up in the rocket?

S Actually, one of the most important things we do is skydiving training. We feel that if you haven't got what it takes to jump out of an airplane with a parachute, you really shouldn't be strapping yourself to the top of a 17-ton rocket.

I These two other people who've already booked their place on your Thunderstar, do you know who they are?

S Absolutely. I've taken their money.

I Right.

S Well, it's a couple. It's 2 people that want to fly in space and they came to me a few years ago and basically they said 'Steve we want to fly in the rocket. Here's the money,' and they paid me half a million pounds for it.

I And how often do you consider the possibility that something might go wrong?

S I think about it every day, you know. I've built a lot of rockets. Most of them have worked really well, some haven't, and I think about that every day.

T 5.8 **Spoken English**

1 A Did your team win?
  B No, but they played pretty well, all the same.
2 A You haven't lost your mobile phone again!
  B Oh, no. I'm pretty sure it's in my bag somewhere.
3 A Do you enjoy skiing?
  B I do, but I'm pretty hopeless at it.
4 A What do you think of my English?
  B I think it's pretty good.

T 5.9 see p119

T 5.10

1 Bob and Jan don't get on at all. They disagree about everything.
2 Money doesn't always lead to happiness.
3 My aunt says today's kids are all rude and impolite.
4 Thanks for your advice, it was really helpful. I really appreciate your kindness.
5 My dad's useless at fixing his computer, I always have to help him.
6 Please don't misunderstand me. I didn't mean to be unkind. I'm really sorry.
7 Timmy fell off his bike and hit his head. He was unconscious for a few hours.
8 What was your wife's reaction when she heard you'd won the lottery?

T 5.11 see p44

T 5.12

1 A The doctors are going to operate on my grandma's knee.
  B Oh, dear!
  A Don't worry, it's not a serious operation.
2 A Did you explain the homework to Maria?
  B I did, but I don't think she understood my explanation.
3 A I couldn't find the book I wanted in the library.
  B Did you ask the librarian? She'll tell you if they have it.
4 A Can I have a copy of that photograph?
  B Yes, of course. I'm not a great photographer but this one's OK, isn't it?
  A It is. Usually I can't stand photos of me.

T 5.13 **Arranging to meet**

G = Gary M = Mike

G Mike, it's me, Gary.
M Gary! Long time no see. How are you doing?
G Good, thanks. Listen, I'm coming up to town next weekend and I was wondering if we could meet?
M Oh dear, I'd love to, but this weekend of all weekends I am *so* busy.
G Look, you must have some free time.
M Yeah, I'll just get my diary. Hang on … OK … shoot!
G Right. What are you doing Friday evening?
M Friday evening? Er …, that's my Spanish class. Our company's going to do a lot of work in Spain, so we're all learning Spanish. But I finish work early on Friday. I could meet you in the afternoon.
G No, I'm afraid that's no good, my train doesn't get in until 7 o'clock. Uh … have you got any free time on Saturday?
M Er … let me see. What about Saturday afternoon? I'm having my hair cut in the morning and then I'm meeting my sister for lunch, but I'm free in the afternoon.
G Oh no, sorry, Saturday afternoon, I can't, I've got an appointment with an estate agent. I'm going to look round one of those amazing new flats by the river. Didn't I tell you? I'm changing jobs and moving back to the big city.
M Hey, great news Gary. I knew the small town life wasn't your thing!
G So, what about Saturday evening? Is Saturday evening any good?
M Sorry, the evening's out for me. I'm going to the theatre with friends. We've had it booked for ages. But … hang on, what time are you leaving on Sunday?
G Late morning. I'm getting the 11.55 train.
M Hey, I've got an idea. Why don't we meet at the station?
G Good idea! We could have coffee together.
M I've got an even better idea. They do a great full English breakfast at the café. Let's meet there for breakfast. Shall we say about 10 o'clock?
G Sounds good to me. But can you make it 10.30? It *is* Sunday.
M Fine. 10.30 it is. I'll see you then. Bye Gary! Hope you like the flat.
G Fingers crossed. Bye Mike. See you Sunday.

T 5.14 **Music of English**

1 I was wondering if we could meet?
2 I could meet you in the afternoon.
3 What about Saturday afternoon?
4 Is Saturday evening any good?
5 Why don't we meet at the station? Let's meet there for breakfast.
6 Shall we say about 10 o'clock?
7 Can you make it 10.30?

UNIT 6

T 6.1 see p46

T 6.2 **Describing places**

1 What's your flat like?
  It's quite modern, but it's cosy.
2 How big is it?
  About 75 sq m.
3 How many rooms are there?
  A kitchen-diner, a living room, and a bedroom.
4 What size is the kitchen?
  Four metres by two.
5 Which floor is it on?
  The fourth.
6 Which part of town is it in?
  It's south of the river.
7 How far is it to the shops?
  Just a five-minute walk.

T 6.3 **Describing things**

1 What make is it?
  Sony.
2 How much does it weigh?
  1.3 kg.
3 What's it made of?
  Carbon and titanium.
4 What's this button for?
  It turns it on.
5 How big is the screen?
  13.2 inches.
6 How long is the battery life?
  Eight hours.
7 What size is the hard disk?
  80 gigabytes.

T 6.4

1 What sort of bread do you have?
2 What flavour ice-cream would you like?
3 Which way do we go?
4 What make is your camera?
5 What kind of food do you like?
6 Whose top are you wearing?
7 How long does it take to get to the airport?
8 How far is your house from the beach?
9 How often do you go to the cinema?
10 How many of you want coffee?
11 What size shoes do you take?

T 6.5

fresh fruit
latest fashions
pretty woman
clear sky
fast food
crowded restaurant
casual clothes
close friend
handsome man
straight hair
cosy room
challenging job

T 6.6

1 Peter and I lived together at university.
2 He's a good student. He tries hard.
3 A Where's the Town Hall?
　B Go straight on.
4 Say that again. I didn't hear you.
5 Don't talk so loud! Everyone can hear you.
6 Why do you drive so fast? Slow down!
7 His wife's name is Sue, not Sally! Get it right.
8 The holiday was a disaster. Everything went wrong.
9 This room is cool, even in summer.
10 A Are you ready?
　B Almost. Give me another five minutes.

T 6.7　My most treasured possession

1 Amie
I would have to save my photo albums. They've got all the photos of my kids, when they were babies, their first steps, you know, when they walked for the first time, their birthday parties, their first day at school. And all the holidays we had together. All those memories are irreplaceable.

2 Jack
I know it sounds a bit sad, but I would have to save my computer. Not very sentimental, but very practical. It's got all my work, all my email contacts, several thousand photos, address books, and my work diary for the next year. I just couldn't live without it.

3 Lucy
I have a matching hairbrush and hand mirror that belonged to my grandmother. She was given them as a wedding present, and she gave them to me before she died. I don't use them, but they're always on the shelf in my bedroom, and every time I see them I think of her. They're solid silver, and they're quite heavy. They're not particularly pretty, but they have immense sentimental value.

T 6.8　My closest relative

Ellie
The person that I'm closest to in my family is probably my mother. She's the kind of person you can talk to about anything. She's very open, my mother, and I can talk to her about boyfriends, stuff that's bothering me at work, friendships, anything. We have our ups and downs of course, but basically we have an easy relationship. We go shopping together. What I like about her is her attitude. She's quite young at heart, like me, not old-fashioned or anything like that.

Simon
I'm closest to my grandmother. Erm, my father, I don't really get on with. We don't really see eye to eye about anything. My mother, uh, I hardly ever see, she's too busy. My grandmother and I like doing the same things. Erm … we like watching TV and uh, having a glass of wine together. We love playing cards. And I think emotionally I'm closer to her than I am to my parents … because she and I have a similar attitude to life. I think we both like people. We're quite outgoing, sociable, and open.

Julia
The person I'm closest to in my family, I think, would be my father. We stay up late listening to music and talking a lot. What I like about him is that he's interesting and interested. He has a curiosity about life. We can talk about anything and everything. We have the same sense of humour, the same love of life. My friends all love him because he's such a good laugh. He doesn't care what people think of him, and I reckon that's great. He's pretty cool, my dad.

Tessa
I think the person that I'm probably closest to is my sister. The thing I love about her is the way everyone knows her. It doesn't matter where we go, everyone says 'Hi, Nina! How you doin'?' I'm just her little sister so people call me 'Baby Nina', but that's fine. We're so different. We have blazing rows. She's so hyperactive and loud, she can't sit still, she has to have people around her, and everyone loves her. In many ways she drives me crazy. She just can't think straight. Me, I'm a lot quieter. I'm happy on my own. But we're so proud of each other.

Chris
I'm closest to my twin, Nick. Obviously we have so much in common. The same friends. The same football team. The same music. We go everywhere together. But we have amazing rows about everything. We're like chalk and cheese. I'm like my Mum – calm and easy-going. Nick's like my Dad – very bad-tempered. They fight like cat and dog. But things have changed between me and Nick now we're older. We appreciate each other more. The biggest difference is probably interests. I'm into all things history and politics, and Nick's interested in science and nature. But of course we're a lot closer than just brothers and sisters. In a way we're like one. I would trust him like I would trust no one else.

T 6.9　In a department store

1 A Morning!
　B Hello. I'd like to try on these shoes, please.
　A Certainly, sir. What size do you take?
　B Nine. That's 41, isn't it?
　A Uh, no, I think you'll find 43 would be more comfortable, sir.
2 A Have you got these football shorts for age 10–11?
　B I'm afraid that's all we have. We've sold out of that size.
　A Will you be getting any more in?
　B We should be getting a delivery by the end of the week.
3 A Do you have any sofas like this in stock?
　B No, Madam. They all have to be ordered.
　A How long does delivery take?
　B It all depends, but on average about eight weeks.
4 A Yes, madam?
　B I'd like this fruit bowl, please.
　A Certainly. Is it a present?
　B Yes, it is.
　A Would you like me to gift wrap it?
　B Ooh, that would be lovely! Thank you so much!
5 A I like this.
　B How does it feel?
　A Really good. I love the colour, but the size is wrong. It doesn't fit me. It's too tight.

　B Shame. It really suits you. What's it made of?
　A Cashmere. It's so soft.
6 A Yes, sir?
　B I'll have this coffee maker, please.
　A Certainly. Have you got a store card?
　B No, just a debit card.
　A That's fine. Uh … PIN number, please. Keep your receipt. That's your guarantee.
　B How long is it guaranteed for?
　A For a year.

 UNIT 7

T 7.1　see p55

T 7.2

1 Where and when was she born?
　She was born near Bristol, in England, in 1965.
2 When did she write her first story? What was it about?
　She wrote her first story when she was six. It was about a rabbit with measles.
3 What was she doing when she had the idea for Harry Potter?
　She was travelling by train between Manchester and London.
4 Where did she teach English?
　In Portugal.
5 When was the first Harry Potter book published?
　In 1997.
6 How long has she been writing the books?
　For nearly 20 years.
7 How many has she written?
　Seven.
8 How many children has she had?
　Three.
9 How many books have been sold?
　Over 300 million copies.
10 Which books have been made into films?
　The first six.
11 How much money has she made?
　She's made over £600 million.
12 How many authors have become billionaires?
　Only one – her.

T 7.3　Jack

I = Interviewer　J = Jack

I So Jack, I know you love Harry Potter. How long have you been a fan of the books?
J I think since I was about five but I was so small I couldn't read yet and my mum read them to me.
I How many of the books have you read?
J I've read them all – well not all exactly.
I What do you mean?
J Well I didn't like *Harry Potter and the Half-blood Prince* so I didn't finish it.
I Which did you like best?
J I liked all the others but not that one. It was too 'samey' – it was boring 'cos it was just like the one before.
I Have you seen any of the Harry Potter films?
J Yes, I have.
I Which have you seen?
J I've seen them all, every one.
I And did you like them *all*?
J Yes, I did. I thought they were fantastic, but my brother didn't, he got scared. He didn't like the *Chamber of Secrets*, the bit where the Basilisk attacked …
I The what?
J The Basilisk. It's kind of a huge snake and it attacked Harry Potter.
I Oh, I bet a lot of children were frightened by it.
J I wasn't.
I Jack, have you any idea how many Harry Potter books have been sold in the world?
J Er – I dunno. Er– millions, maybe 20 million.

I Erm – not quite. It's 300 million.
J 300 million. Wow! That's a lot of books.
I And what do you know about the author?
J I know it's JK Rowling and she's got two children. I wonder if they've read their mum's books?
I She has three children actually. Have a lot of your friends read the books?
J Yes, every single one.
I What *all* your friends?
J Yeah, definitely – all of them.
I That's amazing. Now, I know as well as Harry Potter, you have another passion.
J Yeah, football. I'm a big Blackburn Rovers fan. They're brilliant!
I Are they? And how long have you been playing football?
J Since I could walk. I'd rather play football than do anything else in the world.
I So, if I asked you – what would you rather do this afternoon? Read a Harry Potter or play football?
J You know the answer.

T 7.4 Discussing grammar

1 His plane took off a few minutes ago.
2 The president has resigned and a new president has been elected.
3 I've been working in Dubai since last March. When did you arrive?
4 How many emails have you sent?
5 What have you been doing in the bathroom? You've been in there for ages.
6 A huge snowstorm has hit New York. Over 40 cms of snow has fallen in the past 12 hours. People have been advised to stay at home.

T 7.5 Calvin Klein – a passion for fashion

1 A How long has Calvin Klein been interested in fashion?
   B Since he was about 14. When he was a teenager he spent hours sketching women's suits and dresses.
2 A What different kinds of clothes has he designed in his career?
   B He's designed sportswear and underwear but he's possibly most famous for his jeans which always have his name on the back pocket.
3 A How many times has he been married and divorced?
   B He's been married twice and divorced twice. His first wife was Jayne Centre. He met her when they were both fashion students. His second wife was Kelly Rector – she was a rich New York socialite and photographer.
4 A How many children does he have?
   B Just one. A daughter Marci, who is now a successful television producer.
5 A How many awards has he won?
   B He's won seven fashion awards altogether. He made history because he won awards for both men's and women's fashions in the same year.
6 A How long has he been making his own perfumes?
   B He's been making Calvin Klein perfumes since the late 80s.
7 A What are they called?
   B His first were called *Obsession* and *Eternity*. His most recent is called *Euphoria*. His others include *Truth* and *Crave*, which was designed for men.
8 A Which famous people has he worked with and designed for?
   B He's worked with the model Kate Moss and designed clothes for many stars including Julia Roberts, Gwyneth Paltrow and Helen Hunt. He's also worked with Brooke Shields, who, aged 15, modelled his jeans with the famous line 'nothing comes between me and my Calvins.'
9 A How long has he been selling cosmetics?
   B Since the 1990s. These are only sold in the best department stores such as Harrods, in London, and Bloomingdales in New York.

T 7.6 Spoken English

1 A How long are you here for?
   B Four more days. We came two days ago.
2 A How long have you been here?
   B Since Monday.
3 A How long are you here for?
   B Until Friday. We're leaving Friday morning.
4 A How long have you been here?
   B Over half an hour! Where have you been?
5 A How long have you been here?
   B We're staying a month altogether.

T 7.7 Things I'm passionate about.

Julia

I'm really passionate about playing tennis. I've been playing nearly 20 years. I was about … 7 or 8 when I started having lessons, and I had a fantastic teacher. I think that's why I still love it – she was passionate about the sport and that influenced me. I've played in competitions, mainly when I was at school, I still do sometimes. I enjoy it, I think, because it's a very psychological game. I mean, if you're playing badly you have to push yourself to continue, it's a challenge not to give up. It's also a very sociable sport – I've made lots of friends playing doubles, and, it's a game that doesn't have to be expensive – anyone can play – all you need is a tennis racket. You don't need expensive clothing or equipment, like you do for skiing, and it's a fantastic way to keep fit all year round – there's only about 3 months that you can't play. When I lived in Australia I played every week of the year. I adored that, it was brilliant.

Paul

My passion at the moment is horseriding – it's strange to hear myself say that 'cos I've only been doing it about a year and I never imagined I'd be so keen on it. It all happened because I was talking to someone who rode horses and I said that stupid thing people often say 'Oh, I've always wanted to do that' and she said, 'Why don't you then?'. And I thought, 'Why not?'. I've always liked horses, they're so big and powerful but so beautiful when you see them racing round a field or on a track. It amazes me that they let people ride on their backs. Riding is very physically demanding because your body has to be in harmony … er, it has to move with the horse, but it keeps you fit. Of course, I have fallen off a few times, but it seems that the more you fall, the less it hurts. Also, you have to try and understand your horse. They have moods, you never quite know what a ride is going to be like – a horse you had a fantastic ride on one week can be slow and miserable the next week. I really like that about horses – they have personalities.

Andrew

I'm passionate about poetry – I studied English Literature at university but it wasn't until after I graduated that I really got into poetry and I started writing some myself. And I met some other people who wrote poetry and I heard them read it aloud and that was amazing. I felt the power of the words – the thing I like so much about it is that you can say so much with just a few words. So, little means a lot. Each word, each noun, adjective, preposition has to work hard. There's a poem by Simon Armitage called 'To His Lost Lover'. It's a poem of regret, about not saying the things you should have said in a relationship. It has it all for me. Poetry's all about saying what often goes unsaid, and with passion. It can be such a help in your life – if you feel tired or depressed, you can always find a poem that will help – it can be short or long, it doesn't matter.

James

The thing I'm passionate about, and this may surprise many people, is –erm, British weather. I know lots of people can't stand our weather –er they complain about it all the time but I love it. You see, when I was a child my family lived in California for five years and we had about 365 days of sunshine every year, it was so boring. I was ten when we came back to England and I just loved all the changes in the weather. Here, you really appreciate the sunshine *and* you notice the seasons. For me one of nature's miracles is after a long, hot, sunny day there's a thunderstorm or a downpour of rain and you go out in the garden and you can smell the freshness in the air, the world has been washed clean and bright. It's magic. And you know it's a myth that it rains all the time. Anyway, it's the rain that gives us our green fields. You know that joke 'if you don't like English weather – wait ten minutes' – that's why it's interesting.

Harriet

Something I feel really passionately about is fox-hunting. My grandmother, mother, and uncles have always been keen on hunting and I started when I was about 6. We hunt up in the Welsh mountains, we go out from about 11 a.m. and we don't get back till after dark. And the thing I love best about is that you are away from everything and everyone, up in the hills, and you work together with horses and dogs. And if you're following a clever fox you can see him working out how to lose the dogs – he knows the countryside so well, where the holes are, where to hide. Where we hunt in Wales -erm … it's a sheep farming area, so the farmers contact us if they have a problem with a fox. We only hunt on their land if we are asked. I don't hunt so much now because the laws have changed.

Song: Teacher's Book p154

T 7.8 see p61

T 7.9

Pleasure
That's great!
Lovely!
Agreement
Definitely.
Fair enough.
Fine.
Surprise
You didn't!
You did what?
Sympathy
That's a shame.
That's too bad.
Bad luck.

T 7.10

A My grandfather hasn't been too well lately.
B Oh dear.
A He's 79. Don't you think at his age he should slow down a bit?
B Absolutely.
A But he won't listen to me. He says he wants to enjoy his life to the full.
B Fair enough.
A Last summer he went on a two-week cycling holiday in France.
B You're kidding!
A We're going to give him a big party for his 80th birthday.
B That's great.
A But before that, I'm going to have a word with him and tell him to take things *more easy*.
B Good for you.

T 7.11

1 A My boyfriend's just asked me to marry him.
   B Did he? How fantastic! Did you say yes?
2 A Will spaghetti bolognese be OK for dinner?
   B Of course. That's great! It's one of my favourites
3 A There's a strike at the airport so my holiday's been cancelled.
   B Oh dear. That's a shame. Will you get your money back?
4 A I failed my driving test again.
   B You didn't! That's too bad. Better luck next time.

5 A We're expecting a baby.
  B Are you? Congratulations! When's it due?
6 A So you think I should save to buy a car, not borrow the money?
  B Definitely. You've already got too many debts.
7 A I told him I never wanted to see him again.
  B You're kidding! What a pity. I always thought the two of you were so good together.

UNIT 8

T 8.1 see p62–63

T 8.2

1 When we saw the photos we couldn't help feeling worried.
2 The photos made it look worse than it really was.
3 Your friends must promise to keep their room tidy.
4 It's really kind of you to let them stay.
5 Did Victor help you escape from the crocodile?
6 He warned us not to go swimming.
7 We couldn't help feeling a bit scared.
8 Have you decided to come home yet?

T 8.3 Phoning home

M = Mum   K = Kate

M Kate! It's so good to hear from you. Are you OK?
K Oh Mum, I'm really sorry for worrying you so much. I really didn't mean to.
M We opened our emails and we were so delighted to see all your photos and then we saw that one.
K I didn't want my friends to post it on *Facebook*. I asked them not to.
M But Kate, all that blood, and you went to hospital. We couldn't help feeling worried.
K I know, but honestly Mum, my friends made me go to the hospital, I really didn't need to.
M How is your head now?
K Absolutely fine. Honestly. I'll email you some more photos and you can see for yourself.
M OK. Don't forget to.
K I'll call again soon and I promise to text regularly. Bye.
M Bye. Take care!

T 8.4 Spoken English

1 A Did you post my letter?
  B Oh sorry, I forgot to.
2 A I can't go out with you this evening. Sorry.
  B Oh, but you promised to.
3 A Why did you email your mother again?
  B Because she asked me to.
4 A Do you think you'll apply for that job?
  B Yes, I've definitely decided to.
5 A Are you taking your brother to the airport?
  B Well, I offered to but he said he didn't want me to.

T 8.5 Fears and phobias

1 Jodie
I have a really unusual phobia. It began when I was a little girl. I was staying with my grandmother and she asked me to go upstairs and get her cardigan. I opened the cupboard and saw this big, dark green cardigan with huge, black buttons hanging there – I was terrified. I started screaming. My grandmother rushed upstairs and finally managed to calm me down but from then on it was a problem, it was the buttons – all buttons made me feel uncomfortable. It's difficult for me to buy clothes – I try to find skirts and trousers with just belts and zips, but it's not easy. About a year ago a button came off a colleague's jacket at work and I had a panic attack. I've decided to see a psychotherapist, but I'm embarrassed to say 'I'm scared of buttons.' It sounds silly.

2 Gavin
I'm not sure what first started my phobia, but my dad used to go fishing and afterwards I didn't like watching him cleaning the fish in the kitchen sink. Then when I was about seven I started feeling afraid when I saw him coming home with the fish. He had to stop catching it. As I grew up the problem got worse and worse. I couldn't go into supermarkets – the sight of fish made me feel sick. When I started going out with my wife I had to ask her never to eat fish. I daren't go to restaurants because once I saw someone eating an oyster and I had a panic attack. I can only eat in hamburger bars now. It makes life very difficult for my whole family. I've started to see a psychologist but I haven't succeeded in conquering my phobia yet.

3 Melissa
I'm 13 years old and I've been terrified of balloons since I was five. I was trying to blow one up and it popped in my face. I can remember feeling the rubber on my skin – ugh it was awful. My friends don't understand, they enjoy chasing me around with blown up balloons because they think it's fun to see me cry. Last time, we were in the school playground, and I had a panic attack. At first they refused to believe me and they didn't get the teacher but then they saw how bad it was – I was having difficulty breathing and they got frightened. The worst thing is that I can't go to parties, if I do I have to ask them not to have balloons. I can't imagine ever blowing one up. I can't even look at them on TV, I start to shake. I want to see somebody about it. My teacher says I have to.

T 8.6 The psychologist's view

Human beings are programmed to be afraid of things that can hurt them. Show a baby a picture of a snake or a big, poisonous spider and the baby will show fear. It's in our DNA. We're all afraid of some things and that's good. But a phobia causes absolute terror, with physical symptoms such as a racing heart, sickness and panic attacks. Phobias are usually the result of a bad experience, for example a car crash can cause a fear of driving, but it's often just fear of ordinary things like balloons or a particular food. Some people are more likely to get phobias than others, it's in their genes. My job is to train people to conquer their phobia. First we just talk about it, and help the patient relax. Then we might show just a picture or cartoon of their phobia. After that we sometimes show a film and finally we ask them to touch the object. In this way phobias can normally be treated in just three or four sessions.

T 8.7

1 The cat got up the tree easily enough but I had to climb a ladder to get her down.
2 Daniel, stop staring out of the window and get on with your work!
3 Since you whistled that tune I can't get it out of my head.
4 I hate it when my Aunt Mary hugs me tight. She wears this disgusting perfume, and I smell of it afterwards.
5 Bob's hopeless at all sports. He can't even kick a football.
6 You'd better lick your ice-cream – it's melting.
7 Do people kneel down to pray in all religions?
8 I keep trying to stop biting my nails but I can't. It's a terrible habit.
9 I'm terrified of blowing up balloons in case they go 'pop'.
10 Don't scratch that insect bite. You'll get an infection.
11 By the end of the concert we were all clapping our hands to the music.
12 The tourist guide pointed at a place on the map.
13 My dad's useless at doing DIY. He can't even hit a nail with a hammer.
14 My two-year-old nephew is so cute. He loves marching up and down like a soldier.

T 8.8 see p69

T 8.9 see p69

T 8.10 A = Airline steward   B = Passenger

A Good morning. Where are you flying to?
B Dubai.
A And how many bags do you want to check in?
B Just this one.
A Fine. Put it on the scales please … Oh dear.
B What's the matter?
A I'm afraid it's overweight. It's nearly 30 kilos and you're only allowed 23.
B What can I do?
A Well, you can pay for excess baggage. The rate is erm … £18.75 – that's $37 per kilo.
B So 7 times £18.75 that's –er
A That's £131.25 or $259.
B Goodness. That's a fortune but I'll just have to pay it.
A OK. And just the one piece of hand luggage?
B Yes, just this bag.
A That's fine. Here's your boarding pass. You're boarding from Gate 6 at 9.20. The gate will be open 45 minutes before the flight. Have a good journey.
B Thank you.

T 8.11 A = Passenger   B = Transport Direct employee

A Good morning. Transport direct. Can I help you?
B Oh yes, I was trying to book rail tickets online and it didn't work.
A That's OK. Where and when do you want to travel?
B I want to go from London, King's Cross to Edinburgh on the 13th of March.
A March 30th?
B No, no March 13th. I want to go on the 13th and return on the 30th.
A OK, the 13th to the 30th – so you want a return ticket. And do you want to travel in the morning or the afternoon?
B Well, I want to travel up mid-morning if possible, but I'd like to come back on an evening train.
A Right. There's a train at 10.30 am, it arrives in Edinburgh at 14.53.
B Sounds good. And returning?
A For the return there's one at 19.00, arrives back in London just after midnight.
B Mmm … is there an earlier one?
A There's the 17.30. It arrives back in London at 22.28.
B Er, that sounds perfect. I'll go for that. How much is that?
A It's a saver return, so that's £98.20. Is that OK?
B Fine.
A Can you give me your credit card details?
B Yes, it's a Visa card. The name on the card is Mr K Farnham. The number is 0494 7865 4562 1320
A The expiry date?
B 05/12.
A And your address?
B 15, Kingston Road.
A Did you say 50?
B No, 15, one, five Kingston R …

UNIT 9

T 9.1 Billy's story

1 I'd organize a school day which tried to educate everyone about bullying, and I'd invite social workers, police, and psychologists.
2 I'd get my dad to speak to those … if I was older, I'd speak to them myself!
3 I'd ask Billy to try to understand the bullies. I'd get all the parents to meet together.

4 I'd move house so we could change his school and start again somewhere new.
5 I'd get really angry and bang the bullies' heads together.
6 I'd run away.

T 9.2 see p71

T 9.3
1 If they'd understood, he wouldn't have run away.
2 If he'd gone to *Kidcare*, he could have talked about his problems.
3 If he hadn't left, Billy might have felt more secure.
4 If they hadn't threatened him, he wouldn't have run away.

T 9.4 You're an idiot!
1 'I went walking in the mountains for three days with no food or equipment.'
   'You're an idiot! You could have died! You could have starved to death or died of cold!'
2 'I didn't feel like going to work so I phoned in sick. I went shopping instead.'
   'You're such an idiot! Your boss might have seen you. You could have got the sack.'
3 'I had a temperature of 102, but I went out dancing all night.'
   'That's so stupid! You could have been really ill. You should have gone to bed.'
4 'I told Sally I couldn't see her, then went out to the pub with Danielle.'
   'That was a really dumb thing to do! Sally might have seen you in the pub.'
5 'I used to be really good at tennis, I was an under-14 champion, but then I gave it all up.'
   'That's such a shame! You might have been a champion! You might even have won Wimbledon.'

T 9.5 A social conscience
1 I was in the bank the other day, and waiting in a queue. I'd just reached the front of the queue when this guy jumped in front of me and said 'I just need to ask a quick question.' I wasn't very happy and I hate making a scene, so I let him. But then it started taking ages. He looked back at me and grinned. He was so pleased with himself and I was just furious! What could I do? I said nothing.
2 I was in the park, right, and there was this woman with three kids. She'd obviously had a bad day, yeah, she'd just been shouting at the kids for messing around. One of the kids, the eldest boy, about eight, bumped into his little sister and knocked her over. The mother turned on this kid, the boy, and she hit him really hard. I went over to her and told her to stop. She told me to mind my own business, and said some very rude words and stormed off, screaming at the poor boy. He was just a kid!
3 My neighbour always lets his dog do his … you know … business right by my front door, and I always clean it up, day after day, because it just stinks! So the other day I asked him if he could get his dog to do its business somewhere else, or could he pick it up because I didn't like it right by my front door. He was absolutely horrible, and said he'd put it in my letter box from now on! So I suppose I'll just carry on picking it up. What else can I do?
4 I was on the bus the other day. There was just me and a couple of kids. These two kids had their feet on the seat in front of them, so I asked them to put their feet down. These kids, they must have been about sixteen or seventeen, came over to me, pushed me onto the floor, and started kicking me. I've got bruises everywhere! I've only just been able to walk again!

5 I was walking down the street coming home from work about ten at night, it was dark, and this guy jumped out of nowhere and said 'Gimme your wallet and phone!' He had a knife, which he had right up against my nose. I didn't say anything. I was just terrified! I thought he was going to kill me. I just handed over both and he ran away. I was trembling for ten minutes. I couldn't move. I've never been so frightened in all my life.

T 9.6 Spoken English
1 Alice isn't here. She's just gone.
2 I'm sorry I'm in a bad mood. I'm just tired, that's all.
3 I just love your new coat!
4 I've just finished the most wonderful book. You must read it!
5 I don't want any wine. Just a glass of water, please.
6 John's so generous. I think he's just amazing!
7 'Who's coming tonight?' 'Just me.'
8 Hold on a minute. I'm just going to the loo.

T 9.7 Dealing with money
1 A Here's your bill.
   B Thank you. Is service included?
   A No, it isn't. I hope you enjoyed your meal.
2 A How much is a standard room?
   B £55 per night.
   A Does that include everything?
3 A I'll pay for the tickets with my MasterCard.
   B Can you give me your number?
4 A Could you give me the balance on my account?
   B Sure. Tell me your account number
5 A Can I have a gin and tonic and two glasses of white wine, please?
   B Sure. That's £14.50.
   B Thank you.
   A And here's your change. 50p.

T 9.8
1 A Here's your bill.
   B Thank you. Is service included?
   A No, it isn't. I hope you enjoyed your meal.
   B It was lovely, thank you.
   A Can you put in your PIN number, and then press ENTER? And here's your card and your receipt.
   B Thanks. That's for you.
   A That's very kind of you. I hope to see you again soon.
   B Bye!
2 A How much is a standard room?
   B £55 per night.
   A Does that include everything?
   B That includes the room for two people, but it doesn't include breakfast.
   A That's extra, is it?
   B Yes, I'm afraid it is. But the £55 does include VAT.
3 A I'll pay for the tickets with my MasterCard.
   B Can you give me your number?
   A 5484 6922 3171 2435.
   B What's the expiry date?
   A 09 12.
   B And the start date?
   A 10 07.
   B And the three digit security number on the back?
   A 721.
4 A Could you give me the balance on my account?
   B Sure. Tell me your account number.
   A 4033 2614 7900.
   B Bear with me one moment. The current cleared balance on that account is £542.53 in credit.

5 A Can I have a gin and tonic and two glasses of white wine, please?
   B Sure … That's £14.50.
   A Thank you.
   B And here's your change. 50p.
   A Thanks. Er … How much did I give you? I think you've made a mistake!
   B Sorry?
   A I think you must have made a mistake. I gave you £20, but you've given me change for 15.
   B No, I don't think so.
   A Well, I'm pretty sure I gave you a twenty-pound note.
   B Oh, did you? Er … sorry about that. Here you are.
   A Thanks.

UNIT 10

T 10.1 The first computer
Charles Babbage (1791–1871) was a scientist and an engineer. He had the idea for the first programmable computer. He wanted to build a machine that could do calculations without making the mistakes that human 'computers' made.
He designed a machine called the Difference Engine, and the British Government provided funds. The machine was never completed because Babbage ran out of money.
In 1991, a team of engineers from the Science Museum in London built one of Babbage's machines, using his original designs, and it worked perfectly.

T 10.2 Speaking
1 Where did you have lunch today?
2 Where's your mother at the moment?
3 Do you prefer tea or coffee?
4 What's the name of the river in London?
5 Have you got a pet? What's its name?
6 What's your father's job?
7 How do you get to school?
8 What's the name of the Christian holy book? And the Islamic holy book?
9 Who's sitting nearest the window? Next to the teacher?
10 Where are you going after the lesson?

T 10.3
1 Living in London has its disadvantages.
2 To start with, there's a lot of traffic.
3 Londoners like their parks and open spaces.
4 For them it's important to escape from busy city life.
5 London's full of kids, and they're always on the move.
6 The grown-ups have got their parts of town, and the kids have got theirs.

T 10.4 What do you do on the Net?
1 Tom
I go onto websites about sport. I'm into skateboarding, so I go onto skateboarding websites. I watch a lot of skateboarding videos on *YouTube*. I go on things like *MySpace*, where I can talk to friends from school.
   Err … if I'm doing school work, I use *Google* and *Wikipedia*, which can be really useful. And *BBC Bitesize* helps with revision, and there are tests so you can practise.
   I do quite a lot of shopping – clothes, shoes and stuff. I go to *Amazon* for DVDs, games, CDs. And *eBay* for all sorts of things. I'm trying to buy some tickets for a gig on *eBay*. I'm also selling some of my old stuff on it.

2 Monica
I use the Net mainly for *Facebook*. You post a photo and a profile of yourself. You can say what you want – biography, hobbies, interests, music, films. Easy!

You control who can see your profile. Other people search for friends, people who share common interests. When you identify someone on the site you'd like to meet, you can ask to become a friend.

I also use the Net to look for jobs and flats, and to see what's on at the weekend.

3 Justin
I use Internet banking. It's good 'cos I can get my balance any time of day or night, I can transfer money instantly. So I like paying bills online. I just log on to my bank and click on 'Pay Now', and the bill is paid immediately. Easy!

I'm into American baseball, so I watch live baseball games from the US. And … what else? I book restaurants, cinema tickets, holidays. Oh, I get traffic reports, too. Oh, yes! I do nearly all my shopping online. I do my weekly supermarket shop, and it's all delivered. Clothes, birthday presents, Christmas presents, books, music – the lot!

4 Daisy
I don't like reading onscreen, and I don't like watching DVDs, either, but I do use the Net for three things. I email a lot with *Hotmail*. I get the news every day on *The Guardian* website. And I also check the weather every day. I get up in the morning, and get a weather forecast for my town for early morning, mid-morning, early afternoon, and evening. Then, and only then, I get dressed!

5 David
I've gone onto a website called *Friends Reunited*, and I've met up with people from my school days. And I've researched my family history, and traced my ancestors back over two hundred years. I'm retired, so I have lots of time to do these things.

I like to keep up my languages, so I watch the news in Spanish and in French, too. And I download music onto my MP3 player. And I update my satellite navigation system, as well.

T 10.5 Architecture old and new
1 The new station handles fifty million passengers a year.
2 Eurostar travels at 300 kilometres per hour, or 186 miles per hour.
3 Six thousand men built the original station.
4 The roof is 240 feet, or 75 metres, wide.
5 The new station opened in the twenty-first century.
6 A Eurostar train is a quarter of a mile, or 400 metres, long.
7 The champagne bar is 300 feet long.
8 The Midland Grand Hotel opened in 1873.
9 It closed in 1935.
10 The statue 'The Meeting' is 9 metres tall and weighs 20 tons.

T 10.6 see p84

T 10.7 *I need one of those things …*
1 I need one of those things you use when you want to open a bottle of wine. You know, you pull and it goes pop.
2 I'm looking for some of that stuff you use when you want to clean between your teeth … It's like string. It's white. You use it like this.
3 They're long and thin, and the Chinese use them to pick up food.
4 It's made of plastic, and it's used for killing zzzzzz flies. SHPLAT! SHPLOUFF!
5 They're things you use when you're cooking and you want to pick up something that's hot.

T 10.8 see p85

T 10.9
1 It's one of those things you use in the kitchen. You use it to do the washing-up.
2 It's long and thin and sharp at one end. Usually you have two, one in each hand. You can make things out of wool with them.
3 It looks like a mobile phone, it has buttons you push, but you use it to change channels on the TV.
4 It's the stuff you wash clothes with. You put it in the washing machine. It's a powder. It smells … aaaah!
5 It's used for sticking things on the wall, like pictures or posters. It's soft and sticky.
6 They're made of metal. You can also use them to stick things on the wall, but they're sharp. They make a hole. You use them on a notice board.
7 It's a kind of ruler. You use it to measure things that are very long, like a room. It's made of metal, usually.
8 It's something you use when you're travelling. You put it on your suitcase so no one can get into it. You have a key to open it, to take it off.
9 You know! It's got a round, metal bit at one end, and the other end is made of glass. You put it in a lamp to make light.

T 10.10
1 It's one of those things you use in the kitchen.
2 It's long and thin and sharp at one end.
3 It looks like a mobile phone.
4 It's the stuff you wash clothes with.
5 It's used for sticking things on the wall.
6 They're made of metal.
7 It's a kind of ruler.
8 It's something you use when you're travelling.
9 You know! It's got a round, metal bit at one end.

T 10.11
Conversation 1
A Yes, madam. How can I help you?
B I'm looking for a thing you use in the house …
A Yes, now what do you do with it exactly?
B Well, it's not one thing. It's two things. And they're usually made of plastic.
A Uh huh.
B You know if you make a mess, like you drop bread or smash a glass, and there are bits all over the floor …?
A And you need to pick them up?
B Yes! You go like this … SHUP! SHUP!
A What you're talking about is …

Conversation 2
A Can I help you, sir?
B Yes. I don't know how you say this in English. I'm looking for a thing you use in the kitchen …
A OK.
B It's like a thing with, you know, holes …
A Uh huh. What's it for?
B Well, it's for cheese or vegetables like carrots.
A And what do you do with it?
B If you don't want a big piece of cheese, or a whole carrot, but you want little pieces, you can push … you can move … I don't know how you say it. Like this!
A Ah! OK! What you mean is …

UNIT 11

T 11.1 Optical illusions
A How many colours can you see?
B Er, three, if you don't include white, –er green, pink and red.
A No, look again. There's only two, pink and green. When the pink's next to the green it looks red.
B Really? I don't think so. They can't be the same colour. Well, –er maybe. What about this one, the girl? That must be a candlestick in front of her face.

A Yes, you can see one girl behind a candlestick or two girls looking at each other.
B Oh yes, amazing, three girls then! And that one, it looks like a man playing the saxophone.
A Or … another girl. Look, in the shadows …
B Oh yes, I can see her now – she's wearing a hat and lipstick.
A Do you think so? Can you see any more people?
B Yes, that looks like someone wearing glasses and that one is an old lady, and, I'm not sure, but I think she might be wearing a feather in her hat.
A I can also see a young lady with a feather and a fur coat. And I can see the word 'liar'.
B Really? I can't see either of those.
A OK. Try this. Count the legs on that elephant.
B One, two, three –er, it can't have five legs. That's a clever drawing. So is that one, it could be a duck or a rabbit. It depends how you look at it.
A The square looks strange, don't you think?
B Yeah, it looks wobbly, like a jelly.
A Humh, but the lines are all straight and parallel.
B No, they can't be.
A Well, they are. If you look line by line, you'll see.
B I suppose. The dots must be creating the illusion.
A And the last one. Which line's longer?
B Well, the one on the left must be longer.
A Get your ruler and measure.
B Agh. They're the same size – of course. I should have known!
A Interesting, isn't it, the tricks your eyes can play?

T 11.2 Fact or fiction?
1 Lightning never strikes in the same place twice.
This is completely untrue. Lightning often strikes in the same place over and over again – high trees, tall buildings, mountain tops. In fact the purpose of lightning conductors is to be struck time and time again.

2 Hurricanes always have ladies' names.
This used to be true. From 1953 to 1979 only female names were used but now both men's and women's names are used. One name for each letter of the alphabet. The same lists are reused every six years. These are the first six names for 2012: Alberto, Beryl, Chris, Debby, Ernesto, Florence.

3 Women have a higher pain threshold than men.
Some research suggests the opposite, but most people still believe this to be true because women have to give birth. We will never know how men would cope with this experience.

4 The sea is blue because it reflects the sky.
This is true in a way. The white light from the sun is a mixture of all the colours of the rainbow but the air reflects blue light more than other colours so we see a blue sky. Then, when the sky is brilliant blue, the sea is also, because the water reflects the blue of the sky.

5 A penny dropped from a skyscraper can kill a person.
Not true. It might give you a cut or a bruise but it's not likely to kill you.

6 Hair and nails continue to grow after death.
Not true. This is an optical illusion. After death the body quickly dehydrates and the skin shrinks, which gives the illusion that both nails and hair are still growing.

7 Birds are bird-brained and stupid.
Not true. Some birds are the cleverest animals known to science. For example crows are smarter than chimpanzees and some parrots don't just mimic but understand human speech.

8 No two snowflakes are the same.
This could be true. No one has yet found two identical snowflakes but out of all the zillions that fall it is likely that two may be the same.

9 Bats are blind.
Not true. Bats have excellent eyesight. People think they must be blind because they have a sound radar, which means they can hunt insects at night. But it doesn't mean that they can't see.

1 A I think I've lost my passport.
   B You must be very worried.
2 A Your phone's ringing!
   B It might be Jane.
3 A Paul's taking his umbrella.
   B It must be raining.
4 A Harry and Sally never go on holiday.
   B They can't have much money.
5 A Hannah's not in class.
   B She could be in the coffee bar.
6 A Look! Three fire engines!
   B There must be a fire somewhere.
7 A Tom hasn't seen Zoë for ages.
   B They can't be going out together any more.
8 A Whose jacket is this?
   B It might be John's.
9 A You got top marks in the test!
   B You must be joking!

T 11.4 **What are they talking about?**

1 A A glass of white wine and a mineral water, please.
   B Still or sparkling?
   A Sparkling, please.
   B Do you want ice and lemon with that?
   A Just ice, thanks. How much is that?
2 A I can't believe it. My screen's frozen again.
   B Unplug it and take the battery out. Then start it up again. That sometimes works for me.
   A OK. Here goes.
3 A So how did it go?
   B Not too bad, thanks.
   A Were you very nervous?
   B Yeah, but I tried not to show it.
   A Oh. When will you hear?
   B In a couple of days. They said they'd phone me at the end of the week and let me know if I'd got it.
4 A Have you any idea what to get them?
   B Not really, but it should be something special.
   A Yeah, 25 years is a long time.
   B It would be nice to get something silver.
   A Yeah. Why don't we club together and get something from both of us, then we can afford something really nice.
   B Good idea. Mum and Dad would love that.
5 A Do you come here a lot?
   B What?
   A I said DO YOU OFTEN COME HERE?
   B Yeah, me and my friends come every Saturday night. This your first time?
   A Yeah, here. We usually go clubbing at the Zanzibah.
   B Wow – I've heard the Zanzibah's legend.
   A Yeah, how'd you like to try it with me next Saturday?

T 11.5 see p88

T 11.6

R Hello.
C Rachel? It's me Christina. Something dreadful's happened.
R Hi, Christina, what on earth's wrong? Tell me.
C My flat's just been burgled.
R Oh, no! That's terrible. When?
C Well, I discovered it when I came in from work, two hours ago. The door was wide open.
R They must have known no one was at home. What did they take?
C My laptop, of course, with all my work, and my photos on it.
R Had you saved everything?
C Yes, fortunately, I'd put my work and most of my photos on CD.
R Thank goodness. What else is missing?
C My camera, and a whole load of Ella's jewellery, and her new leather jacket.

R Not your camera! Well at least you still have your photos. Oh, and Ella's expensive leather jacket! Does she know?
C No, she doesn't. She's not back from college yet.
R She's going to get such a shock when she gets back – and she's got her final exams soon.
C I know, but at least she had her laptop with her so they didn't get that.
R Yeah, that's good. I know she always takes it with her to lectures. Have you called the police?
C Oh, yes, they're here now.
R Good. Have they any idea who might have done it?
C Well, they say there've been quite a few burglaries in the area and the flat above me was also done.
R So, it wasn't just *your* flat then? Is there much mess? Did they ransack the place?
C The mess is terrible. Whoever did it emptied out all my drawers and my clothes are all over the bedroom floor.
R Oh how awful! Your lovely clothes. Did they take any of them?
C I don't know, I haven't checked. The police have told me not to touch anything.
R Yes, of course, and anyway, it must be really difficult to see exactly what's missing.
C Oh, it is. Oh, Rachel, *(crying)* it's just chaos here.
R Look, Christina you're obviously really upset. I'm coming round. I'll help you tidy up. I'll be there in 15 minutes.
C Oh, Rach. You're a great friend. Thanks so much.

T 11.7 see p89

T 11.8

1 A I can't carry all these shopping bags.
   B What on earth have you bought?
2 A Tom's broken his arm in three places.
   B How on earth did he do that?
3 A There's someone at the door!
   B Who on earth could it be at this time of night?
4 A My aunt left all her money to a cats' home.
   B What on earth did she do that for?
5 A I can't find my car keys.
   B Where on earth have you put them?

T 11.9 see p89

T 11.10 see p89

T 11.11

1 A I can't find my ticket.
   B You must have dropped it.
2 A John didn't come to school yesterday.
   B He must have been ill.
3 A Why is Isabel late for class?
   B She might have overslept.
4 A I can't find my notebook.
   B You must have left it at home.
5 A The teacher's checking Maria's exercise.
   B She can't have finished already!
6 A Why is Carl looking so happy?
   B He may have done well in the test.

T 11.12 **The Adventures of Sherlock Holmes**
Part 4
SH = Sherlock Holmes   HS = Hilton Soames
G = Mr Gilchrist   W = Dr Watson   B= Bannister
HS Holmes! Watson! At last! Tell me. What have you found out? Can the Greek examination take place?
SH Absolutely, the mystery is solved.
HS Really? But who …? Which student …?
SH Dr Watson, can you please ask Mr Gilchrist to join us.
W Of course. Mr Gilchrist? Mr Gilchrist? Can you join us, please?
G What is it? What's happened?
SH Close the door, Mr Gilchrist. Now, sit down and tell me honestly, why did you do it? How did you do it?

G What! Oh, no! How did you find out? I'm sorry, so sorry.
SH Come, come Mr Gilchrist, perhaps it's easier if I speak. You see, when I learnt that you were an athlete and a long jumper, I worked it out immediately.
HS How? I don't understand.
SH Let me continue. This is what must have happened. Yesterday afternoon you, Mr Gilchrist, were returning from practising your sport. You were carrying your jumping-shoes, which, as we all know, have spikes on their soles. You passed your tutor's window and because you are over six feet tall you could see into his room. You couldn't help but notice the examination papers on his desk. As you passed the door, you tried it. Amazingly, it opened …
HS What? How …?
SH Yes, Bannister had forgotten to lock it. Is that not true, Bannister?
B Oh dear, Mr Holmes. Mr Soames, sir, I'm sorry sir. Mr Holmes could be right, I was in a hurry.
SH So, Gilchrist, you entered the room, put your shoes down on the desk and moved to the window to copy the papers and watch for your tutor. Am I right so far?
G Yes, yes.
SH Suddenly you heard your tutor coming in at the side door. Quickly, you picked up your shoes, scratching the top of the desk with the spikes in your haste and leaving a lump of black mud. You ran into the bedroom. You didn't notice that another lump of mud fell to the floor from your shoes. This morning at 6 a.m., I went to the sports ground and collected a sample of mud. It was the same black mud.
W Brilliant, Holmes! Just brilliant.
SH Elementary my dear Watson. Is this all correct, Mr Gilchrist?
G Absolutely correct. I feel so bad, so guilty and ashamed. But can I just show you this, Mr Soames?
HS What is it?
G It's a letter. I wrote it in the middle of the night. Read it, please. In it I say how sorry I am for what I did.
HS Ah yes. And you say you're not going to take the examination. Oh, and you're going to leave the university and the country.
G Yes, I am. I'm going to work in Africa.
HS Gilchrist, I am really pleased to hear that.
B Oh Mr Soames. Mr Gilchrist. It's all my fault. I'm so sorry.
G Absolutely not your fault, Bannister. I am the guilty one.
SH Well, Mr Soames, Mr Gilchrist, time for Watson and myself to have breakfast, I think. I hope the exams go well, Mr Soames. Good luck in Africa, Mr Gilchrist. Goodbye.
HS Thank you, Mr Holmes. It was such a lucky chance that you were staying in town at this time.

T 11.13

1 You need to learn to relax. Why don't you take up yoga?
2 He's just come up with a brilliant plan to save the business.
3 There's no dessert until you've eaten up all your meat and vegetables.
4 Anne and Tony aren't talking to each other. They must have fallen out. They may even have broken up.
5 Did you hear the news? Three dangerous prisoners have broken out of the local prison.
6 You must learn to sort out your washing into coloureds and whites.
7 We're saving up so we can buy a house.
8 Have you found out why you didn't get the job?

1 A I've just found out that I've won the lottery!
  B Congratulations!
2 A I never eat out because I can't really afford to.
  B Me neither.
3 A I don't ever fall out with my husband.
  B What never? I can't believe that.
4 A I can't work out if I feel warm or cold today.
  B Yeah. It's one of those days.
5 A I'm saving up to take my grandma on holiday.
  B That's kind.
6 A I need to sort out my life. I've got problems at work and I've got problems with my boyfriend …
  B Poor you. Come on, let's go out for a drink. Take your mind off things.
7 A I've just come up with a fantastic idea.
  B Uh! I'll believe it when I hear it.
8 A It's important to make up after an argument.
  B Yeah, kiss and make up. Never let the sun go down on an argument.

T 11.15 see p93

T 11.16

'Did you hear about Marcus? You know, the guy who works in my office. Well apparently, he's going to be promoted. To be honest, I don't understand why. Personally, I think he's hopeless at his job. He never does any work. In fact, all he does all day is chat to his friends on the phone and drink coffee. Unfortunately, his desk is next to mine. Presumably, he'll move to another office now so hopefully I won't have to work with him any more. Anyway, enough about me. How's your work going? Are you still enjoying it?'

T 11.17

1 A Hi! You're Pete, aren't you?
  B Actually, no, I'm not. Pete's over there talking to Robert.
2 A What did you think of the film? Great wasn't it?
  B Personally, I thought it was rubbish. I just don't like all that blood and fighting.
3 A What's the latest gossip about Clara and her boyfriend?
  B Apparently, she's going to dump him. She's met someone else.
4 A What's the weather like in spring?
  B Generally, it's warm during the day but you still need to wear a jumper or cardigan in the evening.
5 A What time will we arrive?
  B Hopefully, in the next hour, unless there's another traffic jam.
6 A I've phoned and left messages for them but no reply.
  B Presumably, they're away on holiday. Try them on their mobile.
7 A What did you do when you saw the accident?
  B Obviously, we called 999 immediately. Then we went to see if we could do anything to help.
8 A How did you feel when they offered you the job?
  B To be honest, I was amazed. I didn't expect to get it but of course I was delighted. It'll be a challenge.

UNIT 12

T 12.1 I read it in the papers …

Look, Mum! I've bought a car on *eBay* for £9,000!

A three-year-old boy used his mother's computer to buy a £9,000 car on the Internet auction site *eBay*.

Jack Neal's parents only discovered their son's successful bid when they received a message from the website.

The message said they had bought a pink Nissan Figaro.

Mrs Neal, 36, said that they couldn't understand it. She explained that she had been on the net the day before, but she hadn't bought anything.

'Jack kept telling us that he was so happy, and that we would soon get a big surprise.'

Mrs Neal, from Sleaford, Lincolnshire, thought Jack was joking. He often used the computer, and she was pretty sure that he knew her password. Her husband, John, 37, phoned the seller of the car, and explained that there had been a mistake.

'Fortunately he saw the funny side and said he would advertise the car again.'

Mr Neal has told Jack to be more careful, and he has asked his wife to change her password.

T 12.2

1 Mrs Neal said her son was very clever.
2 She told me he usually played computer games.
3 His father explained that he had bought the computer for his work.
4 Mrs Neal decided that she wouldn't use *eBay* anymore.
5 Jack said he didn't know how it had happened.
6 He told reporters that he had always liked computers.
7 His mother asked Jack to tidy his room.
8 His father told him to go and play football.

T 12.3 Man throws away £20,000 in town centre

A mystery man started a riot in a busy town centre yesterday by hurling £20,000 in banknotes into the air.

Traffic was stopped at 11.00 a.m. in Alexandra Road, Aberystwyth, mid-Wales, as money rained down from the sky.

Local shopkeeper Anthony Jones, 55, said 'I couldn't understand it, so I asked my neighbour what was happening.' They saw people on their hands and knees grabbing money. 'No one knew where the money came from,' he said. 'They were just stuffing it in their pockets.'

Passer-by Eleanor Morris said, 'I wondered if there had been a road accident, because the traffic was at a complete standstill.'

Flower seller Cadwyn Thomas saw the man, who was wearing a red Welsh rugby shirt. 'I asked him why he was giving away all his money, but he didn't answer. He just laughed.'

Police asked Cadwyn if she knew the man. 'I told them I'd never seen him before. He certainly wasn't from around here.'

Dyfed-Powys Police later confirmed that a forty-year-old man from Aberystwyth had been questioned. 'He refused to tell us why he'd done it,' a spokesman said, 'so it's a complete mystery. He wanted to know if we were going to arrest him, but giving away money isn't against the law.'

T 12.4

A I was coming home from the club the other night and I was stopped by the police.
B Were you? Did they ask you lots of questions?
A They certainly did. They asked me where I was going and where I'd been and they wanted to know if I lived in the area.
B Were you scared?
A You bet!
B What else did they ask?
A Well, they wondered how old I was and they wanted to know if I'd been with friends.
B Huh! I'm glad *I* wasn't with you.
A Then they demanded to know if I'd been drinking.
B And had you?
A No, not much anyway. They also asked if I could remember when I'd left home.
B Do you know why they were asking all this?
A No idea. They wouldn't tell me.

T 12.5 But you said …

1 A Bill's coming to the party tonight.
  B Really? I thought you said he wasn't feeling well.
2 A Have you got a cigarette?
  B I didn't know you smoked!
3 A Oh, no! I've spilt tomato ketchup on my white shirt!
  B I told you to be careful. I knew you'd do that.
4 A Did you get me a drink?
  B Sorry. I didn't realize you were here. What would you like?
5 A I'm 25 today!
  B Are you? I didn't know it was your birthday. Many happy returns!
6 A Oh, no! It's raining!
  B Really? But the weather forecast said it was going to be a nice day.
7 A You left the doors and windows of the flat open this morning.
  B I'm sorry. I was pretty sure I'd closed everything.
8 A Where did Tom go last night?
  B I've no idea where he went.

T 12.6 The interview

They wanted to know how old I was.
They asked me what I was doing at the moment.
They asked me how much I was earning.
They asked where I'd worked before.
They asked me if I liked working in a team.
They wanted to know when I could start!

T 12.7

1 She asked me to help her.
2 He reminded her to post the letter.
3 She promised to work hard for her exams.
4 He invited me to his party.
5 She encouraged me to go travelling.
6 He offered to give me a lift to the airport.
7 He persuaded me to apply for the job.
8 She explained that she'd been very busy.

T 12.8 She didn't say that

1 **Merinda phoning Jenny**
  A Can I speak to Jenny, please?
  B I'm afraid she isn't here at the moment. Who's calling?
  A This is Merinda, from work. Could you give her a message?
  B Sure.
  A Can you ask her to ring me as soon as she's back? It's quite important.
  B I'll pass on your message.

2 **Peter talking to his boss**
  A At the moment we can only offer you the job as Assistant Manager. I hope that's acceptable. The salary is £20,000 a year.
  B That's fine. I'll take the job.
  A There's a possibility of promotion in the next six months, if everything works out.
  B Great!

3 **Caroline talking to her son, Ben**
  A Now Ben, you can play on the bike for a bit, but then you must let Mike have a turn. OK? You have to learn to share your toys.
  B OK, Mum.

4 **Sally leaving a message for James**
  This is a message for James. It's Sally here. I've booked the cinema for 8.00, so I'll see you inside the cinema at about 7.45. Hope that's OK. See you later.

5 **Tom talking to Sally**
  A I'll look at your computer for you, but I can't promise to mend it. I'm not an expert.
  B Will you charge me for it?
  A Don't be silly. Of course not. I'll do it for nothing.

T 12.9 What the papers say

An interview with Jamie Seabrook

Part 1

A And now for my final guest. He's a singer and songwriter who's been in the music business for twenty years. He still performs sell-out concerts in front of fifty thousand people. But his life hasn't all been easy. He's had problems with his family and he's been in trouble with the law. And he's just completed a month's rehab in a clinic in Texas. He's never out of the headlines ... Please welcome Jamie Seabrook!

J Hello, good evening.

A Now Jamie, you're in the newspapers and magazines every day. You are photographed wherever you go. Tell me, what do you think of the press?

J Well, it's kind of nice to have people want to know all about me. Sometimes it gets to be too much, but most of the time I don't mind the press attention. I'm sure there are some reporters who really try to tell the truth, but I'm afraid that most of them make up stories to sell their newspapers.

A Are you saying that the stories aren't true at all?

J That's right! They're completely invented!

A Can you give us an example?

J Sure I can! I can give you hundreds!

Part 2

J Two years ago, reporters said my career was finished, and that I'd never sing again. Some friends, who are now ex-friends, said that my marriage was breaking up, and that my brother and I had fallen out and had an argument about money and weren't speaking to each other. Not one word of that was true!

A And in fact your career is on a high ...

J I've just recorded a new album, and my marriage is fine. Sally and I have just celebrated our fifteenth wedding anniversary ...

J ... and my brother and I get on just fine.

A But things haven't all been easy for you. You spent a month in rehab because it was said that you had a drug and alcohol problem ...

J All that's just lies! I've never had a drug or alcohol problem. People in clubs said they'd seen me taking drugs, but it's simply not true. I take prescription drugs for migraines, that's all. I don't do illegal drugs. And I only drink alcohol on special occasions, like my birthday.

A But you were arrested for drink driving just a few months ago!

J Not so! Police officers thought I'd been drinking, but I was driving home from the recording studios and it was two o'clock in the morning and I'd been working all day and I was exhausted. I fell asleep at the wheel. I checked into a clinic for a month because I was suffering from exhaustion.

A Now, you had another legal problem recently. Your Personal Assistant, Barbara James, said you hadn't paid her for six months, and you made her work seven days a week without a break. Is that true?

J It broke my heart when Barbara, my PA, said those things about me. I treated her like my own family. When I met her she was nothing, and I gave her everything. None of what she says is true.

Part 3

A I read that you have become a Buddhist, that you have stopped eating meat, that you spend four hours a day meditating, and that you are going to give half your future income to charity. Is this true?

J Yes, it is. I've decided that life is too short, and I'm getting old. I don't care what people think. I made up my mind to do something useful with my life.

A Now when this story broke a few days ago, the news presenter on MBC's Morning News refused to read the story, saying that there were much more serious stories that deserved attention, and that you were just a celebrity. What do you say to that?

J I can't control what the press says about me. I have to be true to myself. I live my life as honestly as I can, I try to be nice to everyone around me. If you're in the public eye, then you have to be prepared to have some pretty terrible things said about you. I know what's true about me and what's a lie, but I can't change what is said about me in the newspapers and on the television.

A Well, sadly our time has run out and we've come to the end of the show. A big thank you to my guest, Jamie Seabrook, and good luck with the new album!

J Thank you. It's been a pleasure.

T 12.10 see p101

Grammar Reference

UNIT 1

 1.1 Tenses

Unit 1 aims to review what you know. It has examples of the Present Simple and Continuous, the Past Simple and Continuous, and the Present Perfect. There are also examples of the passive voice.
All these forms are covered again in later units.

Present tenses	Unit 2
Past tenses	Unit 3
Present Perfect	Unit 7
Passive	Units 2, 3, 7

1.2 Verbs

1 There are three classes of verbs in English.

Auxiliary verbs *do*, *be*, and *have*
These are used to form tenses, and to show forms such as questions and negatives.

Modal auxiliary verbs
Must, can, should, might, will, and *would* are examples of modal auxiliary verbs. They 'help' other verbs, but unlike *do, be,* and *have,* they have their own meanings. For example, *must* expresses obligation; *can* expresses ability. (See Units 4, 5, 9, 11.)

Full verbs
These are **all** the other verbs in the language, for example, *play, run, help, think, want, go, see, eat, enjoy, live, die, swim,* etc.

2 *Do, be,* and *have* can also be used as full verbs with their own meanings.

do
*I **do** my washing on Saturdays.*
*She **does** a lot of business in Eastern Europe.*

be
*We **are** in class at the moment.*
*They **were** at home yesterday.*

have
*He **has** a lot of problems.*
*They **have** three children.*

3 There are two forms of *have* in the present.

have as a full verb
*I **have** a job.*
*Do you **have** a flat?*
*He doesn't **have** a car.*

have + got
*I've **got** a job.*
***Have** you **got** a flat?*
*She **hasn't got** a car.*

1.3 Auxiliary verbs and tenses

1 be and the continuous forms

Be + verb + *-ing* is used to make continuous verb forms which describe activities in progress and temporary activities.
*He's **washing** his hair.* (Present Continuous)
*They **were going** to work.* (Past Continuous)
*I've **been learning** English for two years.* (Present Perfect Continuous)
*I'd like **to be lying** on the beach right now.* (Continuous infinitive)

2 be and the passive voice

Be + past participle is used to form the passive.
*Paper **is made** from wood.* (Present Simple passive)
*My car **was stolen** yesterday.* (Past Simple passive)
*The house **has been** redecorated.* (Present Perfect passive)
*This homework needs **to be done** tonight.* (Passive infinitive)
There is an introduction to the passive on p135.

3 have and the perfect forms

Have + past participle is used to make perfect verb forms.
*He **has worked** in seven different countries.* (Present Perfect)
*She was crying because she **had had** some bad news.* (Past Perfect)
*I'd like **to have met** Napoleon.* (Perfect infinitive)

Perfect means 'completed before', so Present Perfect means 'completed before now'. Past Perfect means 'completed before a time in the past'.

1.4 Auxiliary verbs and negatives

1 To make a negative, add *-n't* to the auxiliary verb. If there is no auxiliary verb, use *don't/doesn't/didn't*.

Positive	Negative
He's working.	*He **isn't** working.*
I was thinking.	*I **wasn't** thinking.*
We've seen the play.	*We **haven't** seen the play.*
She works in a bank.	*She **doesn't** work in a bank.*
They like skiing.	*They **don't** like skiing.*
He went on holiday.	*He **didn't** go on holiday.*

2 It is possible to contract the auxiliaries *be* and *have* and use the uncontracted *not*.
*He's **not** playing today.* (= He *isn't* playing today.)
*We're **not** going to Italy after all.* (= We *aren't* going to Italy …)
*I've **not** read that book yet.* (= I *haven't* read that book yet.)
BUT *I'm **not** working.* NOT ~~I amn't working~~.

1.5 Auxiliary verbs and questions

1 To make a question, invert the subject and the auxiliary verb. If there is no auxiliary verb, use *do/does/did*.

	Question
She's wearing jeans.	*What **is she** wearing?*
You were born in Paris.	*Where **were you** born?*
Peter's been to China.	***Has Peter** been to China?*
I know you.	***Do I** know you?*
He wants ice-cream.	*What **does he** want?*
They didn't go out.	*Why **didn't they** go out?*

2 There is usually no *do/does/did* in subject questions.

Who wants ice-cream?	*What flavour ice-cream **do** you want?*
What happened to your eye?	*What **did** you do to your eye?*
Who broke the window?	*How **did** you break the window?*

1.6 Auxiliary verbs and short answers

Short answers are very common in spoken English. If you just say *Yes* or *No*, it can sound rude. To make a short answer, repeat the auxiliary verb. In the Present and Past Simple, use *do/does/did*.

Short answer	
Are you coming with us?	**Yes,** I **am.**
Have you had breakfast?	**No,** I **haven't.**
Does she like walking?	**No,** she **doesn't.**
Did Mary phone?	**Yes,** she **did.**

UNIT 2

2.1 Present Simple

Form

The form is the same for *I/we/you/they*.

*I **work** from 9–5 p.m.*
*They **don't work** full time.*
*Where **do** you **work**?*

He/She/It: add *-s* or *-es*, and use *does/doesn't* in questions and short answers.

*He **doesn't work** at weekends.*
*Where **does** she **live**?*

Short answer

Do you live in Bristol?   **Yes, we do.**
Does he have a car?   **No, he doesn't.**

Use

The Present Simple is used to express:

1 an action that happens again and again (a habit).
   *I **go** to work by car.*
   *She **drinks** ten cups of coffee a day.*

2 a fact that is always true.
   *Ronaldo **comes** from Brazil.*
   *My daughter **has** brown eyes.*

3 a fact that is true for a long time (a state).
   *He **works** in a bank.*
   *I **live** in a flat near the centre of town.*

Spelling of *he/she/it* forms

1 Most verbs add *-s* to the base form of the verb.
   *want**s**   eat**s**   help**s**   drive**s***

2 Add *-es* to verbs that end in *-ss*, *-sh*, *-ch*, *-x*, and *-o*.
   *kiss**es**   wash**es**   watch**es**   fix**es**   go**es***

3 Verbs that end in a consonant + *-y* change the *-y* to *-ies*.
   *carr**ies**   fl**ies**   worr**ies**   tr**ies***
   But verbs that end in a vowel + *-y* only add *-s*.
   *buy**s**   say**s**   play**s**   enjoy**s***

2.2 Adverbs of frequency

1 We often use adverbs of frequency with the Present Simple.

   0% ——————————— 50% ——————————— 100%
   never rarely hardly ever not often sometimes often usually always

2 They go before the main verb, but after the verb *to be*.
   *I **usually** start at 9.00.*   *They're **usually** here by now.*
   *I **rarely** see Peter these days.*   *We're **rarely** at home at weekends.*

3 *Sometimes* and *usually* can also go at the beginning or the end.
   ***Sometimes** we play cards.*   *We play cards **sometimes**.*
   ***Usually** I go shopping with friends.*   *I go shopping with friends **usually**.*

2.3 Present Continuous

Form

am/is/are + verb + *-ing*
*I'm **playing** tennis.*
*He's **cooking** lunch.*

*I'm **not enjoying** my new job.*
*They **aren't working** today.*

*What's he **doing**?*
*Where **are** you **living**?*

Short answer

Are you going by train?   **Yes, I am./No, I'm not.**

Use

The Present Continuous is used to express:

1 an activity that is happening now.
   *Don't turn the TV off. **I'm watching** it.*
   *You can't speak to Lisa. She's **having** a bath.*

2 an activity that is not necessarily happening at the moment of speaking but is happening around now.
   *Don't take that book. Jane's **reading** it.*
   *I'm **doing** a French evening class this year.*

3 a temporary activity.
   *Peter is a student, but he's **working** as a waiter during the holidays.*
   *I'm **living** with friends until I find a place of my own.*

4 a planned future arrangement.
   *I'm **having** lunch with Glenda tomorrow.*
   *We're **meeting** at 1.00 outside the restaurant.*

Spelling of verb + *-ing*

1 Most verbs add *-ing* to the base form of the verb.
   *go**ing**   wear**ing**   visit**ing**   eat**ing***

2 Verbs that end in one *-e* lose the *-e*.
   *smok**ing**   com**ing**   hop**ing**   writ**ing***
   BUT *lie* → *lying*
   Verbs that end in *-ee* don't drop an *-e*.
   *agree**ing**   see**ing***

3 Verbs of one syllable, with one vowel and one consonant, double the consonant.
   *sto**pp**ing   ge**tt**ing   ru**nn**ing   pla**nn**ing   jo**gg**ing*
   If the final consonant is *-y* or *-w*, it is not doubled.
   *play**ing**   show**ing***

2.4 State verbs

1 There are certain groups of verbs that are usually only used in the Present Simple. Their meanings are related to states or conditions that are facts, not activities.

Verbs of thinking and opinions

believe	think	understand	suppose	expect	agree
doubt	know	remember	forget	promise	mean
imagine	realize	deserve	guess		

*I **believe** you.*
*Do you **understand** what I mean?*
*I **know** his face, but I **forget** his name.*

Verbs of emotions and feelings

like	love	hate	care	hope
wish	want	prefer	adore	dislike

*I **like** black coffee.*
***Do** you **want** to go out?*
*I **don't care**.*

Verbs of having and being

belong	own	have	possess	contain	cost	seem
matter	need	depend	weigh	resemble	fit	involve

*This book **belongs** to Jane.*
*How much **does** it **cost**?*
*He **has** a lot of money.*

Verbs of the senses

> look   hear   taste   smell   feel   sound

*The food **smells** good.*
*My hair **feels** soft.*

We often use *can* when the subject is a person.
*I **can** hear someone crying.*
***Can** you smell something burning?*

2   Some of these verbs can be used in the Present Continuous, but with a change of meaning. In the continuous, the verb expresses an activity, not a state. Compare:

*I **think** you're right.* (opinion)	*We're **thinking** of going to the cinema.* (mental activity)
*He **has** a lot of money.* (possession)	*She's **having** a bad day.* (activity)
*I **see** what you mean.* (= understand)	*Are you **seeing** Nigel tomorrow?* (activity)
*The soup **tastes** awful.* (state)	*I'm **tasting** the soup to see if it needs salt.* (activity)

 2.5 THE PASSIVE

Form

***to be** + past participle*
The tense of the verb *to be* changes to give different tenses in the passive.
*Are you **being served**?* (Present Continuous)
*My car **is insured** with ASM.* (Present Simple)
*Were you **taken** to visit the cathedral?* (Past Simple)
*I've **been invited** to a wedding.* (Present Perfect)
*I'd love **to be introduced** to a film star.* (Passive infinitive)

Use

1   Passive sentences move the focus from the subject to the object of active sentences.
*Shakespeare **wrote** Hamlet in 1601 while he was living in London. Hamlet, the most famous play in English literature, **was written** by William Shakespeare.*
The passive is not another way of expressing the same sentence in the active. We choose the active or the passive depending on what we are more interested in.

2   *By* and the agent are often omitted in passive sentences if …
… the agent is not known:
*I **was burgled** last night.*
… the agent is not important:
*This bridge **was built** in 1886.*
… the agent is obvious:
*I **was fined** £100 for speeding.*

3   The passive is associated with an impersonal, formal style. It is often used in notices and announcements.
*Customers **are requested** to refrain from smoking.*
*It **has been noticed** that reference books **have been removed** from the library.*

4   In informal language, we often use *you*, *we*, and *they* to refer to people in general or to no person in particular. In this way, we can avoid using the passive.
***You can buy** stamps in lots of shops, not just post offices.*
***They're building** a new department store in the city centre.*
***We speak** English in this shop.*

❶ Many past participles are used as adjectives.
*I'm very **interested** in modern art.*
*We were extremely **worried** about you.*
*I'm **exhausted**! I've been working hard all day.*

2.6 Present Simple and Present Continuous passive

Form

Present Simple Passive *(am/is/are + past participle)*
*Most workers **are paid** monthly.*
***Is** service **included** in the bill?*
Present Continuous Passive *(am/is/are being + past participle)*
*This road **is being widened**.*
*Are you **being served**?*

Use

The uses are the same in the passive as in the active.
*My car **is serviced** every six months.* (habit)
*Computers **are used** everywhere.* (fact that is always true)
*The house **is being redecorated** at the moment.* (activity happening now)

UNIT 3

3.1 PAST TENSES

We use different past tenses to describe moments and periods of time in the past.
Look at the diagram. Read the sentences.
When Andrea arrived at work at 9.00 …

—— 8.30 —— [9.00] —— 9.30 —— 10.00 ——

… her secretary had opened the post.

… her secretary was opening the post.

… her secretary opened the post.

3.2 Past Simple

Form

The form of the Past Simple is the same for all persons.
*He **left** at three o'clock.*
*They **arrived** three weeks ago.*

*She **didn't finish** on time yesterday.*
*I **didn't visit** my parents last weekend.*

*When **did** he **finish** the report?*
*What time **did** his train **leave**?*

Short answer
Did you enjoy the meal?   **Yes**, we **did**./**No**, we **didn't**.

Use

The Past Simple is used to express:

1   a finished action in the past.
*We **met** in 2000.*
*I **went** to Manchester last week.*
*John **left** two minutes ago.*

2   actions that follow each other in a story.
*Mary **walked** into the room and **stopped**. She **listened** carefully. She **heard** a noise coming from behind the curtain. She **threw** the curtain open, and then she **saw** …*

3   a past situation or habit.
*When I **was** a child, we lived in a small house by the sea. Every day I **walked** for miles on the beach with my dog.*
This use is often expressed with *used to*. See 3.5 on p136.
*We **used to** live in a small house … I **used to** walk for miles …*

Spelling of verb + -ed

1 Most regular verbs add -ed to the base form of the verb.
worked   wanted   helped   washed

2 When the verb ends in -e, add -d.
liked   used   hated   cared

3 If the verb has only one syllable, with one vowel + one consonant, double the consonant before adding -ed.
stopped   planned   robbed
But we write *cooked, seated,* and *moaned* because there are two vowels.

4 The consonant is not doubled if it is -y or -w.
played   showed

5 In most two-syllable verbs, the end consonant is doubled if the stress is on the second syllable.
pre'ferred   ad'mitted
But we write *'entered* and *'visited* because the stress is on the first syllable.

6 Verbs that end in a consonant + -y change the -y to -ied.
carried   hurried   buried
But we write *enjoyed*, because it ends in a vowel + -y.
There are many common irregular verbs.

▶▶ **Irregular verbs p159**

Past Simple and time expressions

Look at the time expressions that are common with the Past Simple.

I met her	last night.
	two days ago.
	yesterday morning.
	in 2001.
	in summer.
	when I was young.

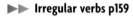 3.3 Past Continuous

Form

was/were + verb + -ing
*I **was learning** French.*
*They **were driving** to Paris.*

*We **weren't waiting** for a long time.*

*What **were** they **doing**?*
*Where **was** he **studying**?*

Short answer

Were you looking for me?   **Yes, I was./No, I wasn't.**
Were they waiting outside?   **Yes, they were./No, they weren't.**

Use

The Past Continuous is used:

1 to express activities in progress before, and probably after, a particular time in the past.
*At seven o'clock this morning I **was having** my breakfast.*
*You made a lot of noise last night. What **were** you **doing**?*

2 for descriptions.
*Jan looked beautiful. She **was wearing** a green cotton dress. Her eyes **were shining** in the light of the candles that **were burning** nearby.*

3 to express an interrupted past activity.
*When the phone rang, I **was having** a shower.*
*While we **were playing** tennis, it started to rain.*

4 to express an incomplete activity.
*I **was reading** a book during the flight. (I didn't finish it.)*
*I **watched** a film during the flight. (the whole film)*

3.4 Past Simple or Past Continuous?

1 Sometimes both tenses are possible. The Past Simple focuses on past actions as complete facts. The Past Continuous focuses on the duration of past activities. Compare:
A *I didn't see you at the party last night.*
B *No. I **stayed** at home and **watched** the football.*
A *I didn't see you at the party last night.*
B *No, I **was watching** the football at home.*

2 Questions in the Past Simple and Past Continuous refer to different time periods. The Past Continuous asks about activities before; the Past Simple asks about what happened after.
A *What **were** you **doing** when the accident happened?*
B *I **was shopping**.*
A *What **did** you **do** when you saw the accident?*
B *I **phoned** the police.*

3.5 *used to*

Used to expresses a habit or state in the past that is now finished.
*I **used to** read comics when I was a kid. (but I don't now)*
*My dad and I **used to** play football together. (but we don't now)*
***Did** you **use to** read comics when you were a child?*
*This town **didn't use to** be a nice place to live, but then it changed.*

3.6 Past Perfect

Perfect means 'completed before'. The Past Perfect refers to an action in the past that was completed before another action in the past.

Form

The form of the Past Perfect is the same for all persons.

Positive and negative

I You We	'd (had) hadn't	seen him before. finished work at six o'clock.

Question

Where had	you she they	been before?

Short answer
Had he already left?   **Yes**, he **had**./**No**, he **hadn't**.

Use

1 The Past Perfect is used to make clear that one action in the past happened *before* another action in the past.
*When I got home, I found that someone **had broken** into my apartment and **had stolen** my DVD player.*
*I didn't go to the cinema because I'd **seen** the film before.*

2 The Past Simple tells a story in chronological order.
Sue met Pete at university. They were together for six years. They divorced last month.

The Past Perfect can be used to tell a story in a different order.
*Sue and Pete divorced last month. They'd **met** at university, and had been together for six years.*

3 Notice the difference between these sentences.
*When I got to the party, Peter **went** home.*
(= First I arrived, then Peter left.)
*When I got to the party, Peter **had gone** home.*
(= First Peter left, then I arrived.)

4 The Past Perfect Continuous refers to longer actions or repeated activities.
*We were exhausted because we'd **been driving** all day.*

3.7 Past tenses in the passive

Form

Past Simple Passive: *was/were* + past participle
*The museum **was opened** in 1987.*
*We **were burgled** last night.*

Past Continuous Passive: *was/were being* + past participle
*The vase **was being restored**.*

Past Perfect Passive: *had been* + past participle
*The house **had been redecorated**.*

Use

The uses are the same in the passive as in the active.
*The bridge **was built** in 1876.* (finished action in the past)
*The bomb **was being defused** when it exploded.* (interrupted past activity)
*The letter didn't arrive because it **had been sent** to my old address.* (one action before another action in the past)

UNIT 4

4.1 *have to*

Form

has/have + to + infinitive
*You **have to go** to school.*
*She **has to study** hard.*

*He **doesn't have to wear** uniform.*
*We **don't have to** take exams.*

***Does** she **have to study** maths?*
***Do** they **have to leave** now?*

Use

1 *Have to* expresses strong obligation.
   *You **have to** work hard if you want to succeed.*

2 *Have to* expresses a general obligation based on a law or rule, or based on the authority of another person.
   *Children **have to** go to school until they are 16.*
   *Mum says you **have to** clean your room before you go out.*

3 *Have to* is impersonal. It doesn't necessarily express the opinion of the speaker.
   *The doctor says I **have to** lose weight.*
   *People all over the world **have to** learn English.*

4 *Have to* has all verb forms. *Must* doesn't.
   *I **had to** work last night.* (Past)
   *You'll **have to** study hard.* (Future)
   *She's rich. She's never **had to** do any work.* (Present Perfect)
   *I hate **having** to get up on winter mornings.* (-ing form)

4.2 *have got to*

1 *Have got to* is common in British English but it is more informal than *have to*. It is more spoken that written.
   *I've **got to** go now. See you!*
   *We've **got to** get up early tomorrow.*
   *I'm in trouble! You've **got to** help me!*

2 *Have got to* expresses an obligation now, or on a particular occasion soon.
   *I've **got to** stop eating ice-cream! It's too yummy!*
   *I usually start work at 9.00, but tomorrow I've **got to** start at 8.00.*
   *Now he's 21, he's **got to** learn to be responsible.*
   *You've **got to** pay me back tomorrow.*

3 *Have to* expresses a general repeated obligation.
   *I always **have to** tell my parents where I'm going.*
   *Teachers **have to** prepare lessons and correct homework.*

4.3 MODAL AND RELATED VERBS

These are the modal verbs:
can, could, may, might, will, would, shall, should, must, ought to.
They are used before other verbs and add meanings, such as certainty, possibility, obligation, ability, and permission.
*You **must** be exhausted.*
*I **can** swim.*
*It **might** rain.*

Form

1 There is no *-s* in the third person singular.
   *She **can** ski.   He **must** be tired.   It **might** rain.*

2 There is no *do/does/don't/doesn't* in the question or negative.
   *What **should** I do?   **Can** I help you?   You **mustn't** steal!*
   *He **can't** dance.   I **won't** be a minute.*

3 Modal auxiliary verbs are followed by the infinitive without *to*. The exception is *ought to*.
   *You **must** go.   I'll **help** you.   You **ought to** see a doctor.*

4 They have no infinitives and no *-ing* forms. Other expressions are used instead.
   *I'd love to **be able to** ski.*
   *I hate **having to** get up on cold winter mornings.*

5 They don't usually have past forms. Instead, we use them with Perfect infinitives.
   *You **should have told** me that you can't swim. You **might have drowned**!*
   Or we use other expressions.
   *I **had to** work hard in school.*

6 *Could* is used with a past meaning to talk about a general ability.
   *I **could** swim when I was six.* (= general ability)

   To talk about ability on one specific occasion, we use *was able to/ managed to*.
   *The prisoner **was able to/managed to** escape by climbing onto the roof of the prison.*

Use

1 Modal verbs express our attitudes, opinions, and judgements of events. Compare:
   'Who's that knocking on the door?'
   'It's John.' (This is a fact.)

   'Who's that knocking on the door?'
   *'It **could/may/might/must/should/can't/'ll** be John.'* (These all express our attitude or opinion.)

2 Each modal verb has at least two meanings. One use of all of them is to express possibility or probability. (See Units 5 and 11.)
   *I **must** post this letter!* (= obligation)
   *You **must** be tired!* (= deduction, probability)

   ***Could** you help me?* (= request)
   *We **could** go to Spain for our holiday.* (= possibility)

   *You **may** go home now.* (= permission)
   *'Where's Anna?'   'I'm not sure. She **may** be at work.'* (= possibility)

4.4 Obligation: *should, ought to,* and *must*

Should, ought to, and *must* are modal verbs. See 4.3 on p137 for form.

Use

1 *Should* and *ought to* express mild obligation, suggestions, or advice. They express what, in the speaker's opinion, is the right or best thing to do. We often use them with *I think/don't think …*
   *You're always asking me for money. I think you **should** spend less.*
   *You **shouldn't** sit so close to the television! It's bad for your eyes.*
   *You **ought to** be more careful with your money.*

2 We often use *Do you think …?* in the question.
   ***Do you think** I should see a doctor?*
   *What **do you think** I should wear to the party?*

3 *Must,* like *have to,* expresses strong obligation. *Must* can express an obligation that involves the speaker's opinion. It is personal.
   *I **must** get my hair cut.*
   *You **must** go and visit your grandmother.*

4 *Must* is also associated with a formal, written style.
   *All visitors **must** show proper ID.*
   *Books **must** be returned on or before the due date.*

have to and must

1 *Have to* and *must* are sometimes interchangeable.
   *I **must** be home by midnight.*
   *I **have to** be home by midnight.*

2 There is sometimes a difference in meaning. *Must* usually expresses the feelings and wishes of the speaker.
   *I **must** buy my mother a birthday card.*
   *Tommy, you **must** look after your toys.*

   Have to often expresses an obligation that comes from somewhere else.
   *You **have to** work hard in this life.*
   *Visitors **have to** report to reception.*

   It is for this reason that you need to be careful when you say *You must …,* because you can sound authoritarian.

   Have to is used more than *must.* If you don't know which to use, use *have to.*

3 Question forms with *have to* are more common.
   *Do I **have to** do what you say?*
   ***Must** I …?* is unusual.

   ! Remember, *have to* has all verb forms. *Must* can only refer to present or future time when used to express obligation.

don't have to and mustn't

1 *Don't have to* and *mustn't* are completely different.
   Don't have to expresses absence of obligation – you can, but it isn't necessary.
   *Some people iron their socks, but you **don't have to**. I think it's a waste of time.*
   *When you go into a shop, you **don't have to** buy something. You can just look.*

2 *Mustn't* expresses negative obligation – it is very important NOT to do something.
   *You **mustn't** steal other people's things. It's wrong.*
   *You **mustn't** drive if you've been drinking. You could kill someone!*

4.5 Permission: *can* and *be allowed to*

Can is a modal verb. See 4.3 on p137 for form.

Use

The main use of *can* is to express ability.
*I **can** swim.*
Can and *be allowed to* express permission. *Can* is more informal and usually spoken.
*You **can** borrow my bike, but you **can't** have the car. I need it.*
*They **can't** come in here with those muddy shoes!*
*You'**re allowed to** get married when you're 16.*
*Are we **allowed to** use a dictionary for this test?*

4.6 Making requests: *can, could, will,* and *would*

1 There are many ways of making requests in English.
   ***Can** I speak to you, please?*
   ***Could** I ask you a question?*

   ***Will** you help me, please?*
   ***Would** you pass me the salt?*

   ***Would you mind** passing me the water?*
   ***Do you mind if** I open the window?*
   ***Would you mind if** I closed the window?*
   Can, could, will, and *would* are all modal verbs.

2 *Could* is a little more formal; *can* is a little more familiar. *Could I …?* and *Could you …?* are very useful because they can be used in many different situations.
   ***Could** I try on this jumper?*
   ***Could** you tell me the time?*

3 Here are some ways of responding to requests:
   A *Excuse me! Could you help me?*
   B *Sure./Of course./Well, I'm afraid I'm a little busy right now.*
   A *Would you mind if I opened the window?*
   B *No, not at all./No, that's fine./Well, I'm a little cold, actually.*

4.7 Making offers: *will* and *shall*

1 The contracted form of *will* is used to express an intention, decision, or offer.
   *Come over after work. I'**ll** cook dinner.*
   *'It's Jane's birthday today.'   'Is it? I'**ll** buy her some flowers.'*
   *Dave'**ll** give you a lift.*
   *Give it back or we'**ll** call the police!*

2 *Shall … I/we …?* is used in questions with the first person, *I* and *we*. It expresses an offer, a suggestion, or a request for advice.
   *'**Shall I** carry your bag for you?'*
   *'**Shall we** go out for a meal tonight?'*
   *'Where **shall we** go?'*

UNIT 5

5.1 FUTURE FORMS

1 There is no future tense in English. Instead, English has several forms that can refer to the future.

I'll see you later. (will)
We're going to see a film tonight. (going to)
I'm seeing the doctor tomorrow. (Present Continuous)
If the traffic's bad, I might be late. (might)
Who knows? You may win! (may)
Take an umbrella. It could rain later. (could)

2 The difference between them is not about near or distant future, or certainty. The speaker chooses a future form depending on how he/she sees the future event. Is it a plan, a decision, an intention, an offer, an arrangement, or a prediction?

5.2 *will/going to* and the Present Continuous

Form

Positive and negative

I'll see you later.
I won't be late.
We're going to stay in a hotel.
We aren't going to rent a cottage.
I'm meeting Jan for lunch.
I'm not seeing her till 2.00.

Question

When will you be back?
Where are you going to stay?
What time are you seeing Jan?

❶ We avoid saying *going to come* or *going to go*.

We're coming tomorrow.
When are you going home?

Facts and predictions

will

1 The most common use of *will* is as an auxiliary verb to show future time. It expresses a future fact or prediction. It is called the pure future or the Future Simple.

We'll be away for two weeks.
Those flowers won't grow under the tree. It's too dark.
Our love will last forever.
You'll be sick if you eat all those sweets!

2 *Will* for a prediction can be based more on an opinion than a fact.

I don't think Laura will do very well in her exam. She doesn't do any work.
I am convinced that inflation will fall to three per cent next year.

going to

1 *Going to* can also express a prediction, especially when it is based on a present fact. There is evidence now that something is certain to happen.

She's going to have a baby.
(We can see she's pregnant.)
Our team is going to win the match.
(It's four–nil, and there are only five minutes left to play.)
It isn't going to rain today.
(Look at that beautiful blue sky.)

2 Sometimes there is no difference between *will* and *going to*.

This government will ruin the country.
This government is going to ruin the country.

Plans, decisions, intentions, and arrangements

will

Will is used to express a decision, intention, or offer made at the moment of speaking.

I'll have the steak, please.	NOT ~~I have the steak …~~
Give me a call. We'll go out for coffee.	NOT ~~We go …~~
There's the phone! I'll get it.	NOT ~~I get …~~

going to

Going to is used to express a future plan, decision, or intention made before the moment of speaking.

When I grow up, I'm going to be a doctor.
Jane and Peter are going to get married after they graduate.
We're going to paint this room blue.

Arrangements

1 The Present Continuous can be used to express a future arrangement between people. It usually refers to the near future.

We're going out with Jeremy tonight.
I'm having my hair cut tomorrow.
What are we having for lunch?

2 Think of the things you put in your diary to remind you of what you are doing over the next few days and weeks. These are the kinds of events that are expressed by the Present Continuous for the future. There is often movement or activity.

I'm meeting Peter tonight.
The Taylors are coming for dinner.
I'm seeing the doctor in the morning.

3 You can't use the Present Simple for this use.

We're going to a party on Saturday night.	NOT ~~We go …~~
I'm having lunch with Sarah.	NOT ~~I have …~~
What are you doing this evening?	NOT ~~What do you do …~~

4 Sometimes there is no difference between an arrangement and an intention.

We're going to get married in the spring.
We're getting married in the spring.

5.3 Future possibility: *may/might/could*

Form

May, *might*, and *could* are modal verbs.

Positive and negative

I	may might could	see you later.		I	may not might not	get the job.

Question

Questions about future possibility are often asked with *Do you think … will …?*

Do you think you'll get the job?

Use

1 *May*, *might*, and *could* all express a future possibility.

It	may might could	rain later.

2 *May* can be more formal.

The government may increase income tax.

3 *Could* suggests something less definite.

I could be a champion if I trained hard.
The house is nice, but it could be beautiful.

UNIT 6

6.1 Information questions

1   *What* and *which* can be followed by a noun.
   What colour *are your eyes?*
   What size *shoes do you take?*
   What sort *of music do you like?*
   Which part *of town do you live in?*
   Which way *do we go?*
   Which one *do you want?*

   We use *which* when there is a limited choice.
   Which one *do you want, the red one or the blue one?*
   Which restaurant *shall we go to?*

   We use *what* when there is (almost) unlimited choice.
   What language *do they speak in Brazil?*
   What car *do you drive?*

   Sometimes there is no difference.
   What/Which newspaper *do you read?*
   What/Which channel *is the football on?*

2   *Whose* can be followed by a noun.
   Whose book *is this?*
   Whose *is this book?*

3   *How* can be followed by an adjective or an adverb.
   How tall *are you?*
   How big *is the memory?*
   How far *is it to the station?*
   How often *do you go to the cinema?*
   How long *does it take you to get ready?*

4   *How* can be followed by *much* or *many*.
   How many *rooms are there?*
   How much *money do you have?*

6.2 *What ... like? How ...?*

1   *What ... like?* asks about the permanent nature of people and things. It asks for a general description.
   What's Indian food like?   *Really tasty.*
   What's Pete like?   *He's a great guy.*

2   *How ...?* asks about the present condition of something. This condition can change.
   How's work these days?   *It's better than last year.*
   How was the traffic this morning?   *It was worse than usual.*

   To ask about the weather, we can use both questions.
   How's the weather
   What's the weather like   where you are?

3   *How ...?* asks about people's health and happiness.
   How's Peter?   *He's fine.*

4   *How ...?* asks about people's reactions and feelings.
   How's your meal?
   How's your new job?

6.3 Relative clauses

1   Relative clauses identify which person or thing we are talking about. They make it possible to give more information about the person or thing.
   The boy has gone to the beach. (Which boy?)
   The boy **who lives next door** *has gone to the beach.*

   The book is very good. (Which book?)
   The book **that I bought yesterday** *is very good.*

   There is a photo of the hotel. (Which hotel?)
   There is a photo of the hotel **where we stayed**.

2   We use *who/that* to refer to people, and *which/that* to refer to things.
   This book is about a girl **who marries a millionaire**.
   What was the name of the horse **that won the race?**

3   When *who* or *that* is the object of a relative clause, it can be left out.
   The person **you need to talk to** *is on holiday.*
   The film **I watched last night** *was very good.*

   But when *who* or *that* is the subject of a relative clause it must be included.
   I like people **who are kind and considerate**.
   I want a computer **that's easy to use**.

4   *Which* can be used to refer to the whole previous sentence or idea.
   I passed my driving test on the first attempt, **which was a surprise**.
   Jane can't come to the party, **which is a shame**.

5   We use *whose* to refer to someone's possessions.
   That's the man **whose wife won the lottery**.
   That's the woman **whose dog ran away**.

6   We can use *where* to refer to places.
   The hotel **where we stayed** *was right on the beach.*
   We went back to the place **where we first met**.

6.4 Participles

Participles after a noun define and identify in the same way as relative clauses.
That woman **driving** *the red Porsche is my aunt.*
The men **seen** *outside were probably the thieves.*

UNIT 7

7.1 THE PRESENT PERFECT

1   The same form (*have* + past participle) exists in many European languages, but the uses in English are different. In English, the Present Perfect links past and present. It expresses the effect of the past on the present.

2   Present Perfect means 'completed before now'. The Present Perfect does not express when an action happened. If we say the exact time, we use the Past Simple.
   In my life, I **have travelled** *to all seven continents.*
   I **travelled** *around Africa in 1998.*

7.2 Present Perfect

Form

has/have + past participle
I've lived in Rome.
She's lived in London.
He hasn't lived here long.
They haven't bought their flat.
How long have they known Peter?
How long has she been married?

Short answer

Have you always lived in Budapest?   **Yes**, I **have**./**No**, I **haven't**.

Use

There are three main uses of the Present Perfect.

1 Unfinished past

The Present Perfect expresses an action that began in the past and still continues.

We've lived in the same house for 25 years.
How long have you known each other?
They've been married for 20 years.

❶ Be careful! Many languages express this idea with a present tense, but in English this is wrong.

Jan has been a nurse for ten years. NOT ~~Jan is a nurse for ten years.~~

Time expressions

Notice the time expressions that are common with this use.

for	two years a month a few minutes half an hour ages	since	1970 August 8.00 I was a child Christmas

We use *for* with a period of time and *since* with a point in time.

2 Experience

The Present Perfect expresses an experience that happened at some time in one's life. The action is finished, but the effects of the action are still felt.

I've been to the United States. (I still remember.)
Have you ever had an operation? (at any time in your life)
How many times has he *been married*? (in his life)

Exactly *when* the action happened is not important. Questions and answers about definite times are expressed in the Past Simple.

When did you go to the United States?
I broke my leg once.

Time expressions

The adverbs *ever*, *never*, and *before* are common with this use.

Have you ever been to Australia?
I've never tried bungee jumping.
I haven't tried sushi before.

3 Present result

The Present Perfect expresses a past action that has a present result. The action is usually in the recent past.

The taxi hasn't arrived yet. (We're still waiting for it.)
What have you done to your lip? (It's bleeding.)

We often announce news in the Present Perfect.

Have you heard? The Prime Minister has resigned.
Susan's had her baby!

Details will be in the Past Simple.

She resigned because she lost a vote of no confidence.
It's a boy. He weighed 3.5kg.

Time expressions

The adverbs *yet*, *already*, and *just* are common with this use.

I haven't done my homework yet. (negative)
Has the postman been yet? (question)
I've already done my homework.
She's just had some good news.

❶ Be careful with *been* and *gone*.

He's been to the United States. (experience – he isn't there now)
She's gone to the United States. (present result – she's there now)

7.3 Present Perfect or Past Simple?

1 The Present Perfect can express unfinished actions. The Past Simple expresses completed actions.

Present Perfect	Past Simple
I've lived in Texas for six years. (I still live there.)	*I lived in Texas for six years.* (Now I live somewhere else.)
I've written several books. (I can still write some more.)	*Shakespeare wrote 30 plays.* (He can't write any more.)

2 The Present Perfect refers to indefinite time. The Past Simple refers to definite time. Notice the time expressions used with the two tenses.

Present Perfect – indefinite		Past Simple – definite	
I've done it	for a long time. since July. before. recently.	I did it	yesterday. last week. two days ago. at eight o'clock. in 1987. when I was young. for a long time.

I've already done it.
I haven't done it yet.

❶ Be careful with *this morning/afternoon*, etc.

Have you seen Amy this morning? (It's still morning.)
Did you see Amy this morning? (It's the afternoon or evening.)

7.4 Present Perfect Simple passive

Form

has/have been + past participle

It They	has been have been	sold.

Use

The uses are the same in the passive as in the active.

Two million cars have been produced so far this year. (unfinished past)
Has she ever been made redundant? (past experience)
'Have you heard? Two hundred homes have been washed away by a tidal wave!' (present importance)

7.5 Present Perfect Continuous

Form

has/have + been + -ing

She's been studying for three years.
They haven't been working here long.
How long have they been living there?

Use

The Present Perfect Continuous expresses:

1 an activity that began in the past and is continuing now.

I've been studying English for three years.
How long have you been working here?

Sometimes there is no difference between the simple and the continuous.

I've played the piano since I was a boy.
I've been playing the piano since I was a boy.

The continuous can express a temporary activity, while the simple expresses a permanent state.

I've been living in this house for the past few months. (temporary)
I've lived here all my life. (permanent)

❶ Remember: State verbs are rarely used in the continuous (see 2.4 p134).

I've had this book for ages.
I've always loved sunny days.

2 a past activity that has caused a present result.
I've been working all day. (I'm tired now.)
Have you been crying? (Your eyes are red.)
Roger's been cutting the grass. (I can smell it.)

The past activity might be finished or it might not. The context usually makes this clear.
Look out of the window! It's been snowing!
(It has stopped snowing now.)
I've been writing this book for two years. (It still isn't finished.)
I'm covered in paint because I've been decorating the bathroom.
(It might be finished or it might not. We don't know.)

7.6 Present Perfect Simple or Continuous?

1 The simple expresses a completed action.
I've painted the kitchen, and now I'm doing the bathroom.
The continuous expresses an activity over a period of time.
I've got paint in my hair because I've been decorating.

We use the simple if the sentence has a number or quantity, because the simple expresses completion. The continuous isn't possible.
I've been reading all day. I've read ten chapters.
She's been eating ever since she arrived. She's eaten ten biscuits already.

2 Some verbs have the idea of a long time, for example, *wait, work, play, try, learn, rain.* These verbs are often found in the continuous.
I've cut my finger. (One short action.)
I've been cutting firewood. (Perhaps over several hours.)

Some verbs don't have the idea of a long time, for example, *find, start, buy, die, lose, break, stop.* These verbs are more usually found in the simple.
I've lost my passport.
Have you started your Christmas shopping yet?

UNIT 8

Verb patterns

The infinitive

1 The infinitive is used after some verbs.
We've decided to move abroad.
I want to go home.
I'm trying to phone Pete.
She'd love to meet you.

2 Some verbs are followed by a person + the infinitive.
They asked me to help them.
I want you to try harder.
He told me to apply for the job.

3 *Make* and *let* are followed by a person + the infinitive without *to.*
She'll make you feel welcome.
I'll let you know when I'm coming.

4 The infinitive is used after some adjectives.
It's impossible to save money.
It's great to see you.
Pleased to meet you.
It was good to hear your news.

The -ing form

1 The -ing form is used after some verbs.
I enjoy reading history books.
He's finished washing the car.
I don't mind helping you.
We like walking.
He goes fishing at weekends.

2 Some verbs are followed by an object + -ing.
I hate people telling me what to do.
You can't stop me doing what I want.
I can hear someone calling.

3 The -ing form is used after prepositions.
I'm good at finding things.
He's afraid of being mugged.
We're thinking of going to Sweden.
I'm looking forward to meeting you.

►► Verb patterns p158

UNIT 9

9.1 CONDITIONALS

There are many different ways of making sentences with *if.* It is important to understand the difference between sentences that express:

possible conditions = first conditional
improbable conditions = second conditional
impossible conditions = third conditional
no condition = zero conditional

Possible conditions
If I see Dave, I'll tell him to call you.
This is a sentence about reality.
If I see Dave … = a real possibility
… I'll tell him to call you. = the result of a possible situation

Improbable conditions
If I had the money, I'd buy a Mercedes.
This is a sentence which is contrary to reality.
If I had the money … = not impossible. The reality is I don't have the money.
… I'd buy a Mercedes. = the result of an improbable situation

Impossible conditions
If I'd known you were coming, I'd have cooked you a meal.
This is a sentence about an impossible situation. It didn't happen, and now it's too late to change the result.
If I had known … = impossible, because I didn't know.
I'd have cooked … = the result of an impossible situation.

No conditions
If I get a headache, I take an aspirin.
If metal is heated, it expands.
These are sentences that are always true. They refer to 'all time', and are called zero conditionals. *If* means *when* or *whenever.*

9.2 Second conditional: improbable conditions

Form
if + Past Simple, *would* + verb
Positive
If I won some money, I'd go around the world.
My father would kill me if he could see me now.

Negative
I'd give up my job if I didn't like it.
If I saw a ghost, I wouldn't talk to it.

Question
What would you do if you saw someone shoplifting?
If you needed help, who would you ask?

! *Was* can change to *were* in the condition clause.

If I If he	were rich,	I he	wouldn't have to work.

Other modal verbs are possible in the result clause.
*I **could** buy some new clothes if I had some money.*
*If I saved a little every week, I **might** be able to buy a car.*

Use

1 We use the second conditional to express an unreal situation and its probable result. The situation or condition is improbable, impossible, imaginary, or contrary to known facts.
*If I **were** the president of my country, I'**d increase** taxes.* (But it's not very likely that I will ever be the president.)
*If my mother **was** still alive, she'**d be** very proud.* (But she's dead.)
*If Ted **needed** money, I'**d lend** it to him.* (But he doesn't need it.)

2 *If I were you, I'd ...* is used to give advice.
*If I **were you, I'd** apologize to her.*
*I'd take it easy for a while if I **were you.***

3 When the condition is understood, it is common to find the result clause on its own.
What would you do if you had lots of money?
*I'd **travel**.*
*I'd give it all **away**.*
*I'd **buy** my mum and dad a nice house. They'**d love** that!*
*You'**d give away** your last penny!*

4 *Would* can express preference.
I'd love a cup of coffee.
*Where **would** you like to sit?*
I'd rather have coffee, please.
I'd rather not tell you, if that's all right.
*What **would** you rather do, stay in or go out?*

5 *Would* can express a request.
***Would** you open the door for me?*
***Would** you mind lending me a hand?*

9.3 First or second conditional?

Both conditionals refer to the present and future. The difference is about probability, not time. It is usually clear which conditional to use. First conditional sentences are real and possible. Second conditional sentences express situations that will probably never happen.
*If I **lose** my job, I'**ll** ...* (My company is doing badly. There is a strong possibility of being made redundant.)
*If I **lost** my job, I'**d** ...* (I probably won't lose my job. I'm just speculating.)
*If there **is** a nuclear war, we'**ll** all ...* (Said by a pessimist.)
*If there **was** a nuclear war, we'**d** ...* (But I don't think it will happen.)

9.4 Third conditional: impossible conditions

Form

***if* + Past Perfect, *would* + *have* + past participle**

Positive

*If I'd (**had**) worked harder, I'd (**would**) have made more money.*
*They'd (**would**) have been here hours ago if they'd (**had**) followed my directions.*

Negative

*If I **hadn't seen** it with my own eyes, I **wouldn't have believed** it.*
*If you'd **listened** to me, you **wouldn't have got** lost.*

Question

*What **would** you **have done** if you'd **been** me?*
*If the hotel **had been** full, where **would** you **have stayed**?*

Use

We use the third conditional to express an impossible situation in the past and its probable result. It is too late! These things didn't happen.
*If she'd known he was cruel, **she wouldn't have** married him.*
*My parents **wouldn't have met if they hadn't** studied at Oxford University.*

9.5 might / could have done

Use

Might have done and *could have done* express possibilities in the past that didn't happen.
*Thank goodness you went to hospital. You **might have died**.*
*She **could have married** anyone she wanted.*

They are found in the result clauses of third conditional sentences.
*If I'd told him I had no money, he **might have given** me some.*
*If I'd really wanted, I **could have been** a professional footballer.*

Might have done and *could have done* can express criticism.
*You **might have told** me it was her birthday!*
*She **could have helped** tidy the flat instead of going out!*

9.6 should have done

Use

Should have done expresses advice for a past situation, but the advice is too late!
*You **should have apologized**. He wouldn't have been so angry.*
*You **shouldn't have said** she looked old. She really didn't like it.*

Should have done can express criticism.
*You **should have asked** me before you borrowed my car.*

UNIT 10

10.1 NOUN PHRASES

A noun phrase is a group of words before and/or after a noun.

book = **noun**
a book
my book
this book
some books
the book that I was reading
my favourite cook book
} = **noun phrases**

Grammatically speaking, these words are:
articles – *the, a/an*
possessives – *my, your, his, her ...*
demonstratives – *this, that, these, those*
determiners – *some, any, all, each, every ...*
relative pronouns – *who, that, which ...*
compound nouns – *notebook, address book ...*

10.2 Articles

Indefinite articles

The indefinite articles *a/an* are used:

1 to say what something or somebody is.
*This is **a** book.*
*Jane's **a** teacher.*
*I'm **an** optimist.*
*He's **an** idiot.*

2 to refer to a thing or a person for the first time.
*She lives in **a** farmhouse.*
*He's going out with **a** model.*
*I bought **a** pair of shoes today.*

3 to refer to a thing or a person when it doesn't matter which one.
   *Can you lend me **a** pen?*
   *Shall we go for **a** drink?*

Definite article

The definite article *the* is used:

1 to refer to a person or a thing known to the speaker and the listener.
   *Have you got **the** car keys?*
   *The children are in **the** garden.*

2 to refer to a person or a thing for the second time.
   *I got **a** book and **a** computer for Christmas. **The** book is about the British Empire. I haven't unpacked **the** computer yet.*

3 when it is clear which one(s) we mean.
   *I'm going to **the** shops. Do you want anything?*
   *Dave's in **the** kitchen.*
   *Did you enjoy **the** party?*
   *What's **the** score?*
   *Have you heard **the** news?*
   *We went to **the** same school.*
   *I'll meet you on **the** corner.*

4 to refer to the only one there is.
   The sky is very grey today.
   The earth is older that we think.
   The government in this country is rubbish.
   The French like all things French.

5 to refer to things in our physical environment that we all know.
   *I love walking in **the** country.*
   *People always talk about **the** weather.*
   *We can see **the** sea from our house.*
   *We're going to **the** cinema tonight.*

6 with superlatives.
   *You're **the** best teacher.*
   *He was **the** first boy I kissed.*

7 with some place names.
   the *United States of America*
   the *Eiffel Tower*
   the *Pyramids*
   the *British Museum*
   the *Empire State Building*

Zero article

No article (–) is used:

1 to refer to things or people in general.
   I like (–) cheese.
   (–) Doctors earn more than (–) teachers.
   I'm afraid of (–) dogs.
   (–) English is spoken all over the world.
   (–) Life is hard.

2 in some common expressions.
   places
   He's at (–) work. She's at (–) home in (–) bed.
   He's at (–) school. She's at (–) university.
   travel
   I travel by (–) car/bus/train ...
   meals
   We had (–) lunch at 12.00.
   What do you want for (–) dinner?
   time
   I'll do it (–) next week.
   I saw her (–) last year.
   academic subjects
   I'm no good at (–) maths.
   games
   I like (–) chess.

3 in some place names.
   I've travelled a lot in (–) Europe and (–) South America.
   I live in (–) Station Road.
   She studied at (–) Oxford University.
   We walked in (–) Hyde Park.
   We had lunch in (–) Carluccio's Restaurant.
   The plane left from (–) Heathrow Airport.
   I'll meet you at (–) St Pancras Station.
   I climbed (–) Mount Everest.

10.3 Possessives

Possessive adjectives and pronouns

1 Possessive adjectives are used with a noun.
   *This is **my** brother.*
   *You must come and see **our** new house.*
   ***Their** teacher is new.*

2 The possessive pronouns are:

mine	yours	his	hers	ours	theirs

They are used on their own.
   *Don't touch that! It's **mine**.*
   *Take it. It's **yours**.*
   *Can you bring those books? They're **ours**.*

Apostrophe *'s* and *s'*

1 *'s* is used with singular nouns.
   *Lorna**'s** dog*
   *Harry**'s** girl-friend*
   *the boy**'s** father (= one boy)*
   *'Whose is this?'   'It's my brother**'s**.'*
   *I've got a week**'s** holiday.*

2 *s'* is used with regular plural nouns.
   *my parents**'** house*
   *the boys**'** father (= more than one boy)*
   For irregular plurals we use *'s*.
   *the children**'s** room*
   Notice we use *'s* with two people.
   *We were at Alan and Carol**'s** house last night.*

3 *'s* is used with some places.
   *I bought it at the chemist**'s**.*
   *I'm going to the hairdresser**'s**.*
   *You can buy stamps at a newsagent**'s**.*

10.4 *all* and *every*

all

All can be used in different ways:

1 *all* + noun
   ***All** men are born equal.*
   *I like **all** kinds of music.*
   *I invited **all** the students in my class.*
   *I've loved the Beatles **all** my life.*

2 *all* + *of* + noun
   *I invited **all of** the students in my class.*
   *'How much did you eat?'   '**All of** it.'*
   *'Who did she invite?'   '**All of** us.'*

3 *all* + adjective/adverb/preposition
   *I'm **all** wet.*
   *She lives **all** alone.*
   *Tell me **all about** your holiday.*

4 pronoun + *all*
*The sweets are for everyone. Don't eat **them all**.*
*She loves **us all**.*

5 *all* + verb
*We **all support** Manchester United.*
*They have **all been** to university.*
*My friends **all love** you.*

every

Every is used with a singular noun.
***Every student** in the class passed the exam.*
*I've been to **every country** in Europe.*

all and every

1 *All* is not usually used to mean everybody/everything.
   ***All** the people came to the party.*   NOT   ~~*All came ...*~~
   ***Everybody** came to the party.*
   *She lost **all** her possessions in the fire.*   NOT   ~~*She lost all in ...*~~
   *She lost **everything** in the fire.*

2 *All* can mean everything, but only in relative clauses.
   ***All** I want for Christmas is you.*
   *That's **all** I need.*
   *I've told you **all** I know.*
   *Love is **all** you need.*

10.5 *themselves* and *each other*

Reflexive pronouns

1 Reflexive pronouns are:

myself	yourself	himself	herself
itself	ourselves	yourselves	themselves

2 We use reflexive pronouns when the subject and object are the same.
   *I cut **myself** shaving.*
   *You could kill **yourself**.*
   *I'm going to buy **myself** something nice.*
   *Make **yourselves** at home.*
   *I hope you're enjoying **yourself**.*

3 They are used after prepositions.
   *You should be ashamed **of yourself**.*
   *She looked **at herself** in the mirror.*
   *I live **by myself**.*
   *Selfish people only think **of themselves**.*
   *I can look **after myself**.*

4 We use reflexive pronouns for emphasis.
   *Do you like the cake? I made it **myself**.*
   *My daughter can dress **herself** now.*
   *The manager **himself** interviewed me.*

each other

Each other expresses the idea of one to another.
*They looked at **each other**.*
*We send **each other** birthday cards.*
*They hate **each other**.*
*We've known **each other** since childhood.*

UNIT 11

MODAL VERBS OF PROBABILITY

Modal auxiliary verbs can express ability, obligation, permission, and request. They can also express probability, or how certain a situation is. There is an introduction to modal auxiliary verbs on p137.

11.1 Probability in the present and future

1 *Must* and *can't* express the logical conclusion of a situation.
   must = logically probable
   can't = logically improbable
   We don't have all the facts, so we are not absolutely sure, but we are pretty certain.
   *He **must** be exhausted. He hasn't slept for 24 hours!*
   *Sue **can't** have a ten-year-old daughter! She's only 24!*
   *He's in great shape, even though he **must** be at least 60!*
   *A walk in this weather! You **must** be joking!*
   *Aren't they answering? They **must** be in bed. They **can't** be out this late!*

2 *May/might/could* express probability in the present or future.
   May/might + not is the negative. *Couldn't* is rare in this use.
   *He **might** be lost.*
   *They **may** be stuck in traffic.*
   *You **could** win the lottery this week. Who knows?*
   *Dave and Beth aren't at home. They **could** be at the concert, I suppose.*
   *We **may** go to Greece for our holiday. We haven't decided yet.*
   *Take your umbrella. It **might** rain later.*
   *I **might not** be able to come tonight. I **might** have to work late.*
   *They **may not** know where we are.*

3 The continuous infinitive is formed with *be* + *-ing*.
   *You **must be joking**!*
   *They **can't** still **be eating**!*
   *Peter **might be working** late.*
   *They **may be coming** on a later train.*
   *I **could be sitting** on a beach right now.*

11.2 Asking about possibilities

Question forms with modal verbs of probability are unusual. To ask about possibility/probability we usually use *Do you think ...?*
'***Do you think** she's married?*'
'*She can't be.*'

'*Where **do you think** he's from?*'
'*He might be Portuguese.*'

'***Do you think** they've arrived yet?*'
'*They may have. Or they might have got stuck in the traffic.*'

11.3 Probability in the past

1 The perfect infinitive is formed with *have* + past participle.
   *He **must have caught** a later train.*
   *They **might have lost** our phone number.*

2 These forms express degrees of probability in the past.
   *He **must have been** exhausted.*
   *She **can't have told** him about us yet.*
   *The letter **may have got lost** in the post.*
   *He **might have changed** his mind.*
   *They **could have moved** house.*

3 The continuous infinitive is formed with *have* + *been* + *-ing*.
   *She must **have been joking**.*
   *They can't **have been trying** very hard.*
   *He could **have been lying** to you.*

UNIT 12

 12.1 Reported speech and thought

1 It is usual for the verb in the reported clause to move 'one tense back' if the reporting verb is in the past tense (e.g. *said, told*).

Present → Past
Present Perfect → Past Perfect
Past → Past Perfect
will → *would*

'I**'m going**.'   *He said he **was going**.*
'She**'s passed** her test.'   *He told me she **had passed** her test.*
'My father **died** when I was six.'   *She said her father **had died** when she was six.*
'I'll **see** you later.'   *She **said she'd** see me later.*

The verb also moves 'one tense back' when we are reporting thoughts and feelings.

*I thought she **was** married, but she isn't.*
*I didn't know he **was** a teacher. I thought he **worked** in a bank.*
*I forgot you **were coming**. Never mind. Come in.*
*I didn't realize you **were** here.*
*I hoped you **would** call.*

2 There is no tense change if …

… the reporting verb is in the present tense (*says*).
'The train **will be** late.'   *He says the train **will be** late.*
'I **come** from Spain.'   *She says she **comes** from Spain.*

… the reported speech is about something that is still true.
'Rain forests **are being destroyed**.'
*She told him that rain forests **are being destroyed**.*
'I **hate** football.'
*I told him I **hate** football.*

3 Some modal verbs change.

can → *could*
will → *would*
may → *might*

'She **can** type well.'   *He told me she **could** type well.*
'I**'ll** help you.'   *She said she'd help me.*
'I **may** come.'   *She said she **might** come.*

Other modal verbs don't change.
'You **should** go to bed.'   *He told me I **should** go to bed.*
'It **might** rain.'   *She said she thought it **might** rain.*

Must stays as *must*, or changes to *had to*.
'I **must** go!'   *He said he **must/had to** go.*

 12.2 Reporting verbs

1 We rarely use *say* with an indirect object.
She said she was going.   NOT   ~~*She said to me …*~~

2 *Tell* is always used with an indirect object in reported speech.

She told	me the doctor us her husband	the news.

3 We can use *that* after *say* and *tell*.
*He told her (**that**) he would be home late.*
*She said (**that**) sales were down from last year.*

4 Many verbs are more descriptive than *say* and *tell*, for example:

explain	promise	invite	insist	admit
complain	warn	offer	refuse	

Sometimes we report the idea, rather than the actual words.
'I'll lend you some money.'   *He offered to lend me some money.*
'I won't help you.'   *She refused to help me.*

5 There are different verb patterns.
verb + *sb* + infinitive
*He **told me to go** away.*
*They **asked me to teach** them English.*
*I **invited her to come**.*
*We **encouraged him to apply** for the job.*
*She **reminded me to post** her letter.*

verb + infinitive
*She **promised to help**.*
*They **offered to lend** me some money.*

verb + *that* + clause
*He **explained that** he would be home late.*
*She **complained that** she never had any free time.*
*They **admitted that** sales were down that year.*
*I **agreed that** it would be best to stop trying.*

6 We use *tell* for reported statements and reported commands, but the form is different.

Reported statements
*He **told** me **that** he was going.*
*She **told** them **what** had been happening.*

Reported commands
*He **told** me **to** keep still.*
*The police **told** people **to** move on.*

7 We use *ask* for reported commands and reported questions, but the form is different.

Reported commands
*He **asked** me **to** open my suitcase.*
*She **asked** me **to** leave.*

Reported questions
*He **asked** me **what** I did for a living.*
*She **asked** me **why** I had come.*

8 For negative commands, use *not* before *to*.
*He told me **not to** tell anyone.*
*The police warned people **not to** go out.*

12.3 Reported questions

1 The word order in questions is different in reported speech. There is no inversion of subject and auxiliary verb and there is no *do/does/did*.
'Why have you come here?'   *I asked her **why she had come** here.*
'What time is it?'   *He wants to know **what time it is**.*
'Where do you live?'   *She asked me **where I lived**.*

2 If there is no question word (*What, Who, Why, Where, …*), use *if* or *whether*.

| She wants to know | if whether | she should wear a dress. |

3 The rules are the same when we report questions that are thoughts.
I didn't know what was happening.
I wondered where she'd bought her dress.
We couldn't understand what they were saying.

Extra class materials

UNIT 1 *p13*

EVERYDAY ENGLISH
Roleplay

4 Work with a partner. Act out the situations.

1 You are with an English friend when you meet another friend. Introduce them to each other.

2 You are in a coffee bar. You asked for a latte and a muffin but the waiter has brought you an espresso and a piece of chocolate cake.

3 You are in a hotel. You ring reception because the television in your room isn't working.

4 You are at the airport and you can't find the check-in desk for your flight to Prague. Ask at the information desk.

5 You are cooking for some friends. They're all having a drink and chatting. You want them to come to the table and help themselves to the food.

 T 1.12 Listen and compare.

UNIT 2 *p17*

4 Work in small groups. Look at the chart. Compare the correct answers with your ideas.

Which salaries do you think are unfair? Are any surprising?

Who earns how much in Britain?	
Doctor	£105,000
Footballer	£1 million
Senior Director	£750,000
Nurse	£12,500
Supermarket cashier	£11,000
Pilot	£65,000
Police Officer	£22,500
Teacher	£32,000
Lawyer	£120,000
Farmer	£36,000

READING – A Shakespearean tragedy

5 Read Shakespeare's lines from *Romeo and Juliet* in more modern English.

Romeo *and* Juliet

1   Tybalt Peace? I hate the word peace like I hate hell, all Montagues, and you.

2   Romeo Did my heart ever love before now? Because I never saw true beauty before tonight.

    Juliet The only man I love is the son of the only man I hate!

3   Juliet Oh, Romeo, Romeo, why are you a Montague? Forget your father and give up your name. … What's a Montague anyway? … A rose would smell just as sweet if it was called any other name.

4   Romeo I have fallen in love with the beautiful daughter of rich Capulet.

    Friar Laurence This marriage may be lucky enough to turn the hatred between your families into pure love.

5   Romeo Now, Tybalt, … Mercutio's soul is above our heads. Either you, or I, or both of us have to join him.

    Tybalt You, wretched boy, are going with him now.

6   Nurse I'll find Romeo to comfort you.

    Juliet Oh, find him! … And tell him to come and say his last goodbye.

7   Juliet Oh, do you think we'll ever meet again?

    Romeo I have no doubt. All these troubles will give us stories to tell in our future life together.

8   Friar Laurence Take this small bottle and drink the liquid. No pulse or breath will show you are alive for forty-two hours.

    Juliet Give it to me! Love will give me strength.

9   Juliet Romeo, Romeo, Romeo! Here's a drink. I drink to you.

    Nurse Oh hateful day! There has never been so black a day as today. Oh painful day!

10   Romeo Eyes, look for the last time! Arms, make your last embrace! … Here's to my love! Oh, honest pharmacist! Your drugs work quickly. So I die with a kiss.

11   Juliet What's this here? A cup, closed in my true love's hand? Poison, I see … I will kiss your lips. Some poison is still on your lips. Your lips are warm. Oh happy dagger! Let me die!

12   Prince There never was a more tragic story than the story of Juliet and her Romeo.

MODERN DILEMMAS

Readers ask, readers reply

2 Read the readers' questions and the full replies.

1 A reader asks

How should I deal with my difficult and disagreeable neighbour? He is in the habit of dumping his garden waste along the public footpath between our two houses.

Jim T. via email

(d) A reader replies

You've got to act with self-control in a situation like this. I don't think you should confront him. Rows between neighbours can get out of hand. If I were you I'd quietly clean up his mess and keep the peace.

2 A reader asks

Is it OK to greet people with a "how are you?"? In California (my home) it's considered friendly, but in London some people react with a cold look. Should I be less friendly in my greetings?

Erica Fleckberg, London

(c) A reader replies

You don't have to be like the English just because you're in England. Be yourself. Be warm. Be American.

3 A reader asks

My new PC automatically picks up wireless networks to gain access to the Internet. This includes the one belonging to my neighbour. Is it right for me to use it?

Richard Dalton, via email

(g) A reader replies

You can stop others accessing your wireless network if you use a password. You must tell your neighbour this. It's the only fair thing to do.

4 A reader asks

My stepfather was disqualified for two years for drink-driving, but we have learnt that he still drives while under the influence of alcohol. Should we keep quiet or inform the police?

Stella Milne, Newcastle

(a) A reader replies

Your stepfather is not allowed to drive by law. He is a danger to himself and everyone else on the road. You must ring 'Crimestoppers' and report him. You don't have to give your name.

5 A reader asks

I am a medical student. After I qualify in June, I have one month before my first house job starts. My fiancée says I am not allowed to claim unemployment benefit for this. I disagree, because I'll be unemployed. The dole is for all those who are out of work. What do you think?

J. R. Collin, via e-mail

(b) A reader replies

Your fiancée's right. You aren't allowed to claim unemployment benefit but I think you are allowed other benefits. You should check online. Perhaps you should claim it and give the money to charity, if you don't need it.

6 A reader asks

Is it wrong for me to record CDs borrowed from my local library? I am not denying anyone the money, as I wouldn't buy the CD anyway.

Pete Rodriguez, via e-mail

(e) A reader replies

It's not only wrong it's illegal. You are not allowed to do this. You should buy the CD.

7 A reader asks

Is it ever permissible to lie to children? I lied to my two-year-old granddaughter to remove her from a fairground ride without a tantrum. I said: 'You must get off now because the man is going for his dinner.' She got down without any fuss. But I'm worried, if she remembers this, she won't trust me in future.

Barbara Hope, Perth Australia

(f) A reader replies

Not only should you lie sometimes, you often have to. Children should be treated with respect but you don't have to explain everything. Also, it's a good way to learn that we often have to tell 'white lies', such as when asked 'What do you think of my new boyfriend?' 'Er- very nice.'

LISTENING AND SPEAKING
Rules for life

4 Work with a partner. Read the song and discuss which word fits best in each of the gaps.

I Believe
by Ian Dury & the Blockheads

I believe in _____ _____
And beauty from within
I believe in saying _____
And fresh _____ on the skin

bottle banks / Barclays Bank

hello / thanks

hair / air

I believe in healthy _____
As tonic for the feet
I believe in serious talks
And _____ _____ to eat

walks / thoughts

just enough / a lot

Chorus
That's what I believe
Surprising as it seems
I believe that happiness
Is well within our dreams

I believe in being _____
In spite of what you think
I believe in good _____
And not too much to _____

nice / polite

manners / advice
eat / drink

I believe in being _____
In everything you try to _____
I believe in me and you
I hope you share my _____

faithful / true
do / say

point of view / opinion

Chorus

I believe in being _____
Especially when it's hard
I believe an open _____
Can show a fine regard

generous / kind

mind / door

I believe that _____ make
A person good to know
I believe in birthday _____
And going _____

manners / kindness

presents / cake
in the snow / with the flow

Chorus

That's what I believe
Although it seems naïve
I believe that _____
Are there to be achieved
That's what I believe . . .

happiness / peace and love

T 4.6 Listen and check.

WRITING – Telling a story

7 Compare your stories with the story below.

THE TROJAN HORSE

The Greeks and the Trojans had been at war for ten years.

The exhausted Greek army was camped outside the city of Troy, when the Greek king Odysseus suddenly had a good idea. He knew that horses were sacred animals to the Trojans, so he decided to build a huge, hollow wooden horse on wheels. A horse big enough for some of his soldiers to hide inside.

The horse was duly built and some of the soldiers climbed inside. The others set fire to the camp and pretended they were going to sail back home to Greece, defeated. In fact they hid nearby.

The Trojans, delighted that the Greeks had left, immediately came out of the city gates and found the horse. They were very curious indeed. As part of the plan, the Greeks had left behind one soldier hiding near the horse. The Trojans soon found him and asked him about the horse. He said it was an offering to the goddess Athena.

EVERYDAY ENGLISH – Objects

4 **T 10.9** Listen again. Which objects are being described?

1 ___ 2 ___ 3 ___ 4 ___ 5 ___ 6 ___ 7 ___ 8 ___ 9 ___

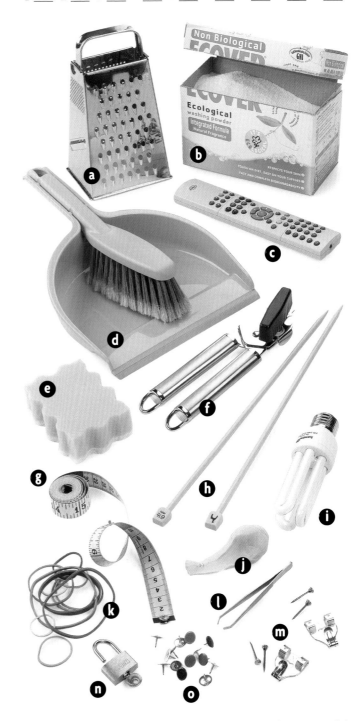

The Trojans tried to pull the huge horse into the city. However, it was so big that they had to tear down part of the city wall to get it in. They took it to the temple of Athena, and had a big party to celebrate victory over the Greeks and the end of the war.

Finally, everyone was exhausted from all the festivities and they fell asleep. Now the Greek soldiers crept out of the horse. They killed all the guards on the walls and then signalled to the Greeks on the other side to attack Troy.

There was a bloody battle and the Greeks won easily. All the Trojan men were killed, and the women and children were taken back to Greece as slaves.

6 Work with a partner. Take it in turns to describe some of the other objects. Point to what your partner describes.

They're made of metal. They're small. You use them to ...

Word list

Here is a list of most of the new words in the units of *New Headway Intermediate, Fourth edition* Student's Book.

adj = adjective
adv = adverb
conj = conjunction
coll = colloquial
n = noun
opp = opposite
pl = plural
prep = preposition
pron = pronoun
pp = past participle
v = verb
US = American English

UNIT 1

alleyway *n* /'æliweɪ/
archaeology *n* /ˌɑːkiˈɒlədʒi/
area *n* /'eəriə/
background *n* /'bækɡraʊnd/
barrel *n* /'bærəl/
Basque *adj* /bæsk/
beat *v* /biːt/
bilingual *adj* /ˌbaɪˈlɪŋɡwəl/
block *n* /blɒk/
brief *v* /briːf/
bright *adj* /braɪt/
cancellation *n* /ˌkænsəˈleɪʃn/
cherish *v* /'tʃerɪʃ/
client *n* /'klaɪənt/
close-knit *adj* /ˌkləʊsˈnɪt/
communal *adj* /'kɒmjənl/
community *n* /kəˈmjuːnəti/
cosmopolitan *adj* /ˌkɒzməˈpɒlɪtən/
cracked *adj* /krækt/
culture *n* /'kʌltʃə(r)/
daylight *n* /'deɪlaɪt/
demolition *n* /ˌdeməˈlɪʃn/
destroy *v* /dɪˈstrɔɪ/
dressmaker *n* /'dresmeɪkə(r)/
earthquake *n* /'ɜːθkweɪk/
elderly *adj* /'eldəli/
end up *v* /ˌend ˈʌp/
equator *n* /ɪˈkweɪtə(r)/
extended family *n* /ɪkˌstendɪd ˈfæməli/
extinct *adj* /ɪkˈstɪŋkt/
fee *n* /fiː/
filling *n* /'fɪlɪŋ/
for good /fə ˈɡʊd/
forbid *v* /fəˈbɪd/
frail *adj* /freɪl/
frugally *adv* /'fruːɡəli/
global warming *n* /ˌɡləʊbl ˈwɔːmɪŋ/
(not) go far /ˌɡəʊ ˈfɑː(r)/
go live *v* /ˌɡəʊ ˈlaɪv/
go on about *v* /ɡəʊ ˈɒn əbaʊt/
a great deal /ə ˌɡreɪt ˈdiːl/
headquarters *n* /ˌhedˈkwɔːtəz/
heritage *n* /'herɪtɪdʒ/
hold *v* /həʊld/
hopefully *adv* /'həʊpfʊli/
hospitality *n* /ˌhɒspɪˈtæləti/
iceberg *n* /'aɪsbɜːɡ/
immediate family *n* /ɪˌmiːdiət ˈfæməli/
kit *n* /kɪt/
life expectancy *v n* /'laɪf ɪkˌspektənsi/
make *v* /meɪk/
means *n* /miːnz/
motto *n* /'mɒtəʊ/

muffin *n* /'mʌfɪn/
municipal *adj* /mjuːˈnɪsɪpl/
neutral *adj* /'njuːtrəl/
nonsense *n* /'nɒnsəns/
noticeable *adj* /'nəʊtɪsəbl/
on the clock *n* /ˌɒn ðə ˈklɒk/
operator *n* /'ɒpəreɪtə(r)/
performance *n* /pəˈfɔːməns/
pin number *n* /'pɪn ˌnʌmbə(r)/
policy *n* /'pɒləsi/
preschool *n* /'priːskuːl/
prestigious *adj* /prɪˈstɪdʒəs/
presumably *adv* /prɪˈzjuːməbli/
profile *n* /'prəʊfaɪl/
propaganda *n* /ˌprɒpəˈɡændə/
provide *v* /prəˈvaɪd/
pyjamas *n* /pəˈdʒɑːməz/
raise *v* /reɪz/
reach *v* /riːtʃ/
regret *n* /rɪˈɡret/
research *n* /rɪˈsɜːtʃ/
rubbish *n* /'rʌbɪʃ/
settle down *v* /ˌsetl ˈdaʊn/
shortly *adv* /'ʃɔːtli/
similarity *n* /ˌsɪməˈlærəti/
slum *n* /slʌm/
storey *n* /'stɔːri/
stressed *adj* /strest/
structure *n* /'strʌktʃə(r)/
stuck *adj* /stʌk/
suburb *n* /'sʌbɜːb/
survey *n* /'sɜːveɪ/
take away *v* /ˌteɪk əˈweɪ/
take home *v* /ˌteɪk ˈhəʊm/
tricky *adj* /'trɪki/
ultimately *adv* /'ʌltɪmətli/
urgent *adj* /'ɜːdʒənt/
vote *n/v* /vəʊt/
well-balanced *adj* /ˌwelˈbælənst/
widely *adv* /'waɪdli/

UNIT 2

accomplish *v* /əˈkʌmplɪʃ/
actually *adv* /'æktʃuəli/
amazing *adj* /əˈmeɪzɪŋ/
ambassador *n* /æmˈbæsədə(r)/
annual *adj* /'ænjuəl/
attend *v* /əˈtend/
bake *v* /beɪk/
banking *n* /'bæŋkɪŋ/
bargain *n* /'bɑːɡən/
be in touch /biː ɪn ˈtʌtʃ/
(surf)board *n* /'sɜːfbɔːd/
boarding school *n* /'bɔːdɪŋ ˌskuːl/
boil *v* /bɔɪl/
broadcaster *n* /'brɔːdkɑːstə(r)/
budget *n* /'bʌdʒɪt/

butler *n* /'bʌtlə(r)/
buzz *n* /bʌz/
cash flow *n* /'kæʃ fləʊ/
cashier *n* /kæˈʃɪə(r)/
casserole dish *n* /'kæsərəʊl ˌdɪʃ/
catch up on *phr v* /katʃ ˈʌp ɒn/
challenging *adj* /'tʃæləndʒɪŋ/
charity *n* /'tʃærəti/
charming *adj* /'tʃɑːmɪŋ/
cheque *n* /tʃek/
chop *v* /tʃɒp/
concentrate *v* /'kɒnsəntreɪt/
concerned *adj* /kənˈsɜːnd/
conservative *adj* /kənˈsɜːvətɪv/
convenient *adj* /kənˈviːniənt/
cope *v* /kəʊp/
day off *n* /ˌdeɪ ˈɒf/
decent *adj* /'diːsənt/
deputy *n* /'depjuti/
documentary *n* /ˌdɒkjuˈmentri/
drill *n* /drɪl/
dutiful *adj* /'djuːtɪfl/
duty *n* /'djuːti/
earn a living /ˌɜːn ə ˈlɪvɪŋ/
earner *n* /'ɜːnə(r)/
eccentric *adj* /ɪkˈsentrɪk/
employee *n* /ɪmˈplɔɪiː/
engagement *n* /ɪnˈɡeɪdʒmənt/
enormous *adj* /ɪˈnɔːməs/
expand *v* /ɪkˈspænd/
extensively *adv* /ɪkˈstensɪvli/
extravagantly *adv* /ɪkˈstrævəɡəntli/
ferry *n* /'feri/
fly by *v* /'flaɪ ˌbaɪ/
food processor *n* /ˌfuːd ˈprəʊsesə(r)/
frustration *n* /frʌˈstreɪʃn/
fry *v* /fraɪ/
get away from it all *v* /ˌget əˈweɪ frəm ɪt ɔːl/
goods *pl n* /ɡʊdz/
handyman *n* /'hændimæn/
hardware *n* /'hɑːdweə(r)/
hard-working *adj* /ˌhɑːdˈwɜːkɪŋ/
head of state *n* /ˌhed əv ˈsteɪt/
heir *n* /eə(r)/
helmet *n* /'helmɪt/
herb *n* /hɜːb/
honey *n* /'hʌni/
host *v* /həʊst/
housekeeper *n* /'haʊskiːpə(r)/
huge *adj* /hjuːdʒ/
human resources *n* /ˌhjuːmən rɪˈzɔːsɪz/
hunting *n* /'hʌntɪŋ/
in charge /ɪn ˈtʃɑːdʒ/
in response to /ɪn rɪˈspɒns tʊ/
include *v* /ɪnˈkluːd/
inconvenience *adj* /ˌɪnkənˈviːniəns/

industry *n* /'ɪndəstri/
invoice *n* /'ɪnˌvɔɪs/
involve *v* /ɪnˈvɒlv/
keep fit *v* /ˌkiːp ˈfɪt/
land *v* /lænd/
laptop *n* /'læptɒp/
lavish *adj* /'lævɪʃ/
lifeguard *n* /'laɪfɡɑːd/
lifetime *n* /'laɪftaɪm/
lively *adj* /'laɪvli/
madly *adv* /'mædli/
maid *n* /meɪd/
managing director *n* /ˌmænɪdʒɪŋ dəˈrektə(r)/
manufacture *v* /ˌmænjuˈfæktʃə(r)/
meditate *v* /'medɪteɪt/
memo *n* /'meməʊ/
mild *adj* /maɪld/
minced meat *n* /ˌmɪnst ˈmiːt/
mix *v* /mɪks/
modernize *v* /'mɒdənaɪz/
monarch *n* /'mɒnək/
negotiate *v* /nɪˈɡəʊʃieɪt/
occupy *v* /'ɒkjupaɪ/
organic *adj* /ɔːˈɡænɪk/
payment *n* /'peɪmənt/
peel *v* /piːl/
personnel *n* /ˌpɜːsəˈnel/
plant *v* /plɑːnt/
politician *n* /ˌpɒləˈtɪʃn/
porter *n* /'pɔːtə(r)/
portray *v* /pɔːˈtreɪ/
praise *v* /preɪz/
product *n* /'prɒdʌkt/
promote *v* /prəˈməʊt/
qualification *n* /ˌkwɒlɪfɪˈkeɪʃn/
racket *n* /'rækɪt/
reception *n* /rɪˈsepʃn/
reckon *v* /'rekən/
recruit *v* /rɪˈkruːt/
redecorate *v* /ˌriːˈdekəreɪt/
ridiculous *adj* /rɪˈdɪkjələs/
riverside *n* /'rɪvəsaɪd/
roast *v* /rəʊst/
sales *pl n* /seɪlz/
screwdriver *n* /'skruːdraɪvə(r)/
serve an ace /ˌsɜːv ən ˈeɪs/
service *n* /'sɜːvɪs/
shift *n* /ʃɪft/
shooting *n* /'ʃuːtɪŋ/
situate *v* /'sɪtʃueɪt/
sketch *n* /sketʃ/
small talk *n* /'smɔːl tɔːk/
soap *n* /səʊp/
socializer *n* /'səʊʃəlaɪzə(r)/
squeeze *v* /skwiːz/
state *n* /steɪt/
stiff *adj* /stɪf/
support *n* /səˈpɔːt/
sweat *v* /swet/

sweetheart *n* /'swi:thɑ:t/
tackle *v* /'tækl/
tantrum *n* /'tæntrəm/
tax *n* /tæks/
tell off *v* /tel 'ɒf/
term-time *n* /'tɜ:mtaɪm/
throne *n* /θrəʊn/
torch *n* /tɔ:tʃ/
trade *n* /treɪd/
training *n* /'treɪnɪŋ/
understanding *n* /ˌʌndə'stændɪŋ/
valet *n* /'væleɪ/
VIP *n* /ˌvi: aɪ 'pi:/
weed *v* /wi:d/
weigh *v* /weɪ/
well intentioned *adj* /ˌwel ɪn'tenʃnd/
workforce *n* /'wɜ:kfɔ:s/
zoom *n* /zu:m/

UNIT 3

according to *prep* /ə'kɔ:dɪŋ tə/
alliance *n* /ə'laɪəns/
apothecary *n* /ə'pɒθəkəri/
art dealer *n* /'ɑ:t ˌdi:lə(r)/
asylum *n* /ə'saɪləm/
ban *v* /bæn/
banish *v* /'bænɪʃ/
beg *v* /beg/
beloved *adj* /bɪ'lʌvɪd/
blind *adj* /blaɪnd/
bury *v* /'beri/
cemetery *n* /'semətri/
clumsy *adj* /'klʌmzi/
collection *n* /kə'lekʃn/
comfort *v* /'kʌmfət/
commit *v* /kə'mɪt/
dagger *n* /'dægə(r)/
dawn *n* /dɔ:n/
declare *v* /dɪ'kleə(r)/
decline *v* /dɪ'klaɪn/
depression *n* /dɪ'preʃn/
despite *prep* /dɪ'spaɪt/
dismiss *v* /dɪs'mɪs/
donate *v* /dəʊ'neɪt/
dynasty *n* /'dɪnəsti/
electric *adj* /ɪ'lektrɪk/
embrace *n* /ɪm'breɪs/
enemy *n* /'enəmi/
entire *adj* /ɪn'taɪə(r)/
eternal *adj* /ɪ'tɜ:nl/
exile *v* /'eksaɪl/
explode *v* /ɪk'spləʊd/
fair *adj* /feə(r)/
fair enough *adj* /ˌfeər ɪ'nʌf/
fall in love *v* /ˌfɔ:l ɪn 'lʌv/
fancy *v* /'fænsi/
farewell *n* /feə'wel/
fellow *adj* /'feləʊ/
feud *n* /fju:d/
fiercely *adv* /'fɪəsli/
friar *n* /'fraɪə(r)/
funny *adj* /'fʌni/
genius *n* /'dʒi:niəs/
glad *adj* /glæd/

go out *v* /gəʊ 'aʊt/
go weak at the knees /gəʊ ˌwi:k
  ət ðə 'ni:z/
grief *n* /gri:f/
hateful *adj* /'heɪtfl/
hatred *n* /'heɪtrɪd/
(fall) head over heels /ˌhed əʊvə
  'hi:lz/
heavily *adv* /'hevɪli/
horrible *adj* /'hɒrəbl/
horrified *adj* /'hɒrɪfaɪd/
identify *v* /aɪ'dentɪfaɪ/
insane *adj* /ɪn'seɪn/
lifeless *adj* /'laɪfləs/
liquor *n* /'lɪkə(r)/
madness *n* /'mædnəs/
move *v* /mu:v/
nature *n* /'neɪtʃə(r)/
nightmare *n* /'naɪtmeə(r)/
nobleman *n* /'nəʊblmən/
on the mend /ˌɒn ðə 'mend/
overwhelmed *adj* /ˌəʊvə'welmd/
pay attention /ˌpeɪ ə'tenʃn/
peace *n* /pi:s/
pleasurable *adj* /'pleʒərəbl/
poison *n* /'pɔɪzn/
porcelain *n* /'pɔ:səlɪn/
precious *adj* /'preʃəs/
pretend *v* /prɪ'tend/
priceless *adj* /'praɪsləs/
psychiatrist *n* /saɪ'kaɪətrɪst/
psychology *n* /saɪ'kɒlədʒi/
publish *v* /'pʌblɪʃ/
pulse *n* /pʌls/
quarrel *v* /'kwɒrəl/
rancour *n* /'ræŋkə(r)/
razor blade *n* /'reɪzə ˌbleɪd/
reciprocated *adj* /rɪ'sɪprəkeɪtɪd/
recognize *v* /'rekəgnaɪz/
regrettable *adj* /rɪ'gretəbl/
reject *v* /rɪ'dʒekt/
rescue *v* /'reskju:/
sense of humour *n* /ˌsens əv
  'hju:mə(r)/
a shame /ə 'ʃeɪm/
shiny *adj* /'ʃaɪni/
slip *v* /slɪp/
slow motion *n* /ˌsləʊ 'məʊʃn/
soul *n* /səʊl/
stab *v* /stæb/
stuff *n* /stʌf/
stunned *adj* /stʌnd/
suicide *n* /'su:ɪsaɪd/
swear *v* /sweə(r)/
tension *n* /'tenʃn/
testify *v* /'testɪfaɪ/
tight *adj* /taɪt/
tomb *n* /tu:m/
tragedy *n* /'trædʒədi/
tragic *adj* /'trædʒɪk/
treasure *n* /'treʒə/
unfortunate *adj* /ʌn'fɔ:tʃənət/
uninvited *adj* /ˌʌnɪn'vaɪtɪd/
unite *v* /ju'naɪt/
unrecognized *adj* /ˌʌn'rekəgnaɪzd/
upside down *adj* /ˌʌpsaɪd 'daʊn/
valuable *adj* /'væljuəbl/
vase *n* /vɑ:z/

vial *n* /'vaɪəl/
vineyard *n* /'vɪnjəd/
voluntarily *adv* /ˌvɒlən'teərəli/
warring *adj* /'wɔ:rɪŋ/
wed *v* /wed/
weep *v* /wi:p/
windowsill *n* /'wɪndəʊsɪl/
woe *n* /wəʊ/
wretched *adj* /'retʃɪd/
yoga *n* /'jəʊgə/

UNIT 4

access *n* /'ækses/
accessory *n* /æk'sesəri/
adjust *v* /ə'dʒʌst/
apparently *adv* /ə'pærəntli/
appreciate *v* /ə'pri:ʃieɪt/
bargain *n* /'bɑ:gən/
battered *adj* /'bætəd/
benefit *n* /'benɪfɪt/
borrow *v* /'bɒrəʊ/
bottle bank *n* /'bɒtl ˌbæŋk/
bring up *v* /ˌbrɪŋ 'ʌp/
chore *n* /tʃɔ:(r)/
claim *v* /kleɪm/
code *n* /kəʊd/
confront *v* /kən'frʌnt/
consider *v* /kən'sɪdə(r)/
council house *n* /'kaʊnsl ˌhaʊs/
cuddly *adj* /'kʌdli/
cut off *v* /ˌkʌt 'ɒf/
deal with *v* /'di:l wɪð/
decorate *v* /'dekəreɪt/
demand *n* /dɪ'mɑ:nd/
dig *v* /dɪg/
dilemma *n* /dɪ'lemə/
disagreeable *adj* /ˌdɪsə'gri:əbl/
discipline *n* /'dɪsɪplɪn/
disqualify *v* /dɪs'kwɒlɪfaɪ/
domestic *adj* /də'mestɪk/
drink-driving *n* /ˌdrɪŋk'draɪvɪŋ/
dump *v* /dʌmp/
electronic *adj* /ɪˌlek'trɒnɪk/
enter *v* /'entə(r)/
equipment *n* /ɪ'kwɪpmənt/
era *n* /'ɪərə/
fair *adj* /feə(r)/
fairground ride *n* /'feəgraʊndraɪd/
fiancée *n* /fi'ɒnseɪ/
footpath *n* /'fʊtpɑ:θ/
freeze *v* /fri:z/
fuss *n* /fʌs/
gadget *n* /'gædʒɪt/
gain *v* /geɪn/
get through *v* /ˌget 'θru:/
gift-wrap *v* /'gɪft ˌræp/
give in *v* /ˌgɪv 'ɪn/
go with the flow /ˌgəʊ wɪð ðə
  'fləʊ/
great-grandmother *n*
  /ˌgreɪt'grænmʌðə(r)/
greet *v* /gri:t/
hi-tech *adj* /ˌhaɪ'tek/
in spite of *prep* /ɪn'spaɪt əv/
iron *v* /'aɪən/

keep quiet *v* /ˌki:p 'kwaɪət/
lift *n* /lɪft/
make *n* /meɪk/
match *n* /mætʃ/
medical *adj* /'medɪkl/
menace *n* /'menɪs/
military service *n* /ˌmɪlətri 'sɜ:vɪs/
missionary *n* /'mɪʃənri/
morals *pl n* /'mɒrəlz/
naïve *adj* /naɪ'i:v/
open *adj* /'əʊpən/
optimist *n* /'ɒptɪmɪst/
out of work /ˌaʊt əv 'wɜ:k/
permissible *adj* /pə'mɪsəbl/
pessimist *n* /'pesɪmɪst/
pick up *v* /ˌpɪk 'ʌp/
point of view *n* /ˌpɔɪnt əv 'vju:/
pump *n* /pʌmp/
punk *n* /pʌŋk/
push up *v* /ˌpʊʃ 'ʌp/
put up with *v* /ˌpʊt 'ʌp wɪð/
qualify *v* /'kwɒlɪfaɪ/
react *v* /ri:'ækt/
regard *n* /rɪ'gɑ:d/
remove *v* /rɪ'mu:v/
retell *v* /ˌri:'tel/
row *n* /raʊ/
scary *adj* /'skeəri/
schooling *n* /'sku:lɪŋ/
servant *n* /'sɜ:vənt/
set an example /ˌset ən ɪg'zɑ:mpl/
set up *v* /ˌset 'ʌp/
share *v* /ʃeə(r)/
spread *v* /spred/
space station *n* /'speɪs ˌsteɪʃn/
stepfather *n* /'stepfɑ:ðə(r)/
strict *adj* /strɪkt/
strip *v* /strɪp/
stuck *adj* /stʌk/
suit *v* /su:t/
take after *v* /ˌteɪk 'ɑ:ftə(r)/
take up *v* /ˌteɪk 'ʌp/
tear *n* /tɪə(r)/
thrift *n* /θrɪft/
token *n* /'təʊkən/
tonic *n* /'tɒnɪk/
transform *v* /træns'fɔ:m/
transport *v* /ˌtræns'pɔ:t/
treat *n* /tri:t/
valuable *adj* /'væljuəbl/
Victorian *adj* /vɪk'tɔ:riən/
wardrobe *n* /'wɔ:drəʊb/
wireless *adj* /'waɪələs/
woodwork *n* /'wʊdwɜ:k/

addiction n /əˈdɪkʃən/
advance n /ədˈvɑːns/
alien n /ˈeɪliən/
amateur adj /ˈæmətə(r)/
astronaut n /ˈæstrənɔːt/
attitude n /ˈætɪtjuːd/
awareness n /əˈweənəs/
beyond your wildest dreams
  /bɪ jɒnd jɔː ˌwaɪldɪst ˈdriːmz/
blackness n /ˈblæknəs/
breakthrough n /ˈbreɪkθruː/
cause for concern /ˌkɔːz fə
  kənˈsɜːn/
cell n /sel/
centenarian n /ˌsentɪˈneəriən/
confidently adv /ˈkɒnfɪdəntli/
confirmation n /ˌkɒnfəˈmeɪʃn/
consciousness n /ˈkɒnʃəsnəs/
controversial adj /ˌkɒntrəˈvɜːʃl/
cookery n /ˈkʊkəri/
current adj /ˈkʌrənt/
curvature n /ˈkɜːvətʃə(r)/
cyber- /ˈsaɪbə(r)/
damage n /ˈdæmɪdʒ/
diseased adj /dɪˈziːzd/
disorder n /dɪsˈɔːdə(r)/
distribute v /dɪˈstɪŋwɪʃ/
drought n /draʊt/
emotion n /ɪˈməʊʃn/
evacuate v /ɪˈvækjueɪt/
evidence n /ˈevɪdəns/
existence n /ɪɡˈzɪstəns/
expand v /ɪkˈspænd/
expect (a baby) v /ɪkˈspekt/
expense n /ɪkˈspens/
extend v /ɪkˈstend/
fiction n /ˈfɪkʃn/
fingers crossed /ˌfɪŋɡəz ˈkrɒst/
flood n /flʌd/
forecast n /ˈfɔːkɑːst/
form v /fɔːm/
galaxy n /ˈɡæləksi/
generate v /ˈdʒenəreɪt/
generation n /ˌdʒenəˈreɪʃn/
get in v /ˌɡet ˈɪn/
give birth v /ˌɡɪv ˈbɜːθ/
glow v /ɡləʊ/
half-time n /ˌhɑːf ˈtaɪm/
heatwave n /ˈhiːtweɪv/
hopeless adj /ˈhəʊpləs/
hurricane n /ˈhʌrɪkən/
infinite adj /ˈɪnfɪnət/
injection n /ɪnˈdʒekʃn/
knowledge n /ˈnɒlɪdʒ/
laboratory n /ləˈbɒrətri/
limb n /lɪm/
major adj /ˈmeɪdʒə(r)/
mammal n /ˈmæml/
mankind n /mænˈkaɪnd/
marvel n /ˈmɑːvl/
melt v /melt/
meteorologist n /ˌmiːtiəˈrɒlədʒɪst/
mission n /ˈmɪʃn/
nuclear energy n /ˌnjuːkliə(r)
  ˈenədʒi/

orbit n /ˈɔːbɪt/
organ n /ˈɔːgən/
parallel adj /ˈpærəlel/
permafrost n /ˈpɜːməfrɒst/
pill n /pɪl/
presence n /ˈprezəns/
primate n /ˈpraɪmeɪt/
prove v /pruːv/
quote n /kwəʊt/
rainfall n /ˈreɪnfɔːl/
rapidly adv /ˈræpɪdli/
realist n /ˈrɪəlɪst/
reassure v /ˌriːəˈʃʊə(r)/
reduce v /rɪˈdjuːs/
regenerate v /riːˈdʒenəreɪt/
regrow v /ˌriːˈɡrəʊ/
replace v /rɪˈpleɪs/
research v /rɪˈsɜːtʃ/
resource n /rɪˈzɔːs/
revulsion n /rɪˈvʌlʃn/
science fiction n /ˌsaɪəns ˈfɪkʃn/
sensational adj /senˈseɪʃənl/
sensor n /ˈsensə(r)/
sink into v /ˌsɪŋk ˈɪntu/
skydiving n /ˈskaɪdaɪvɪŋ/
snowstorm n /ˈsnəʊstɔːm/
spine n /spaɪn/
status n /ˈsteɪtəs/
study n /ˈstʌdi/
suitable adj /ˈsuːtəbl/
supply n /səˈplaɪ/
take for granted /ˌteɪk fə ˈɡrɑːntɪd/
task n /tɑːsk/
technical adj /ˈteknɪkl/
the norm n /nɔːm/
throughout prep /θruːˈaʊt/
thunderstorm n /ˈθʌndəstɔːm/
transplantation n
  /ˌtrænsplɑːnˈteɪʃn/
tropical adj /ˈtrɒpɪkl/
universe n /ˈjuːnɪvɜːs/
vertebrate n /ˈvɜːtɪbrət/
vigorous adj /ˈvɪɡərəs/
virtual adj /ˈvɜːtʃuəl/
weightlessness n /ˈweɪtləsnəs/

appliance n /əˈplaɪəns/
associate v /əˈsəʊʃieɪt/
astronomy n /əˈstrɒnəmi/
attractive adj /əˈtræktɪv/
badly behaved adj /ˌbædli
  bɪˈheɪvd/
basement n /ˈbeɪsmənt/
battery n /ˈbætri/
bomb n /bɒm/
bother v /ˈbɒðə(r)/
brightly adv /ˈbraɪtli/
button n /ˈbʌtn/
cashmere n /ˈkæʃmɪə(r)/
casual adj /ˈkæʒuəl/
cattle n /ˈkætl/
celebration n /ˌselɪˈbreɪʃn/
china n /ˈtʃaɪnə/
clearance n /ˈklɪərəns/
coach n /kəʊtʃ/
consume v /kənˈsjuːm/
cosmetics pl n /kɒzˈmetɪks/
cosy adj /ˈkəʊzi/
cottage n /ˈkɒtɪdʒ/
crumble v /ˈkrʌmbl/
curiosity n /ˌkjʊəriˈɒsəti/
curly adj /ˈkɜːli/
dome n /dəʊm/
dominant adj /ˈdɒmɪnənt/
drive sb crazy /ˌdraɪv ˈkreɪzi/
emigrate v
equipped adj /ɪˈkwɪpt/
file n /faɪl/
fluently adv /ˈfluːəntli/
full-time adj /ˌfʊlˈtaɪm/
fully adv /ˈfʊli/
garlic n /ˈɡɑːlɪk/
get together v /ˌɡet təˈɡeðə(r)/
gigabyte n /ˈɡɪɡəbaɪt/
glassware n /ˈɡlɑːsweə(r)/
good-looking adj /ˌɡʊdˈlʊkɪŋ/
gravitate v
guarantee n /ˌɡærənˈtiː/
hand-made adj /ˌhændˈmeɪd/
handy adj /ˈhændi/
hard disk n /ˌhɑːd ˈdɪsk/
hard-working adj /ˌhɑːdˈwɜːkɪŋ/
homecomings n /ˈhəʊmkʌmɪŋz/
housewife n /ˈhaʊswaɪf/
hut n /hʌt/
hyperactive adj /ˌhaɪpərˈæktɪv/
immense adj /ɪˈmens/
in tune with /ˌɪn ˈtjuːn wɪð/
independent adj /ˌɪndɪˈpendənt/
ingredient n /ɪnˈɡriːdiənt/
insecure adj /ˌɪnsɪˈkjʊə(r)/
irreplaceable adj /ˌɪrɪˈpleɪsəbl/
kitchenware n /ˈkɪtʃənweə(r)/
lentils pl n /ˈlentlz/
like chalk and cheese /laɪk ˌtʃɔːk
  ən ˈtʃiːz/
linen n /ˈlɪnɪn/
long-lasting adj /ˌlɒŋˈlɑːstɪŋ/
low-fat adj /ˌləʊˈfæt/
loyalty n /ˈlɔɪəlti/
massage n /ˈmæsɑːʒ/

medium height n /ˈmiːdiəm ˌhaɪt/
mud n /mʌd/
night-life n /ˈnaɪtlaɪf/
orchard n /ˈɔːtʃəd/
painkiller n /ˈpeɪnkɪlə(r)/
panoramic adj /ˌpænəˈræmɪk/
paradise n /ˈpærədaɪs/
practical adj /ˈpræktɪkl/
premises pl n /ˈpremɪsɪz/
pre-packed adj /ˌpriːˈpækt/
prosecute v /ˈprɒsɪkjuːt/
purchase v /ˈpɜːtʃɪs/
rabbit n /ˈræbɪt/
elieve v /rɪˈliːv/
remind v /rɪˈmaɪnd/
responsible adj /rɪˈspɒnsəbl/
restore v /rɪˈstɔː(r)/
safety n /ˈseɪfti/
seek v /siːk/
sell out v /ˌsel ˈaʊt/
sentimental adj /ˌsentɪˈmentl/
shelter n /ˈʃeltə(r)/
simply adv /ˈsɪmpli/
smart adj /smɑːt/
smartly adv /ˈsmɑːtli/
sociable adj /ˈsəʊʃəbl/
solid adj /ˈsɒlɪd/
staff n /stɑːf/
stationery n /ˈsteɪʃənri/
stone n /stəʊn/
subscribe v /səbˈskraɪb/
take-away adj /ˈteɪkəweɪ/
tempting adj /ˈtemptɪŋ/
terrace n /ˈterəs/
the Ladies n /ðə ˈleɪdiz/
think straight /ˈθɪŋk ˌstreɪt/
tiny adj /ˈtaɪni/
toiletries pl n /ˈtɔɪlətriz/
top floor n /ˈtɒp ˌflɔː(r)/
treasure v /ˈtreʒə(r)/
turmeric n /ˈtɜːmərɪk/
wavy adj /ˈweɪvi/
wear n /weə(r)/
wedding n /ˈwedɪŋ/
well behaved adj /ˌwel bɪˈheɪvd/
well dressed adj /ˌwel ˈdrest/
whisper v /ˈwɪspə(r)/
woollens pl n /ˈwʊlənz/
young at heart /ˌjʌŋ ət ˈhɑːt/

accustomed *adj* /ə'kʌstəmd/
agreement *n* /ə'gri:mənt/
apply for *v* /ə'plaɪ fə/
be fond of *v* /bi 'fɒnd əv/
best-selling *adj* /ˌbest'selɪŋ/
chamber *n* /'tʃeɪmbə(r)/
chaos *n* /'keɪɒs/
common *adj* /'kɒmən/
contact *v* /'kɒntækt/
continent *n* /'kɒntɪnənt/
copy *n* /'kɒpi/
countless *adj* /'kaʊntləs/
create *v* /kri'eɪt/
deathly *adj* /'deθli/
decade *n* /'dekeɪd/
demanding *adj* /dɪ'mɑ:ndɪŋ/
dominate *v* /'dɒmɪneɪt/
don't mind *v* /ˌdəʊnt 'maɪnd/
doubles *pl n* /'dʌblz/
downpour *n* /'daʊnpɔ:(r)/
due *adj* /dju:/
elect *v* /ɪ'lekt/
enthusiastic *adj* /ɪnˌθju:zi'æstɪk/
eternity *n* /ɪ'tɜ:nɪti/
euphoria *n* /ju:'fɔ:riə/
fail *v* /feɪl/
fan *n* /fæn/
fancy dress *n* /ˌfænsi 'dres/
female *n* /'fi:meɪl/
fine *adj* /faɪn/
fox-hunting *n* /'fɒkshʌntɪŋ/
gifted *adj* /'gɪftɪd/
goblet *n* /'gɒblɪt/
ground *n* /graʊnd/
hallow *n* /'hæləʊ/
harmony *n* /'hɑ:məni/
have a word *v* /ˌhæv ə 'wɜ:d/
heated *adj* /'hi:tɪd/
hero *n* /'hɪərəʊ/
horseriding *n* /'hɔ:sraɪdɪŋ/
image *n* /'ɪmɪdʒ/
infectious *adj*
institute *n* /'ɪnstɪtju:t/
introduce *v* /ˌɪntrə'dju:s/
invest *v* /ɪn'vest/
launch *v* /lɔ:ntʃ/
lifestyle *n* /'laɪfstaɪl/
loathe *v* /ləʊð/
longhand *n* /'lɒŋhænd/
make your mark *v* /ˌmeɪk jɔ: 'mɑ:k/
male *n* /meɪl/
measles *n* /'mi:zlz/
medieval *adj* /ˌmedi'i:vl/
mob *n* /mɒb/
musical *n* /'mju:zɪkl/
myth *n* /mɪθ/
name *v* /neɪm/
numerous *adj* /'nju:mərəs/
obsession *n* /əb'seʃn/
once and for all /ˌwʌns ənd fə(r) 'ɔ:l/
orphan *n* /'ɔ:fn/
passionate *adj* /'pæʃənət/
philosopher *n* /fɪ'lɒsəfə(r)/

phoenix *n* /'fi:nɪks/
poverty *n* /'pɒvəti/
producer *n* /prə'dju:sə(r)/
psychological *adj* /ˌsaɪkə'lɒdʒɪkl/
public school *n* /ˌpʌblɪk 'sku:l/
regular *adj* /'regjələ(r)/
resign *v* /rɪ'zaɪn/
respond *v* /rɪ'spɒnd/
rivalry *n* /'raɪvəlri/
slow down *v* /ˌsləʊ 'daʊn/
snap up *v* /ˌsnæp 'ʌp/
soccer *n* /'sɒkə(r)/
socialite *n* /'səʊʃəlaɪt/
sort out *v* /ˌsɔ:t 'aʊt/
stage *n* /steɪdʒ/
statistics *n pl* /stə'tɪstɪks/
sticking point *n* /'stɪkɪŋ ˌpɔɪnt/
strike *n* /straɪk/
sympathy *n* /'sɪmpəθi/
talent *n* /'tælənt/
tattoo *n* /tə'tu:/
the big time /ðə ˌbɪg 'taɪm/
to the full /tə ðə 'fʊl/
totally *adv* /'təʊtəli/
track *n* /træk/
trademark *n* /'treɪdmɑ:k/
try one's luck /traɪ wʌnz 'lʌk/
twinkly *adj* /'twɪŋkli/
underwear *n* /'ʌndəweə(r)/
video game *n* /'vɪdiəʊ ˌgeɪm/
violent *adj* /'vaɪələnt/
waste ground *n* /'weɪst ˌgraʊnd/
wizard *n* /'wɪzəd/

approach *v* /ə'prəʊtʃ/
ascent *n* /ə'sent/
base *n* /beɪs/
battle *n* /'bætl/
bite *v* /baɪt/
blow *v* /bləʊ/
blow up *v* /ˌbləʊ 'ʌp/
body language *n* /'bɒdi ˌlæŋgwɪdʒ/
bold *adj* /bəʊld/
bunk bed *n* /ˌbʌŋk 'bed/
canoe *n* /kə'nu:/
catapult *v* /'kætəpʌlt/
clap *v* /klæp/
cliff *n* /klɪf/
conquer *v* /'kɒŋkə(r)/
crew *n* /kru:/
cross *v* /krɒs/
crossing *n* /'krɒsɪŋ/
cure *v* /kjʊə(r)/
dare *v* /deə(r)/
daring *adj* /'deərɪŋ/
declare *v* /dɪ'kleə(r)/
defeat *v* /dɪ'fi:t/
defeat *v* /dɪ'fi:t/
DIY *n* /ˌdi: aɪ 'waɪ/
DNA *n* /ˌdi: en 'eɪ/
empire *n* /'empaɪə(r)/
face *v* /feɪs/
fearless *adj* /'fɪələs/
ferry *v* /'feri/
fighter *n* /'faɪtə(r)/
force *v* /fɔ:s/
found *v* /faʊnd/
freak out *v* /fri:k aʊt/
gene *n* /dʒi:n/
get out of hand *v* /ˌget aʊt əv 'hænd/
go over someone's head *v* /gəʊ ˌəʊvə ... 'hed/
have a sweet tooth *v* /hæv ə ˌswi:t 'tu:θ/
hit a problem /ˌhit ə 'prɒbləm/
hollow *adj* /'hɒl əʊ/
hug *v* /hʌg/
iceberg *n* /'aɪsbɜ:g/
illiterate *adj* /ɪ'lɪtərət/
infection *n* /ɪn'fekʃn/
initially *adv* /ɪ'nɪʃəli/
innocent *adj* /'ɪnəsnt/
install *v* /ɪn'stɔ:l/
kick *v* /kɪk/
kick up a fuss *v* /ˌkɪk ʌp ə 'fʌs/
kneel *v* /ni:l/
lack *n* /læk/
ladder *n* /'lædə(r)/
leadership *n* /'li:dəʃɪp/
lick *v* /lɪk/
lifeboats *n* /'laɪfbəʊts/
lower *v* /'ləʊ ə/
maiden voyage *n* /ˌmeɪdn 'vɔɪdʒ/
manpower *n* /'mænpaʊə(r)/
military *adj* /'mɪlətri/
nail *n* /neɪl/
numerous *adj* /'nju:mərəs/

overcome *v* /ˌəʊvə'kʌm/
overweight *adj* /ˌəʊvə'weɪt/
oxygen *n* /'ɒksɪdʒən/
oyster *n* /'ɔɪstə(r)/
panic *v* /'pænɪk/
pass *n* /pɑ:s/
perish *v* /'perɪʃ/
phobia *n* /'fəʊbiə/
pitch-black *adj* /ˌpɪtʃ 'blæk/
plain *n* /pleɪn/
playground *n* /'pleɪgraʊnd/
poisonous *adj* /'pɔɪzənəs/
pray *v* /preɪ/
program *n* /'prəʊgræm/
prosperous *adj* /'prɒspərəs/
province *n* /'prɒvɪns/
psychotherapist *n* /ˌsaɪkəʊ'θerəpɪst/
pull someone's leg *v* /ˌpʊl ... 'leg/
put up *v* /ˌpʊt 'ʌp/
raft *n* /rɑ:ft/
recognize *v* /'rekəgnaɪz/
reduce *v* /rɪ'dju:s/
remain *v* /rɪ'meɪn/
remarkable *adj* /rɪ'mɑ:kəbl/
remote *adj* /rɪ'məʊt/
revolutionary *adj* /ˌrevə'lu:ʃənəri/
rule *v* /ru:l/
scar *n* /skɑ:(r)/
scratch *v* /skrætʃ/
see eye to eye *v* /si: ˌaɪ tu 'aɪ/
set off *v* /ˌset 'ɒf/
sickness *n* /'sɪknəs/
silly *adj* /'sɪli/
slide *v* /slaɪd/
slip *v* /slɪp/
snorkel *n* /'snɔ:kl/
soldier *n* /'səʊldʒə(r)/
stack *n* /stæk/
stare *v* /steə(r)/
steerage *n* /'stɪərɪdʒ/
struggle *v* /'strʌgl/
suffer *v* /'sʌfə(r)/
sumptuous *adj* /'sʌmptʃuəs/
superior *adj* /su:'pɪəriə(r)/
swallow *v* /'swɒləʊ/
sweaty *adj* /'sweti/
symptom *n* /'sɪmptəm/
tear down *phr v* /teə 'daʊn/
terrified *adj* /'terɪfaɪd/
terror *n* /'terə(r)/
threaten *v* /'θretn/
trek *n* /trek/
tribesmen *n pl* /'traɪbzmən/
tune *n* /tju:n/
unbelievable *adj* /ˌʌnbɪ'li:vəbl/
unsinkable *adj* /ʌn'sɪŋkəbl/
waste your breath *v* /ˌweɪst jɔ: 'breθ/
whistle *v* /'wɪsl/

UNIT 9

action-packed *adj* /ˈakʃən ˌpækt/
addict *n* /ˈædɪkt/
ages *pl n* /ˈeɪdʒɪz/
arrest *v* /əˈrest/
ashamed *adj* /əˈʃeɪmd/
balance *n* /ˈbæləns/
bear with *v* /ˈbeə wɪð/
blood *n* /blʌd/
bother *v* /ˈbɒðə(r)/
brainstorm *v* /ˈbreɪnstɔːm/
buddy *n* /ˈbʌdi/
bully *v* /ˈbʊli/
bump into *v* /ˌbʌmp ˈɪntu/
burglary *n* /ˈbɜːgləri/
clean up *v* /ˌkliːn ˈʌp/
clear *v* /klɪə(r)/
convict *v* /kənˈvɪkt/
counsellor *n* /ˈkaʊnsələ(r)/
curious *adj* /ˈkjʊəriəs/
determined *adj* /dɪˈtɜːmɪnd/
digit *n* /ˈdɪdʒɪt/
dozen *n* /ˈdʌzn/
dysfunctional *adj* /dɪsˈfʌŋkʃənl/
economize *v* /ɪˈkɒnəmaɪz/
effective *adj* /ɪˈfektɪv/
eldest *adj* /ˈeldɪst/
encounter *n* /ɪnˈkaʊntə(r)/
enter *v* /ˈentə(r)/
explode *v* /ɪkˈspləʊd/
faceless *adj* /ˈfeɪsləs/
find fault *v* /ˌfaɪnd ˈfɔːlt/
fraud *n* /frɔːd/
get through to *v* /ˌget ˈθruː tu/
grin *v* /grɪn/
gym *n* /dʒɪm/
hand over *v* /ˌhænd ˈəʊvə(r)/
head teacher *n* /ˌhed ˈtiːtʃə(r)/
heroin *n* /ˈherəʊɪn/
hit rock bottom /hɪt ˌrɒk ˈbɒtəm/
homeless *adj* /ˈhəʊmləs/
imprisonment *n* /ɪmˈprɪznmənt/
in touch /ɪn ˈtʌtʃ/
jail *v* /dʒeɪl/
knock over *v* /ˌnɒk ˈəʊvə(r)/
letter box *n* /ˈletə(r) ˌbɒks/
light *v* /laɪt/
limit *n* /ˈlɪmɪt/
litter bin *n* /ˈlɪtə(r) ˌbɪn/
locate *v* /ləʊˈkeɪt/
make a scene *v* /ˌmeɪk ə ˈsiːn/
mind your own business /ˌmaɪnd jɔː(r) əʊn ˈbɪznəs/
ordinary *adj* /ˈɔːdnri/
outburst *n* /ˈaʊtbɜːst/
over the moon /ˌəʊvə ðə ˈmuːn/
overdrawn *adj* /ˌəʊvəˈdrɔːn/
passer-by *n* /ˌpɑːsəˈbaɪ/
penniless *adj* /ˈpeniləs/
phone in *v* /ˌfəʊn ˈɪn/
play truant *v* /ˌpleɪ ˈtruːənt/
prison *n* /ˈprɪzn/
protect *v* /prəˈtekt/
punishment *n* /ˈpʌnɪʃmənt/
purpose *n* /ˈpɜːpəs/
pursue *v* /pəˈsjuː/

queue *n* /kjuː/
receipt *n* /rɪˈsiːt/
register *v* /ˈredʒɪstə(r)/
rehabilitate *v* /ˌriːhəˈbɪlɪteɪt/
release *v* /rɪˈliːs/
relieved *adj* /rɪˈliːvd/
restorative justice *n* /rɪˌstɒrətɪv ˈdʒʌstɪs/
rude *adj* /ruːd/
scruffy *adj* /ˈskrʌfi/
shop-lift *v* /ˈʃɒplɪft/
social worker *n* /ˈsəʊʃl ˌwɜːkə(r)/
stitch *n* /stɪtʃ/
stop dead *v* /ˌstɒp ˈded/
storm off *v* /ˌstɔːm ˈɒf/
stuff *v* /stʌf/
stunned *adj* /stʌnd/
suspect *v* /səˈspekt/
temperature *n* /ˈtemprətʃə(r)/
theft *n* /θeft/
timid *adj* /ˈtɪmɪd/
tremble *v* /ˈtrembl/
urban *adj* /ˈɜːbən/
VAT *n* /ˌviː eɪ ˈtiː/
victim *n* /ˈvɪktɪm/
violence *n* /ˈvaɪələns/

UNIT 10

amenity *n* /əˈmiːnəti/
ancestor *n* /ˈæncestə(r)/
appear *v* /əˈpɪə(r)/
arch *n* /ɑːtʃ/
basically *adv* /ˈbeɪsɪkli/
brewery *n* /ˈbrʊəri/
bronze *adj* /brɒnz/
burger *n* /ˈbɜːgə(r)/
calculation *n* /ˌkælkjəˈleɪʃn/
capacity *n* /kəˈpæsɪti/
censorship *n* /ˈsensəʃɪp/
chairman *n* /ˈtʃeəmən/
coal *n* /kəʊl/
code *n* /kəʊd/
commerce *n* /ˈkɒmɜːs/
complex *adj* /ˈkɒmpleks/
crystal *adj* /ˈkrɪstl/
daily *adv* /ˈdeɪli/
decoration *n* /dekəˈreɪʃn/
democracy *n* /dɪˈmɒkrəsi/
depict *v* /dɪˈpɪkt/
device *n* /dɪˈvaɪs/
diagnose *v* /ˈdaɪəgnəʊz/
digital *adj* /ˈdɪdʒɪtl/
distinctive *adj* /dɪsˈtɪŋktɪv/
district *n* /ˈdɪstrɪkt/
efficient *adj* /ɪˈfɪʃnt/
embrace *n* /ɪmˈbreɪs/
error *n* /ˈerə(r)/
estate agent *n* /ɪˈsteɪt ˌeɪdʒənt/
ethnic group *n* /eθnɪk ˈgruːp/
facilities *pl n* /fəˈsɪlətiz/
feat *n* /fiːt/
feature *n* /ˈfiːtʃə(r)/
flash *v* /flæʃ/
float *v* /fləʊt/
found *v* /faʊnd/
gig *n* /gɪg/
glide *v* /glaɪd/
Gothic *adj* /ˈgɒθɪk/
haircut *n* /ˈheəkʌt/
halt *n* /hɒlt/
handcuffs *pl n* /ˈhændkʌfs/
headlight *n* /ˈhedlaɪt/
headphones *pl n* /ˈhedfəʊnz/
headquarters *pl n* /ˌhedˈkwɔːtəz/
headstone *n* /ˈhedstəʊn/
headway *n* /ˈhedweɪ/
high tech *adj* /ˌhaɪ ˈtek/
home-made *adj* /ˌhəʊmˈmeɪd/
influence *n* /ˈɪnfluə ns/
inner-city *n* /ˌɪnəˈsɪti/
instantly *adv* /ˈɪnstəntli/
laundry *n* /ˈlɔːndri/
log onto *v* /ˌlɒg ˈɒntu/
major *adj* /ˈmeɪdʒə(r)/
motorbike *n* /ˈməʊtəbaɪk/
motorway *n* /ˈməʊtəweɪ/
mouth (of a river) *n* /maʊθ əv ə rɪvə/
Net *n* /net/
newsagent *n* /ˈnjuːzeɪdʒənt/
nickname *n* /ˈnɪkneɪm/
notice board *n* /ˈnəʊtɪsbɔːd/
online dating *n* /ˌɒnlaɪn ˈdeɪtɪŋ/

onscreen *n* /ˌɒnˈskriːn/
operate *v* /ˈɒpəreɪt/
outdated *adj* /ˌaʊtˈdeɪtɪd/
penthouse *n* /ˈpenthaʊs/
perfectly *adv* /ˈpɜːfektli/
plumbing *n* /ˈplʌmɪŋ/
poster *n* /ˈpəʊstə(r)/
print *v* /prɪnt/
programmable *adj* /ˈprəʊgræməbl/
regeneration *n* /rɪˌdʒenəˈreɪʃ/
remote *n* /rɪˈməʊt/
restoration *n* /ˌrestəˈreɪʃn/
revolving door *n* /rɪˌvɒlvɪŋ ˈdɔː(r)/
satellite navigation *n* /ˌsætəlaɪt ˌnævɪˈgeɪʃn/
sharp *adj* /ʃɑːp/
silicon *n* /ˈsɪlɪkən/
skateboarding *n* /ˈskeɪtbɔːdɪŋ/
skyline *n* /ˈskaɪlaɪn/
social networking *n* /ˌsəʊʃl ˈnetwɜːkɪŋ/
span *n* /spæn/
statue *n* /ˈstætjuː/
stick *v* /stɪk/
sticky *adj* /ˈstɪki/
storage *n* /ˈstɔːrɪdʒ/
supply *v* /səˈplaɪ/
surface *n* /ˈsɜːfɪs/
surgeon *n* /ˈsɜːdʒən/
switch *v* /swɪtʃ/
thriving *adj* /ˈθraɪvɪŋ/
trace *v* /treɪs/
traffic jam *n* /ˈtræfɪk ˌdʒæm/
traffic lights *pl n* /ˈtræfɪk ˌlaɪts/
traffic warden *n* /ˈtræfɪk ˌwɔːdn/
transfer *v* /trænsˈfɜː(r)/
transistor *n* /trænˈzɪstə(r)/
treat *v* /triːt/
triumph *n* /ˈtraɪʌmf/
tube *n* /tjuːb/
undivided *adj* /ˌʌndɪˈvaɪdɪd/
unsupported *adj* /ˌʌnsəˈpɔːtɪd/
waiting room *n* /ˈweɪtɪŋ ˌruːm/
wallpaper *n* /ˈwɔːlpeɪpə(r)/
wool *n* /wʊl/
wrapping paper *n* /ˈræpɪŋ ˌpeɪpə(r)/

acquaintance *n* /ə'kweɪntəns/
afford *v* /ə'fɔːd/
agitated *adj* /'ædʒɪteɪtɪd/
anniversary *n* /ˌænɪ'vɜːsəri/
apparently *adv* /ə'pærəntli/
available *adj* /ə'veɪləbl/
battery *n* /'bætri/
bird-brained *adj* /'bɜːdbreɪnd/
break out of *v* /ˌbreɪk 'aʊt əv/
break up *v* /ˌbreɪk 'ʌp/
bruise *n* /bruːz/
burgle *v* /'bɜːgl/
candlestick *n* /'kændlstɪk/
cheers *interj* /tʃɪəz/
chimpanzee *n* /ˌtʃɪmpæn'ziː/
club together *v* /ˌklʌb tə'geðə(r)/
clue *n* /kluː/
come up with *v* /kʌm 'ʌp wɪð/
cricket *n* /'krɪkɪt/
crow *n* /krəʊ/
culprit *n* /'kʌlprɪt/
dehydrate *v* /ˌdiː'haɪdreɪt/
dot *n* /dɒt/
dreadful *adj* /'dredfl/
dump *v* /dʌmp/
eat out *v* /ˌiːt 'aʊt/
eat up *v* /ˌiːt 'ʌp/
elementary *adj* /elɪ'mentri/
eyesight *n* /'aɪsaɪt/
fall out *v* /ˌfɔːl 'aʊt/
feather *n* /'feðə(r)/
gamble *v* /'gæmbl/
have around *v*
hopefully *adv* /'həʊpfəli/
hurriedly *adv* /'hʌrɪdli/
identical *adj* /aɪ'dentɪkl/
impatiently *adv* /ɪm'peɪʃntli/
intruder *n* /ɪn'truːdə(r)/
investigation *n* /ɪnˌvestɪ'geɪʃn/
irritably *adv* /'ɪrɪtəbli/
jelly *n* /'dʒeli/
lecture *n* /'lektʃə(r)/
liar *n* /'laɪə(r)/
lightning *n* /'laɪtnɪŋ/
lightning conductor *n* /'laɪtnɪŋ
  kənˌdʌktə(r)/
long jump *n* /'lɒŋ dʒʌmp/
look like *v* /'lʊk ˌlaɪk/
lottery *n* /'lɒtəri/
lump *n* /lʌmp/
make sth up *v* /ˌmeɪk 'ʌp/
make up (w sb) *v* /ˌmeɪk 'ʌp/
mimic *v* /'mɪmɪk/
mineral water *n* /'mɪnərəl
  ˌwɔːtə(r)/
motive *n* /'məʊtɪv/
naturally *adv* /'nætʃrəli/
No kidding! /ˌnəʊ 'kɪdɪŋ/
obviously *adv* /'ɒbviəsli/
on tiptoe /ɒn 'tɪptəʊ/
optical illusion *n* /ˌɒptɪkl ɪ'luːʒn/
oversleep *v* /ˌəʊvə'sliːp/
parrot *n* /'pærət/
personally *adv* /'pɜːsənəli/
presumably *adv* /prɪ'zjuːməbli/

promote *v* /prə'məʊt/
radar *n* /'reɪdɑː(r)/
ransack *v* /'rænsæk/
really *adv* /'rɪəli/
reflect *v* /rɪ'flekt/
refuse *v* /rɪ'fjuːz/
responsible *adj* /rɪ'spɒnsəbl/
rugby *n* /'rʌgbi/
save up *v* /ˌseɪv 'ʌp/
scandal *n* /'skændl/
shrink *v* /ʃrɪŋk/
skyscraper *n* /'skaɪskreɪpə(r)/
snowflake *n* /'snəʊfleɪk/
sole *n* /səʊl/
solve *v* /sɒlv/
sort out *v* /ˌsɔːt 'aʊt/
spare *v* /speə(r)/
spike *n* /spaɪk/
strike *v* /straɪk/
suspicious *adj* /sə'spɪʃəs/
take up *v* /ˌteɪk 'ʌp/
threshold *n* /'θreʃhəʊld/
tidy up *v* /ˌtaɪdi 'ʌp/
to be honest /tə bi: 'ɒnɪst/
translation *n* /trænz'leɪʃn/
trick *n* /trɪk/
tutor *n* /'tjuːtə(r)/
undoubtedly *adv* /ʌn'daʊtɪdli/
unplug *v* /ˌʌn'plʌg/
work out *v* /ˌwɜːk 'aʊt/
work sth out *v* /ˌwɜːk 'aʊt/
wobbly *adj* /'wɒbli/
zillions *pl n* /'zɪliənz/

abandon *v* /ə'bændən/
absurd *adj* /əb'zɜːd/
accuse *v* /ə'kjuːz/
adapt *v* /ə'dæpt/
adolescent *adj* /ˌædə'lesənt/
agnostic *n* /æg'nɒstɪk/
alienate *v* /'eɪliəneɪt/
angle *n* /'æŋgl/
auction *n* /'ɔːkʃn/
bid *n* /bɪd/
bulk *n* /bʌlk/
chain *v* /tʃeɪn/
charge *v* /tʃɑːdʒ/
clinic *n* /'klɪnɪk/
concept *n* /'kɒnsept/
conditions *pl n* /kən'dɪʃnz/
contradict *v* /ˌkɒntrə'dɪkt/
contrary to *adj* /'kɒntrəri tu/
creationist *n* /kri'eɪʃnɪst/
descended from *v* /dɪ'sendɪd frəm/
disorder *n* /dɪs'ɔːdə(r)/
encourage *v* /ɪn'kʌrɪdʒ/
equality *n* /ɪ'kwɒləti/
evolve *v* /ɪ'vɒlv/
ex- /eks/
existence *n* /ɪg'zɪstəns/
expert *n* /'ekspɜːt/
force-feeding *n* /ˌfɔːs'fiːdɪŋ/
gossip *n* /'gɒsɪp/
healer *n* /'hiːlə(r)/
heresy *n* /'herəsi/
heretical *adj* /hə'retɪkl/
heroine *n* /'herəʊɪn/
highs and lows *pl n* /ˌhaɪz ən
  'ləʊz/
hip *n* /hɪp/
hunger strike *n* /'hʌŋgə ˌstraɪk/
hurl *v* /hɜːl/
hysterical *adj* /hɪ'sterɪkl/
in the public eye /ɪn ðə ˌpʌblɪk 'aɪ/
incapable *adj* /ɪn'keɪpəbl/
indifferent *adj* /ɪn'dɪfrənt/
individually *adv* /ˌɪndɪ'vɪdʒuəli/
influential *adj* /ˌɪnflu'enʃl/
insoluble *adj* /ɪn'sɒljəbl/
irresponsible *adj* /ˌɪrɪ'spɒnsəbl/
ketchup *n* /'ketʃʌp/
law-breaker *n* /'lɔːbreɪkə(r)/
many happy returns /ˌmeni ˌhæpi
  rɪ'tɜːnz/
mediocre *adj* /ˌmiːdi'əʊkə(r)/
meditate *v* /'mediteɪt/
mesmerize *v* /'mezməraɪz/
method *n* /'meθəd/
migraine *n* /'miːgreɪn, 'maɪgreɪn/
militant *adj* /'mɪlɪtənt/
motivation *n* /ˌməʊtɪ'veɪʃn/
natural selection *n* /ˌnætrəl
  sɪ'lekʃn/
notion *n* /'nəʊʃn/
observe *v* /əb'zɜːv/
opponent *n* /ə'pəʊnənt/
originate *v* /ə'rɪdʒɪneɪt/
password *n* /'pɑːswɜːd/
persuade *v* /pə'sweɪd/

planet *n* /'plænɪt/
presenter *n* /prɪ'zentə(r)/
process *n* /'prəʊses/
promotion *n* /prə'məʊʃn/
protest *v* /prə'test/
put forward *v* /ˌpʊt 'fɔːwəd/
railings *pl n* /'reɪlɪŋz/
rain down *v* /ˌreɪn 'daʊn/
rational *adj* /'ræʃənl/
recommend *v* /ˌrekə'mend/
recording studio *n* /rɪ'kɔːdɪŋ ˌstjuː
  diəʊ/
remind *v* /rɪ'maɪnd/
reputation *n* /ˌrepju'teɪʃn/
reverse *v* /rɪ'vɜːs/
rhythm *n* /'rɪðəm/
right *n* /raɪt/
right-wing *adj* /ˌraɪt'wɪŋ/
riot *n* /'raɪət/
rotate *v* /rəʊ'teɪt/
sell-out *n* /'selaʊt/
sensational *adj* /sen'seɪʃənl/
sex symbol *n* /'seks ˌsɪmbl/
shake *v* /ʃeɪk/
significance *n* /sɪg'nɪfɪkəns/
simply *adv* /'sɪmpli/
slash *v* /slæʃ/
species *n* /'spiːʃiːz/
spill *v* /spɪl/
standstill *n* /'stændstɪl/
struggle *n* /'strʌgl/
suffragette *n* /ˌsʌfrə'dʒet/
suffragist *n* /'sʌfrədʒɪst/
tactic *n* /'tæktɪk/
telescope *n* /'telɪskəʊp/
theory *n* /'θɪəri/
threat *n* /θret/
unaware *adj* /ˌʌnə'weə(r)/
undermine *v* /ˌʌndə'maɪn/
unverifiable *adj* /ʌn'verɪfaɪəbl/

Verb patterns

Verbs + *-ing*	
adore can't stand don't mind enjoy finish imagine loathe	doing swimming cooking

Note

We often use the verb *go* + *-ing* for sports and activities.

    *I **go swimming** every day.*
    *I **go shopping** on weekends.*

Verbs + preposition + *-ing*	
give up look forward to succeed in think of	doing

Verbs + *to* + infinitive	
afford agree choose dare decide expect forget help hope learn manage mean need offer plan promise refuse seem want would hate would like would love would prefer	to do to come to cook

Notes

1 *Help* and *dare* can be used without *to*.
    *We **helped clean up** the kitchen.*
    *They didn't **dare disagree** with him.*

2 *Have to* for obligation.
    *I **have to wear** a uniform.*

3 *Used to* for past habits.
    *I **used to smoke**, but I quit last year.*

Verbs + sb + *to* + infinitive		
advise allow ask beg encourage expect force help invite need order persuade remind tell want warn would like	me him them someone	to do to go to come

Note

Help can be used without *to*.
    *I **helped** him **do** the dishes.*

Verbs + sb + infinitive (no *to*)		
help let make	her us	do

Notes

1 *To* is used with *make* in the passive.
    *We were **made to work** hard.*

2 *Let* cannot be used in the passive. *Allowed to* is used instead.
    *She was **allowed to leave**.*

Verbs + *-ing* or *to* + infinitive (with little or no change in meaning)	
begin continue hate like love prefer start	doing to do

Verbs + *-ing* or *to* + infinitive (with a change in meaning)	
remember stop try	doing to do

Notes

1 *I **remember posting** the letter.*
    (= I have a memory now of a past action: posting the letter.)

    *I **remembered to post** the letter.*
    (= I reminded myself to post the letter. I didn't forget.)

2 *I **stopped drinking** coffee.*
    (= I gave up the habit.)

    *I **stopped to drink** a coffee.*
    (= I stopped doing something else in order to have a cup of coffee.)

3 *I **tried to sleep**.*
    (= I wanted to sleep, but it was difficult.)

    *I **tried counting** sheep and **drinking** a glass of warm milk.*
    (= These were possible ways of getting to sleep.)

Irregular verbs

Base form	Past Simple	Past participle	Base form	Past Simple	Past participle
be	was/were	been	leave	left	left
beat	beat	beaten	lend	lent	lent
become	became	become	let	let	let
begin	began	begun	lie	lay	lain
bend	bent	bent	light	lighted/lit	lighted/lit
bite	bit	bitten	lose	lost	lost
blow	blew	blown	make	made	made
break	broke	broken	mean	meant	meant
bring	brought	brought	meet	met	met
build	built	built	must	had to	had to
buy	bought	bought	pay	paid	paid
can	could	been able	put	put	put
catch	caught	caught	read /riːd/	read /red/	read /red/
choose	chose	chosen	ride	rode	ridden
come	came	come	ring	rang	rung
cost	cost	cost	rise	rose	risen
cut	cut	cut	run	ran	run
dig	dug	dug	say	said	said
do	did	done	see	saw	seen
draw	drew	drawn	sell	sold	sold
dream	dreamed/dreamt	dreamed/dreamt	send	sent	sent
drink	drank	drunk	set	set	set
drive	drove	driven	shake	shook	shaken
eat	ate	eaten	shine	shone	shone
fall	fell	fallen	shoot	shot	shot
feed	fed	fed	show	showed	shown
feel	felt	felt	shut	shut	shut
fight	fought	fought	sing	sang	sung
find	found	found	sink	sank	sunk
fit	fit	fit	sit	sat	sat
fly	flew	flown	sleep	slept	slept
forget	forgot	forgotten	slide	slid	slid
forgive	forgave	forgiven	speak	spoke	spoken
freeze	froze	frozen	spend	spent	spent
get	got	got	spoil	spoiled/spoilt	spoiled/spoilt
give	gave	given	spread	spread	spread
go	went	been/gone	stand	stood	stood
grow	grew	grown	steal	stole	stolen
hang	hanged/hung	hanged/hung	stick	stuck	stuck
have	had	had	swim	swam	swum
hear	heard	heard	take	took	taken
hide	hid	hidden	teach	taught	taught
hit	hit	hit	tear	tore	torn
hold	held	held	tell	told	told
hurt	hurt	hurt	think	thought	thought
keep	kept	kept	throw	threw	thrown
kneel	knelt	knelt	understand	understood	understood
know	knew	known	wake	woke	woken
lay	laid	laid	wear	wore	worn
lead	led	led	win	won	won
learn	learned/learnt	learned/learnt	write	wrote	written

Phonetic symbols

Consonants

1	/p/	as in	**pen** /pen/
2	/b/	as in	**big** /bɪg/
3	/t/	as in	**tea** /tiː/
4	/d/	as in	**do** /duː/
5	/k/	as in	**cat** /kæt/
6	/g/	as in	**go** /gəʊ/
7	/f/	as in	**four** /fɔː/
8	/v/	as in	**very** /'veri/
9	/s/	as in	**son** /sʌn/
10	/z/	as in	**zoo** /zuː/
11	/l/	as in	**live** /lɪv/
12	/m/	as in	**my** /maɪ/
13	/n/	as in	**near** /nɪə/
14	/h /	as in	**happy** /'hæpi/
15	/r/	as in	**red** /red/
16	/j/	as in	**yes** /jes/
17	/w/	as in	**want** /wɒnt/
18	/θ/	as in	**thanks** /θæŋks/
19	/ð/	as in	**the** /ðə/
20	/ʃ/	as in	**she** /ʃiː/
21	/ʒ/	as in	**television** /'telɪvɪʒn/
22	/tʃ/	as in	**child** /tʃaɪld/
23	/dʒ/	as in	**German** /'dʒɜːmən/
24	/ŋ/	as in	**English** /'ɪŋglɪʃ/

Vowels

25	/iː/	as in	**see** /siː/
26	/ɪ/	as in	**his** /hɪz/
27	/i/	as in	**twenty** /'twenti/
28	/e/	as in	**ten** /ten/
29	/æ/	as in	**stamp** /stæmp/
30	/ɑː/	as in	**father** /'fɑːðə/
31	/ɒ/	as in	**hot** /hɒt/
32	/ɔː/	as in	**morning** /'mɔːnɪŋ/
33	/ʊ/	as in	**football** /'fʊtbɔːl/
34	/uː/	as in	**you** /juː/
35	/ʌ/	as in	**sun** /sʌn/
36	/ɜː/	as in	**learn** /lɜːn/
37	/ə/	as in	**letter** /'letə/

Diphthongs (two vowels together)

38	/eɪ/	as in	**name** /neɪm/
39	/əʊ/	as in	**no** /nəʊ/
40	/aɪ/	as in	**my** /maɪ/
41	/aʊ/	as in	**how** /haʊ/
42	/ɔɪ/	as in	**boy** /bɔɪ/
43	/ɪə/	as in	**hear** /hɪə/
44	/eə/	as in	**where** /weə/
45	/ʊə/	as in	**tour** /tʊə/

OXFORD
UNIVERSITY PRESS

Great Clarendon Street, Oxford OX2 6DP

Oxford University Press is a department of the University of Oxford. It furthers the University's objective of excellence in research, scholarship, and education by publishing worldwide in

Oxford New York

Auckland Cape Town Dar es Salaam Hong Kong Karachi Kuala Lumpur Madrid Melbourne Mexico City Nairobi New Delhi Shanghai Taipei Toronto

With offices in

Argentina Austria Brazil Chile Czech Republic France Greece Guatemala Hungary Italy Japan Poland Portugal Singapore South Korea Switzerland Thailand Turkey Ukraine Vietnam

OXFORD and OXFORD ENGLISH are registered trade marks of Oxford University Press in the UK and in certain other countries

© Oxford University Press 2009

The moral rights of the author have been asserted
Database right Oxford University Press (maker)
First published 2009

2013 2012 2011 2010 2009
10 9 8 7 6 5 4 3 2 1

ISBN: 978 0 19 476864 1

Printed in Spain by Orymu S.A.

ACKNOWLEDGEMENTS

The authors and publisher are grateful to those who have given permission to reproduce the following extracts and adaptations of copyright materials: p10 'Welcome to Our World: The Qus: Beijing, China'; The Guardian, 21st October 2006. Copyright Guardian News and Media Ltd 2006; p11 'Welcome to Our World: The Kamaus Ongata Rongai, Kenya'; The Guardian, 21st October 2006. Reproduced by kind permission of Xan Rice; p12 'A world in one family': interviews reproduced with kind permission of Ana Reynoso and family; pp19–20 Adapted extracts from 'The Best of Times'; Majesty Magazine, November 2006. Reproduced by kind permission of Majesty Magazine; p24 'Smash! Museum visitor trips on lace and destroys priceless vases'; The Daily Telegraph, 30th January, 2006. Copyright The Telegraph Media Group Ltd; pp26–7 Extracts from 'Romeo and Juliet', Oxford World Classics; © Oxford University Press 2000; pp33 and 150 'I Believe' Words and Music by Ian Dury and Michael Gallagher © Templemill Music and Mute Song. All rights on behalf of Templemill Music administered by Warner/Chappell Music Ltd, London W6 8BS. Reproduced by permission; p35 'You don't know you are born', The Sunday Times, 11th February 2007 © NI Syndication, London (2007) p41 'Rocket Man, Steve Bennett'; BBC-Saturday Live, 10/03/2007. © BBC Radio. Reproduced with kind permission of Steve Bennett, Starchaser Plc and BBC Radio. pp42–3 'Year 2025: We'll find aliens, talk to animals and be sprightly at 100'; from

Daily Mail, 16/11/2006 © Daily Mail 2006; pp58–9 'How a book of rules gave the world the beautiful game'; Sunday Times, 19/03/02006. © NI Syndication, London (2007); p65 'Don't panic, Its only a Fish' by Lucy Elkins, Daily Mail, 17/04/2007. © Daily Mail 2007; pp74–5 'I am sorry: How a burglar and his victim became best of friends', Daily Mirror, 19/03/2007. © Daily Mirror 2007.

Although every effort has been made to trace and contact copyright holders before publication, this has not been possible in some cases. We apologize for any apparent infringement of copyright and if notified, the publisher will be pleased to rectify any errors or omissions at the earliest opportunity.

Illustrations by: Tim Branch p28 (yin yang); Gill Button pp25, 36, 44, 62, 76, 80, 92, 102; Mark Duffin p86 (all optical illusions except duck-rabbit, elephant re-drawn after Roger N. Shepard, the Ray Lyman Wilbur Professor Emeritus of Social Science, Stanford University, California); Melvyn Evans p41 (rocket); Leo Hartas pp105, 110, 111, 150–1; Detmeer Otto pp6–7, 61; Gavin Reece pp16, 26–7, 108, 148; Keith Robinson pp90–1; Martin Saunders p66; Jason Stavron p65; Lorna Aps Woodland pp70–1.

Commissioned photography by: Gareth Boden pp8 Ruth, Nick and Lily, 14 (Jenny & Mike), 64, 77 (restaurant, bar), 103, 107, 117, 147 (waiter); Paul Freestone p12 (Ana Reynoso and family); Mark Mason pp85, 151.

We would also like to thank the following for permission to reproduce the following photographs: Alamy pp9 (dog/Jeremy Pardoe), 9 (saxophone/i love images), 13 (Jupiterimages/Creatas), 14 (Vicky/Travelshots.com), 20 (cooking/A Room with Views), 20 (gym/Buzz Pictures), 20 (tennis/moodboard), 20 (music/the box studio), 20 (cycling/Ingram Publishing/Superstock Limited), 38 (rainforest/Ern Mainka), 41 (Space Shuttle Discovery/KPA/Galaxy/Content Mine International), 48 (Mamma Mia jar/Martin Lee/Mediablitzimages (UK) Ltd), 49 (Devon cottage/Elizabeth Whiting & Associates), 49 (watch/Synthetic Alan King), 53 (shoppers/Ian Dagnall), 59 (fans/Felipe Rodriguez), 65 (Jodie/Dynamic Graphics/Jupiterimages/Creatas), 65 (Melissa/Leland Bobbe/Photodisc), 69 (bus stop/TNT Magazine), 69 (bananas/picturesbyrob), 69 (football ticket/Nick Cobbing), 90 (skyline/Tim Gaine); Lorna Aps Woodland p71 (Billy small photo); Steve Baxter p24 (fallen visitor); Pearl Bevan p84 (sunglasses); Mahesh Bhat p51 (Lakshmamma); Chris Boon p59 (modern football and boots), 94 (Nissan); The Bridgeman Art Library pp22 (Vincent van Gogh, Self Portrait, 1889, Private Collection), 22 (Vincent van Gogh, Irises, 1889, Private Collection), 22 (Vincent van Gogh, Red Vineyards at Arles, 1888, Pushkin Museum, Moscow), 23 (Vincent van Gogh, Sunflowers, 1888. Neue Pinakothek, Munich, Germany), 54 (David Nolan, The Princess Elizabeth Storms North in All Weathers, Private Collection), 66 Chinese School (20th c.), Revolutionary Ideal is Supreme: The Long March of 1935, Private Collection, Archives Charmet), 98 (Justus Sustermans (1597-1681), Portrait of Galileo Galilei, Galleria Palatina, Palazzo Pitti, Florence; Camera Press pp18 (H.R.H. Prince Charles/Photography by Ian Jones/Gamma), 19 (H.R.H. Prince Charles and H.R.H. Camilla, Duchess of Cornwall/Richard Gillard); Casio Electronics Company Limited p34 (Casio EXLIM Zoom EX-Z9 digital compact camera); Christie's Images p59 (old football boots and football); Corbis pp9 (canoeing/David Madison), 9 (Big Ben/Alexander Benz), 28 (Ole Graf/zefa), 38 (Kalahari bushmen/Drew Gardner), 39 (polar bears/epa), 41 (Jules Verne rocket, From the Earth to the Moon, 1872/Bettmann), 49 (father and son/Alexander Scott/zefa), 55 (Jack/Andrew Fox), 56 (Calvin Klein/Jesse Frohman), 56 (shop front/James Leynse), 59 (World Cup/John Van Hasselt), 66 (Mao/Swim Ink), 77 (credit card/LWA-Dann Tardif), 81 (Tom/Little Blue Wolf Productions), 98 (Darwin/Richard Milner/Handout/epa), 98 (Freud/Bettmann), 106 (Mother Teresa smiling/Reuters), 106 (Mother Teresa serious/JP Laffont/Sygma); Creative Technology Ltd p34 (Creative Zen Vision MP3 Player); Stephen Daniels/www.danpics.com p94 (Jack Neal); Dorling Kindersley p 49 (Teddy bear); Reproduction by permission of the Syndics of the Fitzwilliam Museum, Cambridge p24 (Chinese porcelain vases c. 1680–1720); Getty Images pp14 (Dave/Peter Dazeley/The Image Bank), 15 (Sean Davey), 18 (The Royal Family on the balcony /Daniel Berehulak), 19 (Prince Charles with Princes William and Harry/Tim Graham Photo Library), 20 (LWA/Photodisc), 21 (Liverpool/Suzanne & Nick Geary/Stone), 29 (John Cumming/Iconica), 30 (questions/Jed Share/Photographer's Choice), 33 (Millie/Photographer's Choice), 33 (Frank/Marc Romanelli/Photographer's Choice), 39 (coral/Jeff Hunter/The Image Bank), 43 (galaxy/Ian Mckinnell/Photographer's Choice), 50 (tarts/Heidi Coppock-Beard/Stone), 51 (Elizabeth Anne Hogan/Stephanie Diani), 52 (Grant Faint/The Image Bank), 53 (coffee/Sergio Pitamitz/Iconica), 53 (escalator with couple/Justin Pumfrey/Iconica), 57 (Nicho Sodling), 58 (woodcut

mob football 1721/Rischgitz/Hulton Archive), 60 (Julia/Ron Krisel/The Image Bank), 60 (James/Stock4B), 60 (Paul/David Lees), 61 (couple/Paul Thomas/Taxi), 62 (globe/George Diebold/Stone), 63 (group in Amazon/Ghislain & Marie David de Lossy/Riser), 67 (elephant crossing river/Hulton Archive), 69 (petrol pump/Daniel Berehulak), 72 (Hulton Archive), 73 (Taxi), 73 (bank/Christopher Bissell/Stone), 81 (Daisy/Jerome Tisne), 82 (St Pancras today/Cate Gillon), 82 (St Pancras 1958/Leonard G. Alsford/Fox Photos/Hulton Archive), 100 (Jamie Seabrook/Paul Bradbury), 101 (T-shirts/Roger Wright/Stone), 103 (Dublin/Charles Bowman/Robert Harding World Imagery), 112 (running/Regine Mahaux), 115 (cityscape/Siegfried Layda/Photographer's Choice), 115 (Panoramic Images), 147 (introducing/Somos/Veer), 147 (hotel room/Johannes Kroemer), 147 (dinner party); Huw Evans/www.huwevansimages.com p95 (man throws away money); Courtesy of Gibson Guitars p49 (ES335 guitar); Grazia Neri pp51 (Santina Corvaglia/Franco Origlia), 106 (young Mother Teresa /Giovanbattista Brambilla); iStockphoto pp9 (paperclip and paper/Christoph Weihs), 9 (laptop/muharrem öner), 13, 20 (painting/Thye Aun Ngo), 20 (gardening/Alex Hinds), 20 (photography/blackred), 30 (mannequin and question/Palto), 31 (two mannequins/emmgunn), 31 (sign post/Vasiliy Yakobchuk), 32 (paper/Clayton Hansen), 32 (lined paper/Bruce Lonngren), 47 (camera/fajean), 47 (laptop/shapecharge), 48 (Kos boat/Alfred Rijnders), 48 (newspaper ad/Bruce Lonngren), 48 (Mamma Mia illustration), 49 (pills/Bill Fehr), 50 (tablecloth), 55 (bats/Govinda Trazo), 55 (wand/Mihail Glushkov), 58 (football knocked back/Ron Sumners), 62 (email icon/Can Gürbüz), 66 (mountain/Brandon Laufenberg), 69 (20:25/Nikada), 69 (Euros/imagestock), 76 (Taipei/tcp), 81 (computer/Emrah Turudu), 84 (handcuffs/Ivan Mateev), 88 (Christina/Nicole Weiss), 90 (paper/Gaffera), 98 (compass/Olga Samoylova), 100 (paper/christine balderas), 100 (paper/Trevor Hunt), 100 (paper/Christopher Hudson), 114 (Statue of Liberty/Kjell Brynildsen), 114 (taxi/Markanja), 149 (Palto), 149 (emmgunn); Joseph Jastrow, Fact and Fable in Psychology, 1901, p295, p86 (duck-rabbit); Dave King p35 (The Gregory family); Courtesy of London and Continental Railways p82 (St Pancras Hotel); MTV Networks UK & Ireland p34 (robot I SOBOT ROBOT); Mary Evans Picture Library p32 (schoolchildren), 66 (Hannibal), 98 (Pankhurst/The Women's Library); Masterfile p45 (Pierre Tremblay); Ben McMillan p11 (The Qus family); Mirrorpix p75 (John Ferguson); Courtesy of Molecular Expressions/Michael W. Davidson, National High Magnetic Field Laboratory/http://microscopy.fsu.edu p78 (smurf/Photo Karl E. Deckart); National Motor Museum p35 (camper van); Nixon p34 (Nixon bag); PA Photos pp41 (Steve Bennett/Owen Humphreys/PA Archive), 59 (Cristiano Ronaldo/Joe Giddens/Empics Sport); Panos Pictures p10 (The Kamaus family/Sven Torfin), 59 (boys playing/Chris Stowers); Philips p34 (Philips widescreen TV), 34 (Philips DC200 IPOD dock); Punchstock pp11 (map/BLOOMimage), 14 (Terry/image100), 17 (Stockbyte), 20 (camping/Radius Images), 21 (Stockbyte), 33 (Richard/Anthony-Masterson/Digital Vision), 37 (BLOOMimage), 38 (Hannah and Dan/Sven Hagolani/fStop), 38 (gorilla/Gerry Ellis/Digital Vision), 38 (ice and snow/Eastcott Momatiuk/Digital Vision), 43 (running/Colin Anderson/Blend Images), 43 (Chad Baker/Digital Vision), 46 (Stockbyte), 60 (Andrew/Image Source Pink), 60 (Harriet/Noel Hendrickson/Digital Vision), 65 (Gavin/Image Source Pink), 77 (hotel/Digital Vision), 78 (microchip/PhotoAlto Agency/Laurent Hamels), 81 (Monica/Glow Images), 81 (Justin/Photodisc), 81 (David/Digital Vision/Andrew Olney), 87 (John Lund/Digital Vision), 88 (Rachel/IS307/Image Source Pink), 109 (Stockbyte), 112 (bored child/Photodisc); Rex Features pp33 (Ian Dury/Brian Rasic), 54 (J K Rowling signing books/Richard Young), 55 (three fans reading/James Fraser), 98 (Presley/SNAP), 150 (Ian Dury/Brian Rasic); Anna Rianne p32 (sign); Science Photo Library pp38 (Venice/Mauro Fermariello), 40 (NOAA), 41 (Apollo 11/NASA), 68 (Gustoimages); Science & Society Picture Library p79 (Babbage computer/Science Museum); Seiko Europe Limited p34 (Orange Monster Watch); Kate Soars p62 (Kate), 62 (Dan's friends); Sony Computer Entertainment Europe p34 (Playstation 3); Sony Ericsson UK & Ireland p34 (Sony Ericsson W910i mobile phone); Sony UK Limited p34 (Sony Vaio notebook computer); Tomy Corporation p34 (Rock Band Guitar (based on a Fender Stratocaster used for Rock Band computer game published by MTV Games); Troika Photos p83 (The Meeting Place, St Pancras Railway station, by Paul Day/Photo Michael Walter); WeSC - WeAretheSuperlativeConspiracy p34 (headphones); www.all-the-flags-of-the-world.c.la p12 (Bolivia), (Union Jack), (Basque); BAA Aviation Photolibrary, www.baa.com/photolibrary p147 (airport information).